BWANA GAME

The Life Story of
George Adamson

Collins & Harvill Press

LONDON

1968

Printed in Great Britain by Collins Clear-Type Press
London and Glasgow

To the Creatures of the Wild

Acknowledgements

I wish to thank my wife; Bill Travers; Columbia Picture Corporation and Murray Ritchie for kindly letting me use their excellent photographs to illustrate this book.

I should also like to express my gratitude to Bill Travers for making a trip to Kenya to record additional material; to Captain Charles Pitman, the former Game Warden of Uganda, for the trouble he has taken in checking the proofs; and to Mr William Collins and Mrs George Villiers for the encouragement they have given me and the interest they have shown in the preparation of the manuscript.

Contents

List of Illustrations

Author's Note

Several people have urged me to write an account of my twenty-three years' experiences as a Game Warden in the Northern Province of Kenya. Although there is plenty of material collected over the years which might be of interest to lovers of the wild, I feel very diffident about inflicting upon the public yet another book about Africa.

The nature of my profession often entailed the killing of animals, sometimes accompanied with a certain amount of risk, but it is my intention to avoid, as much as possible, burdensome accounts of big game hunting, hair-breadth escapes . . .

What I would like to convey to readers is something of the atmosphere of a way of life which, in this age of artificial living, has almost disappeared. I have spent my best years trying to protect our wild fellow creatures and it is my hope that this book may stimulate interest in and sympathy for them.

In this period of evolution the wild heritage of the human race needs for its protection the active help and sympathy of every civilised man. I am convinced that, as we progress further into an age governed by the 'machine', our hunger for the unspoilt beauty of nature is going to increase and that it would be a tragedy if there were nothing left with which to satisfy that hunger. Every year communications grow swifter and easier and people have more leisure in which to relax. Soon it will be possible for a man of moderate means, in any part of the world, to board an aircraft and be transported in a few hours from the glittering and noise-bedevilled cities into the midst of peace and quiet and find himself among creatures who have not changed since the dawn of time.

It is the plain duty of man to guard and to protect what is at his mercy, and at the same time guarantee the survival of creatures which have so much to contribute to his knowledge and pleasure.

PART ONE
Looking for a Way of Life

1: *Many ways of earning a living*

1916

UNTIL I WAS TEN I lived in India, in Dholpur, one of the princely states, where my Father, an Irishman, was responsible for organising the Rajah's army and building a railway. He was a man of adventurous spirit who had been a sailor in the days of sailing ships and I remember the exciting stories he told us about going round the Horn; he was a very able man as can be imagined since, though only a self-taught engineer, he not only planned the Dholpur railway but realised many other engineering projects. When he left the Royal Navy he started an indigo plantation in India, which was doing well until the discovery of aniline dyes had a severe effect upon the trade in indigo. It was at this point that he took a post in the State of Dholpur, and also married.

My Mother's family had been in India for many years, indeed *her* Mother had, as a small child, lived through the Indian Mutiny. There were just two of us children, myself and my brother Terence who was the younger by a year. Our parents had very different temperaments, Mother being highly strung, very tidy, methodical and observant and Father extremely placid and even-tempered. I think that I have inherited his characteristics, whilst Terence certainly derives his great power of observation from our Mother.

The country was in many ways similar to the semi-desert parts of Northern Kenya. Except for a few missionaries there were no Europeans where we lived, but we made friends among the Rajput soldiers who guarded our house and among the servants.

Sometimes we had the excitement of going on pig-sticking expeditions and in the very hot weather, when the shade temperature reached a hundred and twenty degrees, we went to

Simla where we met other European children. I thoroughly enjoyed the life in India. Later I went to England, to Dean Close School, Cheltenham.

My Father intended to settle in South Africa when he retired from the Rajah's service, but, on his way there, he stopped in Kenya and was so taken by the country that he changed his plans and bought a small coffee plantation in the Highlands. He knew nothing about coffee planting but in those days there were always people around who were ready to advise a new arrival. The plantation was not a great success because the land was at too high an altitude for coffee to thrive; probably tea would have done better, but at that time no one in Kenya had thought of tea-planting.

In spite of the not very satisfactory return on the coffee plantation the plan was that Terence and I should work on it but when, at the age of eighteen, I came to Kenya to join my family I did not take to the endless rows of coffee bushes. My father soon realised that I wasn't cut out to work on the plantation, so he suggested that I should become a ploughman. Those were the early days of tractors and he believed it would be a good thing for me to know something about mechanical ploughing. There were two of us on the job, a man called Ingles and myself. It was hard work, we started at dawn and worked till dark and sometimes went on through the night with a lamp attached to the Bates Steel Mule, as the tractor was called. We slept in a wooden caravan; Ingles, as the older man, on the bunk and I on the floor. In the morning we washed in a nearby stream. That job certainly toughened me up. My pay was fifteen pounds a month.

When I had had enough of ploughing I went to a sisal plantation. I didn't expect sisal to be more exciting than coffee, in fact it was still duller, but the plantation was in much wilder country where game was plentiful and this seemed to me in its favour.

Sisal fibre is used for making rope, bags, fibre board and other things of that type. My job was to cut the plants; they were then carried by light railway to the factory where they were processed, dried, baled and then exported. For my task my pay was twenty pounds a month. David Hobden was the manager of the estate and became a good friend of mine, but I didn't like sisal, so I left to become a farm bailiff on a property of close on one hundred thousand acres which was up for sale.

My job was to ride around and see whether poaching was going on on a large scale and whether timber was being felled. It was an interesting piece of country. On the lower-lying land there were Kikuyu settlements and higher up in the forest Dorobo tribesmen. It was not long however before the property was sold and my job came to an end.

Just then I happened to meet David Hobden again. He had started up a milk round in the neighbourhood of Nairobi; he asked me to join him and I did so. We used to cart round hundreds of gallons of milk in whisky bottles—the only ones available. Sometimes people would complain about this thing and that and I would say 'Yes, Madam', or 'No, Madam', but I never had any complaint that the milk tasted of alcohol! We had some rough journeys, for the roads were not even gravelled in those days and when it rained we would get bogged down and have to spend the night out. It was hard on the truck and hard on the bottles, and we had a lot of breakages.

Later, I worked with David Hobden in other capacities. For instance, he set up a small store with a bar attached to it in Limuru, and I often acted as barman. Then he thought it would be a good thing to start a bus service between Arusha and Nairobi, as at the time there was no means of communication between them; I joined in this enterprise. At first we had quite a lot of passengers but, as there was no road and the track went across black cotton soil, when the rains came we were often bogged down and our unfortunate passengers were obliged to spend the night in the bus. It was quite an exhausting job, David and I shared the driving, with a bottle of neat whisky between us to see us over the journey. Even so, when, as sometimes happened, we had to drive night and day and dig ourselves out as well, though it was a lot of fun, we got pretty tired.

In the end we gave it up, because the wear and tear on the vehicles was so great that it didn't pay.

By now Terence had come out to join my Father and was working on the plantation. Social life had little attraction for either of us; whenever we had a free moment we went off hunting. Our first expeditions—hunts after buffalo and lion—were not very successful, which may have been just as well as our equipment consisted of a rather antiquated 405 Winchester rifle and a shotgun.

The range of our hunting was limited by the transport available to us, a motor cycle and a side-car. I doubt whether the makers of the 'Henderson' had ever envisaged their product being subjected to the treatment we gave it. At the end of a strenuous weekend we would set off for home with a hartebeest weighing some three hundred pounds in the side-car, the camp gear tied on wherever possible and my brother clinging on to the pillion. Fortunately, the machine was a powerful one, with four cylinders, but, even so, when we came to a steep hill we had to carry the load to the top. Later we borrowed my Father's car.

We were usually away for a couple of nights which we spent sleeping in the forest under tarpaulins with a good fire going nearby to keep us warm and discourage predators. On these expeditions we were always accompanied by an old Dorobo tracker called Masondu. I used to collect him from his home where he lived with his Kikuyu wife. They cultivated a little patch of ground but probably lived mostly on the results of Masondu's poaching. He was a wizened little man, about five foot high with white hair, and must have been about sixty— very old for a Dorobo. His only clothing was a scrap of blanket which he wound around his middle. When he came with us he carried nothing but a small stick, though no doubt when he went out on his own he had a bow and poisoned arrows. (These bows are very light; it is the poison that kills.) When we had shot any beast that provided good eating he would collect his friends and they would camp round the carcase until they had finished it, rather like lions sitting over a kill.

Masondu was incredibly good in the bush—in fact he was as familiar with it as any wild animal. He could always tell whether a beast had been lightly or badly wounded, or if it were dying.

He taught me how to test the wind and also a great deal about reading spoor; for instance, he made me observe whether leaves or grass had been bruised, whether there was dew on the spoor, whether ants had made runs over it. Another very useful tip I got from him was that when following a wounded buffalo one must exercise extreme care as these animals have a habit of circling back and waiting to ambush one.

It is many years since I went out with Masondu, but I still often think of him and remember what a wonderful hunter and great character he was.

My first trading venture was in partnership with two friends, Hugh Grant and Roger Courtney, both older than myself. Grant, a fair, tall Highlander, was an active World War I soldier with a double M.C. to his credit; I had met him on hunting expeditions. Courtney, a ginger-haired, stocky rugger player, had been an unsuccessful gold miner. We established our base camp on the shores of Lake Baringo, a shallow stretch of brackish water, some one hundred and fifty square miles in extent, situated in the Rift Valley. Here it was possible to buy goats and sheep from the local Njemps tribesmen for between four and five shillings apiece. Our idea was to buy as many as we could afford and transport them by truck to the Highlands, a distance of about a hundred miles, where it was possible to sell them for between twenty and twenty-five shillings each. The project started with a swing; there was no lack of goats and sheep and soon we had a truck load. I set off with one African assistant, the vehicle packed tight with bawling livestock. All went well until we came to a particularly steep hill up which the truck refused to go, so there was nothing for it but to unload, drive the flock to the top of the hill and re-load. Quite reasonable and simple—in theory. Unfortunately, the animals had had their fill of motoring and their one desire was to escape, and this they did in all directions as soon as their feet touched the ground.

Young and active as I was, after three hours of chasing goats through the surrounding thorn bush, I was nearly exhausted. At last we collected the beasts into a reasonably subdued flock at the top of the hill. Then the problem of re-loading arose. Each goat had to be caught, clasped to one's bosom, carried to the truck and pushed in. But those already loaded had by no means lost their craving for the open spaces, so, as soon as the door was opened to put in another passenger, there would be a concerted rush for freedom. It was late evening by the time we were ready to get going again; by then we were reeking of goat and tired out and we still had another fifty miles to go. Our first load sold well and we had visions of expanding the business, buying more trucks and employing African drivers. But it was not to be. The animals already disposed of could not stand the sudden change of climate, they began to sicken and die and, after a short time, there were no more buyers.

The camp by the shores of the lake was most attractive and interesting. There were plenty of fish in the water and duck in the marshy areas to the north, also an abundance of crocodile and some hippo. At that time, the Njemps fishermen had no knowledge of nets and caught their fish by means of crude barbless hooks attached to a short cord fastened to a pole; they used a species of small dragonfly as bait. In order to attract the fish a series of sticks would be stuck into the bottom of the lake, their ends protruding a few inches above its surface, on these the dragonflies settled and the fish would jump up to them. The fisherman stood waist-deep between the sticks. Crocodiles could often be seen a few feet away from him but he ignored them completely. The fish caught by this method are a species of tilapia (*Tilapia nilotica*); scaling about a pound, they are the best eating fish in Africa.

On one occasion, I walked along the shore accompanied by a Njemps looking for crocodile. Not meeting with any success I was about to turn back when the Njemps motioned me to hide behind some rocks. Then he lay down in the reeds by the water's edge and began to call 'Imm-imm-imm . . .' from deep down in his throat, while his breath lasted. After a few minutes, I was astounded to see the heads of some dozen crocodiles, all making towards the sound, some from more than two hundred yards away. They came up to within a few feet of the man, then became suspicious, apparently, at not finding what they had expected. I was never able to discover just what the crocodiles did expect to find. The imm-imm-imm sound is quite unlike any made by these creatures or any other animal I know of. It has been suggested that it may resemble the piping of newly hatched baby crocodiles, and it is said that, attracted by the noise, the parents and other friends and relations gather around and eat the young. If true, in the case of crocodile, this is a commendable habit. After some practice I too became able to call crocodile and I have since done so successfully on many lakes and rivers.

The only craft on the lake were canoe-shaped rafts made of ambatch stems bound together. The ambatch (*Aeschynomene elaphroxylon*) is a curious plant. It grows in water and stands about twelve feet high. It has bulbous, pithy stems six to ten inches in thickness. The wood when dry is said to weigh about ten to twelve pounds per cubic foot, which is lighter than cork. The rafts are propelled by means of scoop-shaped pieces of wood about eight inches in length, used as paddles.

In the year 1928 there were still many elephant around Lake Baringo. Courtney and I had been camping near together, but on this occasion I was alone, as he had gone off to sell a lot of goats. During the night a small herd came close and caused the goats to burst out of their enclosure and scatter. These Baringo elephant were inclined to be aggressive, probably because they had been hunted by Europeans and poached by Africans. One day when I shot an antelope for meat a herd came charging towards the sound of the shot and it was over an hour before I could recover the carcase. On the east side of the lake was the grave of an Administrative Officer who had actually been killed by an elephant, a testimony to their aggressiveness.

Just when the goat venture was failing and we had made up our minds to abandon it large swarms of locusts invaded Kenya from the north and I was able to enrol as a government locust officer in the Baringo District.

In those early days, before much research had been carried out on this pest, the only effective method of dealing with locusts was to attack the young, or hoppers as they are called, before they grew wings and took to the air. We used stirrup-pumps and

sprayed with a solution of arsenic and, where suitable, poisoned
bait in the form of bran contaminated with arsenic was put down.
Undoubtedly, these methods led to considerable mortality among
wild birds and harmless, or even beneficial, insects, and owing to
the carelessness of the herders, livestock sometimes also suffered.
The danger to the locust control team was considerable, for
arsenic can be absorbed through the skin, so, we always had to
see that the Africans, when spraying, had greased their hands
and any part of their body that was exposed. It was also most
important to be very careful not to spray into the wind; I got
poisoned in this way more than once and suffered from diarrhoea
and vomiting. So far as the Africans were concerned the cans
themselves were also a grave danger. The arsenide of sodium
arrived in small five pound tins, and as the Africans were very
keen on empty cans I was continually warning them of the danger
involved in making any use of them. All the same, they would
steal them and use them as food containers or drinking vessels
without even bothering to clean them out, and so quite a lot of
Africans went sick. Of course, we always carried ferric chloride
and bicarbonate of soda with us as antidotes for arsenical poisoning, and thanks to them no one died, but many were ill for a time.

In the early days, the locust campaigns attracted an extremely
varied assortment of characters: the work-shy, the drunks, the
remittance men—but there was also a leavening of adventurous
spirits who joined for the same reasons as myself. Each locust
officer was allotted an area which it was his responsibility to endeavour to clear of hoppers. Much to my delight, I was posted to
Karpeddo, the northernmost point of the operation, some thirty-
five miles north of Lake Baringo. I was on the border between
the Suk and Turkana tribesmen. Karpeddo itself was an abandoned military post situated near the foot of an extinct volcano
called Silarli in the trough of the Rift Valley. Its most remarkable
features are the almost boiling hot springs which form the
source of the Sugota River. Soon after issuing out of the bowels of
the earth the water goes over a fall of about thirty feet into a
gorge lined with palm trees. Not more than five hundred yards
downstream, where the water is still hot, fish, including tilapia

and barbus, abound in the pools and even an occasional crocodile is to be seen in the clear water. I bathed in the pools and found the temperature that of an uncomfortably hot bath.

My labour force consisted of about fifty men. Half were Suk and half Turkana; they were almost identical in appearance and could only be distinguished by the fact that the Suk are circumcised and the Turkana are not. As they wore no clothes recognition was not difficult.

The Turkana were always pestering me to shoot crocodile and baboon, both of which they considered good eating. I, personally, never tried them out; crocodile flesh looks like chicken but smells very fishy, and I should have felt rather like a cannibal eating baboon. Besides providing food, baboon pelt is much in demand by the Turkana elders who use it as a short cape which falls down the back and provides efficient protection against the blistering sun.

I came to like and admire the Turkana. Theirs must be the toughest lives lived by any human beings; their country is a barren wilderness of sand, lava and thorn bush and they are chronically on the brink of starvation. Yet, in spite of their hard lot, they are fine specimens physically; the men are often six feet and over in height and the women correspondingly well developed.

The Turkana are among the unlucky tribes which were halted in a desert by Pax Brittanica. A Nilotic tribe, they probably came from somewhere in the Sudan. When, early in the century, the British administrators arrived in Kenya, owing to the incidence of tribal warfare, they felt obliged to halt nearly all the tribes in the territory they then occupied. Later, demarcation lines were drawn. So, just when the Turkana's eyes were turned to the South on lands of plenty, from which, being war-like and courageous, they would no doubt have ousted the sedentary agriculturalists who occupied them, they were compelled to settle in the desert.

A Turkana family on the move is a fine sight. The men, carrying only a brace of long spears, a stool or head-rest and a container for tobacco, drive their flocks and herds; the women and children follow with donkeys lightly laden with a few water gourds and skins. Unlike most pastoral tribes, the Turkana do not carry prefabrications for their dwellings: in fact, a Turkana village hardly deserves the name, for all it consists of is an enclosure for livestock and a few rough shelters made out of sticks with grass and skins thrown over the top as roofs.

During the First World War the Turkana, owing to their propensity for raiding their neighbours, caused a good deal of trouble and it was deemed necessary to carry out punitive measures against them. Almost without exception, the officers, mostly soldiers who took part in the early administration of the country, developed a liking and admiration for their charges, and in return gained their respect and even their grudging affection. The warlike Turkana were able to recognise the need for the military measures taken against them and bore no grudge for the defeats and casualties they sustained.

Unfortunately, the Government decided to deprive them of their firearms. This put them at a disadvantage, since there were still tribes moving into their territory from Ethiopia who did not suffer this handicap.

The result of all this is that today there is a destitute section of the tribe which, in order to exist, has to live by poaching and thieving and often infiltrates into other tribal areas to the South, or on to European farms and, the Turkana being a remarkably fertile race, the problem they present becomes more acute every year.

In a couple of months the locusts had matured and taken wing and the campaign was over. Fortunately for me, my services were retained as a reconnaisance officer with instructions to cover as much of the country as possible and to report on locust movements and signs of breeding. Nothing could have pleased me more. I had the run of the entire region and could go where I wanted to. At that time most areas were road-less, so the only way to see the country properly was on foot.

I sent for Narro, the secondary Paramount chief, a man in his late forties, and ordered him to supply a dozen donkeys complete with native *sogis*; these are donkey pack-saddles made in the shape of a W of raw hide. I also asked for two drovers. Donkeys were our only means of transportation. In those days they cost about twelve shillings; today the price is up to three pounds. Ours had great personalities and became real friends.

Narro was a pleasant character and a fine specimen of middle-aged manhood. I grew very fond of him and often he would tell me stories about the cattle raiding forays of the past. One day he confided to me that he felt his powers were waning and enquired whether the white man had any medicine to stimulate potency. I replied that there was nothing suitable in my medicine chest but suggested he might try rhino horn powdered, the Asiatic elixir of rejuvenation. I never discovered whether he followed my suggestion.

At length, the donkeys arrived together with a fat sheep. The latter was a gift from Narro to help me on my way. Leaving the government lorry and all non-essential gear at Karpeddo, I set off with twelve well-laden donkeys, two Suk drovers, my cook Yusuf and two locust scouts. The safari lasted a month, our slow pace was due to the fact that the country had been eaten out by the locusts and there was scarcely a blade of grass or leaf left for the poor donkeys to eat. Also, owing to the prevalence of hyena, and even lion, it was impossible to leave them out at night to pick up food. Instead, as soon as it was dark, they had to be secured in a strong thorn enclosure. On this occasion, we were lucky to find plenty of thorn; if there isn't much around and one can only build a flimsy hedge there is always the danger that a predator may stampede the donkeys which will then break out. We sometimes also used hurricane lamps which are more of a deterrent to lion than fires to protect the donkeys—not that these lamps are a hundred per cent guarantee of safety, for, in bad lion country, I have known *bomas* to be attacked in spite of having hurricane lamps burning.

The hyenas in these parts were very bold indeed as this example shows: a few days before leaving Karpeddo I learnt that an Indian trader had died at Nginyang, an evil-smelling water-hole some miles to the south. His men, perhaps afraid to touch the body, surrounded the tent with a strong thorn enclosure and sent word to his fellow countrymen at the next trading centre to collect it. The following night hyenas broke into the tent and by morning there was no trace left of the corpse.

After a few days our donkeys grew so weak from hunger that it became necessary to rest them every third day and to reduce the marches to not more than three or four hours per day and stop and off-saddle on the way, wherever there happened to be some feed. As there was no set time-table, the delay mattered little and gave me ample opportunity to explore the country.

One evening, while out on a solitary walk, I heard a great cackling from a flock of Baringo tufted guinea-fowl; they were perched in the tops of trees, their interest focused on some object below. Going forward cautiously I came on a fine leopard which had evidently been stalking the birds. During the night the same leopard came close to camp, causing me some uneasiness on account of the donkeys.

On the tenth day after leaving Karpeddo, having crossed the rugged Kamasia hills from east to west, I made camp at Kolosia on the wide Kerio river-bed. Kolosia was an administrative post that had been abandoned a few years previously. It was a desolate place, rendered all the more forlorn by the rapidly disintegrating mud buildings and the lonely grave of an English officer. It is said that he committed suicide during the First World War after receiving a letter from his fiancée enclosing a white feather. Yet, in my opinion, it takes more courage to live among wild tribes in a place like Kolosia, completely cut off for months on end from one's own kind, than to fight a war surrounded by thousands of comrades who are in the same boat as oneself. Anyway, for one reason or another, Kolosia had gained a sinister reputation as a *cafard* station and seemed to have a bad effect on its white incumbents. It is related that after prolonged residence one of these sent a challenge to a colleague at Kacheliba, some seventy miles away across the Rift Valley, daring him to bring his fighting men to the border of the district where he would be met by the challenger with an equal force of Turkana spearmen to settle the dispute by force of arms. Needless to say the officer concerned was hurriedly recalled and sent on indefinite home leave.

The main building in the station was still habitable and I made my camp in it, the donkeys were stabled in another. During the night the hungry animals managed to break out and were set on by a pack of at least six hyenas. Four were killed and devoured and by the morning there was nothing left of them, not a shred of skin or a splinter of bone—only blood-stained ground and stomach contents to mark the place where they had been killed. The remaining eight animals were recovered but they were in no state to carry the additional burdens of the four we had lost. I sent word to the Turkana chief, Abong, to produce replacements. In due course he arrived, a man of fine presence and dignity with considerable influence over his people. He brought a fat sheep as a present and, in return, I gave him a quantity of native tobacco. In those days the Turkana would sell their souls for the weed and anything from a gourd of milk to a wife could be purchased for tobacco. It was certainly their only luxury. When they set off on an expedition which might well last up to ten days, naked and with no luggage except for their spears and stool, they carried no food but lived on what they could find on their way; they might spear some animal, or find a tortoise and roast it; more often they were obliged to live on berries or on the pounded husk of doam palm nuts. What food value this flour has I don't know; it smells like cocoa and has an insipid taste, but baboon and elephant, as well as the Turkana, seem to like it.

By the time the new donkeys arrived the Kerio River had come roaring down in flood and there was no question of fording it, however, after a delay of three days the water subsided sufficiently to attempt the crossing. All the donkey loads had to be carried across. The torrent was breast-high and we were only just able to keep our feet. A good deal of effort was required to persuade the donkeys to enter the water. When they did so the current took hold of them and they were swept down the river. But, once out of their depth, donkeys are good swimmers and to my relief they made the opposite bank some three hundred yards downstream. The following morning I set off ahead of the safari and came to a place where the trail forked. Foolishly, instead of waiting for the transport to catch up, I decided to take the right fork and scored a furrow in the path indicating my direction and carried on until the early afternoon, crossing much rhino spoor and the pug marks of a big lone lion. But as by four p.m. there was no sign of the safari I then turned back along the path. By nightfall I reached the fork where I found the imprints of donkey hooves taking the left trail.

It was too dark to see the way or to collect fuel for a fire, so I had to sit with my back against a tree and my rifle across my knees and wait for morning. Sleep was out of the question owing to the swarms of mosquitoes; also, I could hear a lion calling and gradually drawing nearer until it was only fifty or sixty yards away, and I thought that as there was little game in the locality it might not be averse to picking up a solitary sleeper. That night was a tiring one because, knowing that if the lion meant to get me he would creep up very silently and all I would hear would be a pebble being moved or a twig breaking, I had to strain my ears sorting out a potentially dangerous sound from the buzzing of mosquitoes, the chirping of the crickets and the other night noises of the bush; for instance, if I heard a francolin give a squawk, then, since these birds sleep on the ground all through the night, I knew that something, possibly the lion, had put it up. When it was light I started off again on the donkey spoor which was easy to follow. Soon I met two of my men, much perturbed at my long absence, hurrying back to look for me.

During the next five days I re-crossed the Kamasia Range and returned to Karpeddo. In the latter part of the safari I came on extensive signs of egg-laying by locusts. As a result of my reports an anti-locust campaign was organised and ten officers sent to Baringo to deal with the situation. Not long afterwards I arrived at one of the newly established camps and found the two officers in charge clad in towels, tied around their waists, seated at a table set in the middle of the Sugota river under the shade of overhanging doam palms, groaning under a burden of assorted bottles of liquor. Judging by the number of empty bottles bobbing downstream, the party had been in progress some time—and this in the middle of the day at a shade temperature of a hundred and five degrees. But, although some of the men played hard, they also worked hard.

After three months of more or less successful effort against the locusts the campaign came to an end. The remaining hoppers had developed into locusts and taken wing and, as in those days we could only deal with the hoppers, I was once again unemployed; but not for long, as I very soon got another job.

The locust campaign had revealed that in order to be really effective it was necessary to open up a number of new tracks for motor transport into hitherto inaccessible parts of the country, and I was set the task of making a road through from Karpeddo to the Kerio Valley. The first thirty miles offered no great difficulty as the route lay along the Sugota river flats. At intervals it was necessary to make crossings of the beds of dry rivers which, when the rains came, would flow into the Sugota from off the hills to the west. The work consisted of digging sloping ramps into and out of the river-beds, and in places, clearing away loose sand or, where this was too deep, overlaying it with palm fronds of which there were plenty nearby.

The Sugota Valley is part of the Rift and carries the river from its source at Karpeddo, northwards for a distance of about eighty miles to a vast barrier of recently active volcanoes, that blocks the valley and prevents the river flowing into the southern part of Lake Rudolf. At its end the river forms a shallow lake heavily impregnated with natron. This brackish water is much favoured by great flocks of lesser flamingos (*Phoeniconaias minor*) because the underlying mud contains organic matter on which they feed. The Sugota Valley must be about the hottest place in East Africa with a shade temperature in the region of a hundred and twenty degrees. Luckily it is dry heat, but it is of such intensity that during the hot hours practically all movement stops; the birds don't move about, human beings don't move about and all animals seek shade. It is at night that the whole place comes alive. Most of the animals are nocturnal. We too became nocturnal in our habits, neither eating nor drinking during the heat of the day.

My lorry was probably the first motor vehicle to venture into this remote corner of Africa. Many of the local Turkana had never before seen one and at first, when it approached, they would take to their heels. On one occasion, when a strong gale drowned the sound of the engine, I drove up close behind a solitary, naked Turkana who was marching purposefully along. When I was within twenty feet of him he sensed that something was following him and, reacting like lightning, spun round with his spear poised to throw. I could not have blamed him if he had thrown it. The incident evoked roars of laughter from my Turkana passengers, in which the victim finally joined.

One morning, I went up into the hills to prospect for a suitable route for the road to take, leaving my truck at the bottom in charge of a tribesman. When I returned, hot and tired, truck and guard were gone. It was not difficult to follow the tyre marks leading towards the river-bank and to reconstruct the crime. Later I found the vehicle stuck in a sand drift almost overhanging the water. A few days afterwards the culprit was marched into camp by a headman with the recommendation that he should be soundly beaten; he looked very sheepish. I did not carry out the recommendation for I considered that the man had already had a big enough fright. Ever afterwards he was known as 'dreber' (local pronunciation of driver).

Soon afterwards the truck broke down and had to be left behind and I was obliged to continue the road-work over the range of hills with only donkey transport. It was a slow job as the ground was a mass of lava boulders, each of which had to be dug out and moved away by hand. At one point rations ran out owing to the non-arrival of a donkey convoy. After two days without food I suggested to the Turkana labour force that they might kill one of the transport donkeys and eat it. They agreed that it was a sound plan and I told them to go ahead but after a time a deputation came to me saying it couldn't be done. Since the Turkana have no objection to eating almost anything that moves, I was surprised and asked why they couldn't eat the donkey. They replied that they quite enjoyed the taste of donkey but that it was against their custom to kill one; on the other hand, should one happen to die they would have no scruples about eating it. I then enquired whether, supposing I were to engineer the death of a donkey, this would be all right? They agreed that a white man killing a donkey would be the equivalent of an act of God and no responsibility of theirs. The unfortunate donkey was then led in front of my tent. In deathly silence I walked up and presented my pistol at its head and pulled the trigger. The solemnity of the occasion was marred by the fact that the donkey, upon receiving the bullet in its brain, reared up and I was only saved from being knocked over by very quick foot work.

The road progressed until finally it reached the Kerio River where Eric Davies, the District Officer from Lokichar, a post west of the Kerio, arrived to celebrate the occasion. He was the first white man I had seen for fifty-two days. I felt very proud of my road and hoped to be among the first to motor over it. But this was not to be, for only a few days later orders arrived recalling me to Nairobi. At least I have the satisfaction of knowing that parts of my road are still in use today.

After a short leave I was sent to the Tana River where a fresh outbreak of locust-hatching on a large scale necessitated a new campaign. Together with several other officers, I spent Christmas Day 1929 among the Emberra and Tharaka tribesmen. Although mostly heathen the convivial Emberra and Tharaka needed no urging to celebrate the festival in their own fashion. A couple of fat oxen, contributed by us, and uncounted gallons of native beer, supplied by local brewers, provided fuel for a three-day non-stop *ngoma* (dance). Young people from far and wide assembled. The Tharaka competed against the Emberra, and a number of Wakamba from across the Tana River joined in. There were competitions in drumming and dancing and some of the contortionist acrobatics of the Wakamba girls would have made twist experts turn green with envy or seek retirement.

Towards the end of the festivities we Europeans decided to have a quiet day's fishing, and had a good haul. But after we had retired to our camp overlooking the river for refreshment, a *toto* (small boy) arrived breathless to say that a giant *nyoka* (snake) had snatched the catch away as it was being cleaned at the water's

edge and had disappeared with it into the depths of the river.
This was a challenge which could not be ignored. We all trooped
down to the river. I cast a stout line baited with a large chunk of
meat into the pool indicated by the *toto*. A huge flat head appeared
and engulfed the bait. The line parted as if it had been a thread.
This was too much! I doubled the remaining line and handed it
to a colleague while I took up station on a boulder in mid-stream
with a sharp *panga* (long knife) poised. Again the great head
broke surface. With a wild swing of the *panga* I missed the *nyoka*,
cut the line and fell into the river on top of the monster. Huge
coils writhed about me, then it was gone. Undoubtedly it was an
enormous eel, at least seven feet in length. As there was no more
line left we again repaired to camp to view the waning cele-
brations. Loud snores interspersed with an occasional girlish
giggle could be heard from the surrounding bush. So ended a
memorable Christmas.

2: *I deal in insurance, hams, transport and prospect for gold*

EARLY IN THE NEW YEAR the locust campaign ended and I was assigned the job of store keeper at Nairobi headquarters. Not liking this static form of employment I resigned after a few days; in any case, I was suffering from malaria and badly in need of a rest, so I went home. My Father had died three years earlier, at the age of sixty-one from a heart attack, but my Mother and Terence continued to live on the coffee plantation, in the stone house—successor to the original grass *banda*. It was a charming place, for my Mother was a keen gardener and the house was surrounded by plum, peach and other fruit trees, while on one side we had a view of Kilimanjaro, and on the other of Mount Kenya.

If one suffers from malaria any shock is liable to bring on a bout of the fever. Mother, wishing to celebrate the return of her prodigal son, asked me to fill a soda-water syphon, of the type activated by means of a gas cartridge known as a sparklet; I screwed the sparklet in. As, with some impatience, I watched the bubbles of gas subside, I gave the bottle a few vigorous shakes. Suddenly it burst in my face sending flying splinters of glass in all directions. Some lodged in my eyes; I thought I had been blinded. However, after the blood had cleared I found that I could still see, but, as it was impossible to remove some of the deeply buried fragments, I had to go to a doctor to have them taken out. This shock brought on a bad attack of malaria and for over two months, in spite of receiving injections, I had a high temperature.

When at length I was better, David Hobden who was now an insurance agent, first insured my life and then invited me to accompany him to Uganda on a business trip. It proved to be a

35

most amusing and interesting expedition. Hobden had developed an almost uncanny nose for victims and could tell at a glance whether a prospect was worth pursuing. His chief opponent, representing a rival company, was an unfrocked priest who also had great experience. However, Hobden had the advantage of extreme mobility over his rival who was often immobilised for long periods at wayside taverns by frequent recurrences of delirium tremens.

My colleague would condition himself to the exact level of his quarry. A hard-swearing road foreman would be introduced to the advantages of life insurance by an agent surpassing him in invective. A young and earnest newly-wed would be lectured on his duty to make provision for the future. Drunks would be admonished and advised that their probable early demise rendered it imperative to think of sister, mother or other loved ones at home. But I thought he had gone too far when he tried to insure a planter who was obviously in the last stages of blackwater fever.

Our final objective was a small town on the northern borders of Uganda. We arrived late in the evening at an attractive little hotel. The sole occupant of the lounge appeared to be a young man of pleasing appearance. Some time later I realised that our companion was a lady; she was a geologist. We became very friendly and while Hobden went out on his insurance errands among the local planters, I went out sight-seeing with Miss L, in her car. We had several pleasant days together and at the end of our stay decided to have a farewell party. I retired early as I felt a bout of fever coming on. Miss L and Hobden continued the party until the early hours. In the morning I was informed that it had been decided, by the two of them, that Miss L and myself should get married. There was to be no argument and everything had been arranged. We were all to go forthwith to the local magistrate's office for the civil ceremony. Never having considered matrimony at such an early stage of my life I was somewhat staggered at all the implications. While Miss L was a very charming girl she was unusually powerful and determined. Had I not seen her clout an African who had been insolent and send

him reeling? I suggested that Miss L and Hobden should go
ahead in their car and that I would meet them at the magistrate's
office. As soon as they were out of sight I headed south at full
speed; when later we met the atmosphere was distinctly chilly.

On our way back to Nairobi we stopped at a little station called
Elburgon where Hobden successfully insured a pig farmer who,
as a side line, cured hams. The farmer was anxious to get his
product onto the market and asked us to assist on a commission
basis. We readily agreed and were presented with an enormous
ham as a sample to show to prospective buyers. Three days later
we stopped at a small hotel and after a few drinks with the proprietor suggested that he might be interested in hams? We ex-
tolled the soundness of the curer and the excellence of his product.
At length, having aroused the interest of the hôtelier and of the
other inmates of the bar, we produced our large parcel and dumped it with a flourish on the bar counter; heads craned around
while Hobden undid it. There was a devastating stench of decayed pig and out fell a mass of wriggling maggots. That was
the beginning and end of the ham agency. It took several more
drinks to mollify the proprietor.

During the next three years I was engaged mainly on motor
transport work. One venture consisted in conveying spirits,
(mostly whisky) and other luxury items, (mostly scent) from the
port of Mombasa to Kampala in Uganda, a distance of about
eight hundred miles. I also sometimes carried matches, because
the freight charge was so high; but I didn't care for this load as
the bulk was tremendous and so was the risk because of the
possibility of spontaneous combustion. Indeed, on one trip, the
matches in one of the big cartons I was carrying did ignite, but
fortunately, because they were so tightly packed, they went out
when the air was exhausted.

I had a two-ton truck for haulage purposes. The road between
Mombasa and Kampala was little better than a cross-country
track through dense bush and over lava flows and rolling plains
and when rain fell it would turn in many places into a quagmire

and make it necessary for me to camp until the ground dried. The whole journey, under favourable conditions, took five days. It was a hard life with long hours at the wheel and many hazards on the way, such as elephant and rhino, broken bridges and impassable morasses. On one occasion a friend and I undertook to deliver two new trucks at Kampala. We soon discovered that it was necessary to negotiate curves at reduced speed, otherwise the wooden spokes of the front wheels were apt to collapse; we left this for the receiving agent to find out for himself.

My motor transport days taught me to become a reasonably good mechanic, for there were then only a few garages in Kenya mostly run by Englishmen and a few by Greeks. As for spare parts, one had to make them. The wheels were of wood, so they were no problem for if the worst came to the worst one just made a spoke out of a piece of hardwood, but if the axle got bent, all one could do was to get a heavy log and two men to pound at it.

Not least of the hazards was the unfailing hospitality of people along the way—farmers, policemen, railway employees and others—and, if the wherewithal of a merry evening ran out, there was always my cargo to fall back on. Hospitality, at that time, was of the old-fashioned and all-embracing type, not infrequently including, for those who felt so inclined, a companion for the night. There was a wonderful spirit of comradeship; in those days people were much less critical, accepted strangers and liked them for their good qualities. It was more important to have friends than company and it didn't matter a damn where a stranger came from or what his background was; if he was in a fix anyone would go to any amount of trouble to help him.

One evening at a little township in Uganda I was asked to dinner at the camp of a veterinary officer and a road engineer. As usual, there were plenty of sundowners and as the night wore on my two hosts grew belligerent and came to blows. Finally, one seized a guttering oil lamp (the only source of illumination) with a view to crowning his companion. In the nick of time I snatched it away, otherwise the grass building would have gone up in flames. Having established peace I left the two weeping on each other's necks and went supperless away.

On one occasion, I met a lone traveller and invited him to share my meal. He was fat and bald and in his fifties, and complained bitterly of his treatment at the hands of the railway authorities, for he had just been discharged from a construction camp because one night, when after dining with a neighbour, he was trying to find his way back home by the aid of matches, he had inadvertently struck one against the grass wall of the camp hospital. It seemed to be a case of being lit up and lighting up!

Another incident of this period which I can never forget is the kindness of a Roman Catholic missionary Father who found me lying by the roadside with a severe attack of malaria. Several cars had passed without stopping; perhaps the occupants thought I was a drunk. The Father immediately got off his motor-cycle and came over to enquire. He insisted on my removal to his mission station a few miles away where I was carefully nursed for three days until the fever had left me.

At that time malaria was the plague of Africa, and large doses of quinine did little to help. In fact there is now some evidence to suggest that the drug may have been a contributing factor in the many fatal cases of blackwater fever which were then common in Uganda and the low-lying parts of Kenya. Certainly, it is significant that since quinine was superseded by such drugs as paludrine, blackwater fever is seldom heard of in East Africa. Another inconvenience of taking large doses of quinine is that it makes one deaf, and if I am a little deaf today I am sure this is because of the vast amount of quinine I have taken in my lifetime.

During this period, being more or less my own master, I was able to indulge my passion for the wild and went out on many hunting expeditions. On one of these my life was nearly brought to a premature end by a hippopotamus. A friend, Bill Thompson, and myself had been on a long walk after elephant and arrived on the banks of the Tana River. We had a bathe and were sitting unclad on a sand spit; I was trying to take a photograph of a big bull hippo which was behaving in an unusual manner, rearing out of the water and plunging back, not more than thirty yards off. Suddenly, as I was peering into the view-finder of my old-

fashioned camera, the hippo broke surface a few feet in front of
me, his cavernous mouth agape, with distinctly unfriendly intent.
I leapt up and started to run along the sandbank with the hippo
after me. Then I tripped and fell in the loose sand and felt the
monster's breath on my bare back. I threw myself aside and the
hippo's impetus carried him past me. I got up and made for the
river bank across what I thought was shallow water; it proved
to be six feet deep, and I went under still clutching the camera.
Luckily, the hippo, after seeing me off his sandbank, re-entered
the river on the opposite side of the spit. Had he followed me into
the water there would have been no George to write this story.
Bill who, having regained the bank well ahead of me, witnessed
the incident, said he thought the hippo had got me when he saw
me fall. Bill was a great character with whom I often went out
hunting, until he left the area and I believe took up medical
research.

Gold had recently been found at Kakamega, near the north-east
corner of Lake Victoria. Always ready to try my hand at anything
new, I joined in the rush together with Nevil Baxendale. He was
rather younger than me and twice my size—a veritable tower of
strength both physically and psychologically. With high hopes of
making our fortunes, we set off late in the year. Most of the
prospectors, like ourselves, had no experience of gold mining.
Many were farmers and small businessmen, not a few of whom had
sold up and put their all into the venture. At the beginning there
was wonderful comradeship among the prospectors and it was not
difficult to learn the rudiments of gold prospecting as almost
everyone with any knowledge was willing to help with advice.
We also acquired books on the subject.

The elementary principles of searching for gold are: first, to
take samples of the river gravels, choosing suitable places such as
rock bars where free gold is likely to be held up; then, having
found traces, it is necessary to work up-stream and try to locate
the source of the gold. This might be an auriferous quartz reef
several miles away from the main river to discover which required patient following-up of tributary water courses. Our
equipment was primitive. A couple of pans for washing gravel,

a dolly, (pestle and mortar) for crushing quartz samples, an earth auger (a pot hole drill) for taking underground samples and a few picks, shovels and hammers.

The method was to drill a hole about twelve foot deep and then take a hand-pan sample. If this looked promising a trench was then dug to the gold bearing gravel or sand and a ton or more put through the sluice boxes till the gravel was concentrated, then it would be washed in an ordinary pan until it was even more concentrated, afterwards mercury was put into the pan and this would take up the gold. The resulting amalgam of mercury and gold was placed in a retort and cooked.

Finally one was left with a lump of spongy gold that looked enormous, but was actually very light. These lumps we took to the bank at Kisumu and received an advance based on its quality as assessed by the bank clerk. After it had been assayed, one might get a further payment. With our advance in our pocket we would get some essential stores and then go back to the job.

After a month of extremely hard work we discovered an old river bed which showed promising traces of alluvial gold. We decided to work it and pegged our claims. Many and weird were the devices we used for extracting the gold from the gravel. There were the conventional sluice boxes which wobbled from side to side shaking up the gravel as it traversed the riffles and also an ingenious raking device which stirred up the gravel in each riffle. We managed to produce sufficient gold to keep us going for ten months—that would be about an ounce or an ounce and a half a week.

During this period, apart from hard labour, disappointments, minor triumphs and frequent bouts of malaria, we had our lighter moments. The Yala river valley where we had our claim was infested by venomous snakes. The most common were the black-lipped cobra, (*Naja melanoleuca*) and the horned viper, (*Bitis nasicornis*) also a few mambas, (*Dendroaspis jamesoni kaimosae*). On one occasion a large cobra came down the sluice box scattering our labours. On another, I almost stepped on one which suddenly reared up at my feet. I was carrying a pan containing gravel concentrates and, dropping the lot on top of the snake, fled. Often we would come on the beautifully marked rhinoceros horned viper which is said to possess a particularly deadly venom both neurotoxic and haemotoxic in its effects. Fortunately, this snake is not by nature aggressive and, unless actually trodden on, is unlikely to strike. We were anxious to obtain a good specimen and offered a small reward for one brought in alive. Soon afterwards an infant of about four years appeared at our camp dragging an enormous viper by a length of grass tied around its neck. In spite of the undignified treatment to which it had been subjected the snake did not appear to be unduly angry—perhaps being partially strangled it was in no shape to make any very strong protest. The viper was a good three feet in length and enormously thick—out of all proportion to its length. We called it Cuthbert Gandhi, the last name signifying its predilection for 'fasting unto death'. For the first three weeks of its sojourn among us it did not eat anything in spite of being offered milk, eggs and dead rats. At length, in desperation, when Cuthbert Gandhi was showing distinct signs of malnutrition, we thrust a large live rat into his box whereupon he woke up and struck like lightning. In a few moments the rat was dead. But it was not until we concealed ourselves out of his view that he started to swallow it, head first. At this time there was a good deal of thieving by local Africans and many miners had had their camps burgled, so we let it be known that Cuthbert Gandhi would be set to guard our grass hut at night by being tethered to the door post. We were never molested.

Periodically we made trips to Kakamega, the principal township of the area, to attend miners' meetings. Enterprising people had built two hotels there, 'The Golden Hope' and 'The El Dorado'. To these everyone repaired after the meetings to see their friends, swap yarns and learn of the latest finds. It was a break from the monotony of hard work and we all enjoyed ourselves.

Most of the time we were very hard up and could seldom afford such luxuries as a bottle of whisky. In the circumstances, we decided to make our own still--strictly illegal of course. As bananas were cheap and plentiful, we filled a large earthenware pot with the fruit and set it to ferment for several days. When the smell of decaying bananas had become almost unbearable, we stopped up the mouth of the pot with a wooden plug which had a long pipe leading out of it, then we put it over a fire. In due course a colourless liquid dripped out of the end of the tube. The taste was revolting, but it certainly possessed the required kick and when mixed with lime juice it was not impossible to swallow. Large flocks of guinea-fowl kept us going in meat.

After a time the pay sheet (miners' term for gold-bearing gravel), containing the alluvial gold began to grow thinner, and the over-burden of soil deeper until it became uneconomical to continue working the claims. So, regretfully, we decided to abandon work. By then we were financially just about where we had started (which was a good deal better than the luckless majority of miners).

The return home was made difficult by the heavy rains which had turned the earth roads into muddy tracks. At one point, late at night, our truck became hopelessly bogged and we had to unload it. We opened the back door of the vehicle and became conscious of a low hissing sound; this came from Cuthbert Gandhi. At the start of the journey we had put him into his rather flimsy travelling box in a comatose condition due to a heavy meal of rat. Evidently the violent jolting over the uneven roads had woken him up and he sounded angry. What we were not at all sure about was whether he was still in his box, or roaming at large in the back of the truck. As neither of us was anxious to be the first to find out, we prudently waited until dawn to investigate the situation. Daylight revealed Cuthbert wrapped in slumber still in his box. On arrival at Nairobi we presented him to the Coryndon Museum (now the National Museum), where he reposes to this day, inside a large glass jar.

In spite of our lack of success on the Kakamega gold fields, Nevil and I still had the gold fever, so, after a few weeks spent at our respective homes, we decided to set off on another prospecting safari into the country north of Lake Baringo and on to the Kerio Valley, which I had visited some four years previously while on locust work. As our resources were at a low ebb, we started with less than the bare minimum, hoping to live on the country. We made our base camp at Karpeddo, my former camping place, where the truck was to be left. With the help of my old friend Narro, the Suk secondary Paramount Chief, we purchased a dozen donkeys complete with their *sogis*. After two days, spent in dividing up the loads and mending the pack-saddles, we started off; Nevil, myself, two Suk donkey boys and my pointer dog Hindoo. The safari lasted for eighty-four days, during which we were hungry and ill with malaria. Fortunately, the bouts of fever attacked us alternately, leaving one fit enough to look after the other. We had no tent, only a small tarpaulin which had to be used to cover the loads. When it rained, as it did on several nights, we just got wet, which was not much fun, particularly for the one ill with fever. Most of the country we crossed was thick thorn bush and practically uninhabited, so there was no question of being able to buy food, and we had to rely on what game could be shot. Dikdik are good eating but it seemed a pity to shoot them since they are so small and only provide a mouthful, and I never did so unless it was absolutely necessary, and Grant's gazelle were rare in those parts.

While crossing the Kamasia hills a week after starting, we were joined by Yusuf, who had been my cook on earlier expeditions, including the locust campaign. He had heard that I was in the country and had walked over a hundred miles to join me. He was a valuable addition to our force for, besides being an excellent and ingenious cook, he was an expert with donkeys. The son of an old-time Swahili safari porter, he could produce a reasonable meal out of a stringy guinea-fowl, a pound of *posho* (maize meal) and wild spinach and mushrooms collected on the march. During one part of the safari we had reconciled ourselves to the inevitable dish of *posho* when Yusuf, undefeated, produced a store of dried buck meat which he had stowed away in one of the pack-saddles for just such an emergency. I wonder how many of the early explorers and travellers owed their successes and even lives to the never-failing brotherhood of Yusuf—the safari *mpishi* (cook). The African's staple diet consisted then, as it does today, of a couple of pounds of maize meal taken in the form of porridge, plus, of course, vegetable and meat when obtainable.

At one stage of our safari we camped under the Marakwet escarpment. Some two thousand feet above us was a small township and a mission station overlooking the Kerio Valley. I thought it might be a good idea for me to visit the station and perhaps buy some fresh vegetables from the missionaries and other stores from the Indian traders. Poor Nevil was completely incapacitated by chafed testicles, caused by marching for long periods in sweat-drenched trousers, which modesty forbade him from discarding. On such occasions the most comfortable form of wear is a loin-cloth or, better still, a shirt without nether garment. But those were the days when the white man felt it incumbent on him to present a façade of imperturbable dignity, regardless of personal discomfort. Earlier they must have had worse to endure; imagine those explorers in their Norfolk jackets, breeches and leggings!

It was out of the question to expect Nevil to accompany me dressed as comfort dictated and appear before the missionaries in a shirt, but—we wanted the vegetables. So off I set with the faithful Yusuf, and after three hours' climb arrived at the mission. I think the good couple were a little aghast when they saw a gaunt and heavily bearded apparition, but they were kindly people and after an excellent lunch they loaded us with as much as we could carry back. I excused the non-appearance of my friend by saying that he was suffering from sore feet. On the way down a sudden attack of fever took hold of me and I had to lie shivering beside the path for two hours until it passed off.

Hindoo thoroughly enjoyed the first part of the safari. At times there were so many game birds everywhere that he was quite bewildered, and looked at me reproachfully for not taking more interest in his pointing. We owed him a lot for on more than one occasion he saved the safari from blundering unsuspectingly into rhino. After a month he began to lose condition rapidly and there could be little doubt that he had been infected with trypanosomiasis by tse tse fly. There was nothing I could do for him other than watch him grow weaker and weaker day by day. One

evening he seemed restless and came and put his head on my
knee, then staggered away a few paces, and fell into a fit of con-
vulsions. I had to put him out of his suffering.

Hindoo was one of the keenest dogs I ever had. He would point
at anything, even a tortoise; when there were a lot of francolin
around he seemed to expect me to shoot every bird and appeared
much disappointed when I failed to do so, and with all the wild
life of the bush around, he used to be quite exhausted by the end
of the day.

Somehow, in the circumstances, and perhaps because of the
remoteness of the place, the loss of my friend was unutterably sad
and had I been alone I think I would have abandoned the safari
and turned back.

A few days later we reached a fairly large stream called the
Marrun coming out of the hills on the western side of the Rift
Valley. Here we found promising traces of gold in the river
gravel. But by this time our supplies were nearly exhausted and
we had to return, with the determination to revisit the Marrun
and prospect it thoroughly on a future trip.

We spent Christmas 1933 at a dismal little water-hole called
Jesotit, not far from the Kerio River. For the occasion we had
carefully saved up the half bottle of brandy which my mother had
given me with the customary strict instructions that it was to be
used in case of emergency only, and a tinned plum-pudding.
Yusuf rose to the occasion and produced an excellent dinner of
soup, smoked catfish, beautifully roasted guinea-fowl garnished
with wild spinach and mushrooms, and *posho* sauce, followed by
the plum-pudding. By New Year's Eve we were back in civilisation.

A month at our respective homes in the Highlands near Nairobi
found us as keen as ever to set forth and follow up the gold traces
we had discovered on our last safari. We were also beset by
visions of finding the fabled 'Queen of Sheba's Mines' which a
vague tradition suggested might lie in the far north of Kenya near
the Ethiopian border, somewhere in the vicinity of Lake Rudolf.

On the 5th of February, two days after my twenty-eighth
birthday, Nevil Baxendale, Yusuf and I set off in my old truck

which was loaded to capacity with provisions and gear. After a journey of about two hundred miles we arrived at Kapenguria, the then headquarters of Turkana Province; here we saw Arthur Champion, the Provincial Commissioner. He was a man of great experience and a qualified geologist. At one time he had served in the famous Corps of Guides on the North-West Frontier of India. After preliminary reticence while sizing us up, he became very helpful, gave us much valuable advice and issued us with a permit to prospect along the Kerio River as far as its mouth on Lake Rudolf. Champion was one of the old school of 'pukka sahibs'. An irreverent junior has related that on one occasion he found himself on the wrong side of a flooded river which it was necessary to cross. The safest way to cross a flooded river is to take everything off, thus lessening the drag of encumbering clothing, but Champion, a stickler for convention, was dressed in breeches, riding boots and jacket, and it was only after much persuasion that he consented to discard these. Nothing, not even the fear of drowning, would make him part with his shirt and helmet. Eventually the crossing was accomplished with the help of a naked Turkana and the loss of the helmet, and Champion, much embarrassed, landed safely on the opposite bank, busily trying to control his flapping shirt tails.

We made our first camp at the head of the Marich Pass along-side the Marrun River, where the road ended, not far from the place at which we had found the gold on our last safari. For a whole month we worked along this river and its tributaries, searching for the source of the gold. In the end we had to admit defeat and concluded that the reef which had originally shed the gold had long ago ceased to exist. Yusuf was sent off to purchase donkeys from the Turkana in the Kerio Valley while Nevil and I busied ourselves making pack-saddles from *gunny* (ordinary sack-cloth) bags, a long and tedious job. At last, Yusuf returned with a dozen strong but wild-looking donkeys and a couple of equally wild-looking Turkana and all was ready for us to start loading up the donkeys. Each had to be caught, no mean task. All went more or less well until the last donkey was loaded up with the kitchen gear which consisted of pots, pans and two empty four-gallon petrol cans or debbies. Meanwhile the other loaded donkeys were ahead grazing along down the steep trail leading to the plains below. The kitchen donkey, no doubt observing that he was being left behind, set off at a smart trot which soon changed into a headlong gallop, the pots, pans and debbies banging and clattering. This was too much for the other donkeys who, in their turn, set off down the pass at their best pace, shedding their loads as they went. Soon they disappeared out of sight. It was enough to make angels weep, especially the sight of Nevil's bed-roll careering down the steep hillside, and falling with a splash into the river below. It took us the rest of the day to collect the loads and to carry them down to the bottom of the pass where we found our transport grazing peacefully by the river's bank.

Three days later we reached Kolosia on the Kerio River and began our march to Lake Rudolf, stopping a day or two here and there in order to prospect the country. For three weeks we followed the sandy bed of the Kerio which for the most part is lined with doam palms (*Hyphaene coriacea*), and fine acacia trees (*Acacia elatior*), which afforded us welcome shade from the burning sun. At some points along the river there were shrubs (*Cordia gharaf*), which bore clusters of orange-coloured, rather glutinous berries. We ate quantities of them, not because we liked them but because we thought they might act as an antiscorbutic—in this we were probably right. Water could usually be obtained by digging a hole in the sandy river-bed.

Although game was not abundant, there was sufficient to keep us in meat. The commonest were guinea-fowl and the handsome Grant's gazelle (*Gazella granti*). At a water-hole called Lokaturr we met William Hale, the District Officer from Lodwar, the district headquarters. He had arrived in Kenya a year or so previously, and was very interested in wild life and a keen photographer. He had come to Lokaturr by camel safari and was touring the southern part of his area. We had a pleasant evening together and next morning went to look for elephant which Hale wanted to photograph. We found the tracks of a large bull in the river-bed and followed the spoor into a small acacia grove, where we came on him. While Hale was taking pictures the elephant must have got our wind, for he swung around facing us and advanced with his great ears outspread. As we had no wish to molest the old gentleman we took to our heels. Little did I realise that in the future William Hale and myself were to be closely associated.

3: *Exploring the shores of Lake Rudolf*

FOUR DAYS LATER our safari reached Lake Rudolf, the place where legend led us to hope the Queen of Sheba's mines might be found. Across the waters of the lake we could see the mass of Mount Kulal beckoning us from the east. This was supposed to be the end of our safari but we had found no traces of gold worth following up, and could not contemplate the thought of turning back. In spite of having no permit to visit the east side of the lake which was in another province, we decided to risk official displeasure and go and have a look at the mountain. (Permits were imposed because the area was so remote and also subject to raids by armed bandits from across the border and the authorities didn't want to take responsibility for people who might get into trouble and occasion the need for search parties.)

Our stock of food was almost finished, but, with the help of the local chief, Ebert, or Egbert as we called him, we managed to buy two loads of coarse hand-ground *sorghum* meal from Turkana who had small patches of cultivation along the lake shore. It was interesting to observe their method of cultivation. Girls threw short sharp stakes into the soft ground and poured a few seeds into the resulting holes; these they would then cover over with the aid of their toes.

The method of fishing which the Turkana used here was also unusual. A line of men would enter the water carrying inverted, saucer-shaped, open-work baskets about four feet in diameter. At a given signal these would be plunged into the lake and held down on the bottom with one hand. The fisherman thrust his other hand through an opening in the top of the basket and groped around for the catch, if any. It was some years later that a benevolent government instructed the Turkana in the use of nets.

50

In order to establish friendly relations with the meat-hungry Turkana, and to provide ourselves with cooking fat, Nevil shot a hippo. Unfortunately, unlike most of these creatures, it was as lean as a greyhound; none the less it was enjoyed by the Turkana.

As soon as our intention of going round the south of the lake to the east side became known to the Turkana, several of the younger men told us they wished to come with us. We chose only two, one was called Tobosh; we made it clear that we were not in a position to pay them a wage or to give them rations. They said this did not matter as they felt confident that we would shoot enough game to keep them filled with meat. Tobosh was a young man of about twenty years, well over six feet in height and perfectly proportioned. He came with us, as he had come into this world, without a stitch of clothing, nor any possession, not even a spear or sandals on his feet. The other, a smaller and older man whose name I no longer recall, claimed to know the east side of the lake, having been there on a raid some years previously; both proved invaluable.

The march to the south end of the lake was the hardest we had yet encountered. In many places cliffs came down to the water's edge, obliging us to make wide detours inland over the desolate and waterless Loriu Hills. At one stage it took the donkeys nine hours to cover a distance of six miles, as they crossed a waste of giant lava boulders. One poor brute died of sheer exhaustion and another had to be put out of its misery as it could go no farther. As we toiled to get the donkeys along, the intense heat was reflected on to our faces from off the never-ending lava. At last we left this terrible lava oven behind and reached a pleasant little cove called Nangwal at the south-west corner of the lake. Here there was plenty of coarse green grass for the poor animals to eat, shade under palm trees and a small pool of sweet water; (the water of Lake Rudolf is undrinkable owing to its chemical content). Since we had had nothing to eat for two days, apart from a glutinous mess of *sorghum* porridge, I shot two cormorants, but after a few mouthfuls neither of us could stomach the rank, fishy meat and gladly handed the remains over to our hungry Turkana. Here we gave the exhausted donkeys a rest for two days and spent the time fishing. Nevil caught a Nile perch (*Lates niloticus rudolfianus*), of about forty-four pounds and I a smaller one; they were sufficient to give all of us a good feed.

Leaving Nangwal on the third day we crossed two lava flows issuing from Teleki's volcano. The flows were so recent that we saw charred tree stumps along the edges. The volcano, which we climbed, was a huge heap of cinders about three hundred feet in height, with a small, partially filled-in, crater at the top. Five days' easy march brought us to Loingalane, an abandoned military post situated by a spring of good, slightly warm, water and set in the midst of a beautiful grove of palms.

Lake Rudolf, particularly the southern part, is often swept by the most violent gales which blow, night and day, from a south-easterly direction. Von Hohnel, who, with Count Teleki, discovered the lake, has written about the abnormal ferocity of the wind here. It is unbelievably powerful, the usual velocity being forty miles per hour but sometimes reaching over eighty miles per hour. Our food was often blown from our plates before reaching our mouths, or so covered in grit as to be inedible, and at some of our camps the only way to get rest at night was to sleep behind a parapet of stones. Teleki and von Hohnel too had been obliged to build parapets, and I think we came across some of them. Even so, by morning, our eyes, ears and clothing were covered with a layer of sand. Sometimes in the early afternoons the wind suddenly dropped. Then the heat would strike like the breath from a furnace. In spite of these discomforts our marches along the lakeshore were always full of interest. There was a great variety of birdlife, there were many crocodile and an occasional hippo was to be seen, and besides, there was the constant excitement of venturing into the unknown. In addition, there was the danger, more real than we realised at the time, of running into armed raiders from across the Ethiopian border, which kept us alert.

Little did we imagine that twenty-five years later there would be a hotel at Loingalane and bathing belles, iced drinks at their elbows, disporting themselves in a blue-tinted swimming pool, fed by the warm springs.

Since leaving the southern end of the lake we had met no inhabitants and the country appeared completely deserted but at Loingalane we were visited by a party of El Molo fishermen led by their young chief Kurru. All were naked except for Kurru, who sported a red fez and a striped pyjama jacket, possibly a legacy from the military occupation. He was an unusual looking African, light in colour with arms and chest covered with red hair. Perhaps he, too, was a legacy from the same source?

The El Molo tribe numbered barely a hundred souls and lived at this time on off-shore islands. Their sole diet was fish with an occasional crocodile or hippo. As a result, many, particularly the men, were malformed and rickety. They were the last human beings we were to see till the end of the safari.

I was very lucky to have Nevil as my companion on this exciting expedition; nothing ever got him down and often, during our long safari, when everything seemed to be going wrong and I was in the Slough of Despond, he would see the funny side of the situation—and most situations have one.

Loingalane lies about twelve miles due west from the foot of Mount Kulal. As we had come all this way to look at the mountain, we turned aside and followed up a broad stony river-bed, although by now we were almost certain that the mountain was volcanic and barren of gold. Near the slopes the stony ground was covered in good grazing and we wondered why there were no inhabitants. There was a fair amount of game about, such as Grant's gazelle, gerenuk (*Lithocranius walleri walleri*), oryx (*Oryx beisa annectens*), the beautiful Grevy's zebra (*Equus grevyi*), and a few reticulated giraffe (*Giraffa reticulata*). All were exceedingly shy and difficult to approach.

Soon there was no doubt that the mountain was worthless so far as finding gold was concerned, so we returned to Loingalane. The prudent course would have been to declare the safari at an end and to retrace our steps. Our stores were practically finished, we had only one load of *sorghum* meal and a little sugar left: all our tea and coffee and other forms of European food had been consumed, and our clothes and footwear were in tatters. In fact, I had taken to wearing a loin-cloth in order to save the remnants of my trousers for re-entry into civilisation. However, both of us had kept remarkably fit, so we decided to carry on and trust to luck. For the next eleven days we followed the lake-shore northwards, stopping a day or two on the way to prospect. For the most part the country was volcanic and, except for one valley, there was no chance of finding gold; here, however, there were outcrops of granitic rocks and quartz veins. They proved barren. At length we reached Moite Hill, about half-way up the lake, and found that it, too, was volcanic. On the 1st of June we had to turn back as by then even our *sorghum* meal was finished. We were also a little worried in case our long absence should come to the notice of the authorities and cause complications, such as search parties, which might lead to awkward questions.

During the last few days game had increased and was less shy and we shot a Grevy's zebra which provided several pounds of excellent cooking fat. Since leaving Loingalane we had not seen a living soul. It was only long afterwards that we learnt the reason. Apparently, shortly before our safari, a large band of Galubba raiders from across the Ethiopian border had terrorised the country along the lake, killing many Rendile tribesmen and carrying off women and stock.

At our last camp the donkeys were stampeded at night by lion. We had not been able to make a thorn enclosure, for lack of thorn bushes, and as the grazing was good we did not expect them to stray very far. Also, so far as we knew, there were no lion in the area and very few hyenas. But when day broke there was no sign of our donkeys so we all turned out to search in different directions. Tobosh finally found them: they were being stalked by two lions. Without hesitation, though quite unarmed, Tobosh got between the lions and their prey and drove the donkeys back, closely followed by the lions until he neared camp. One donkey was still missing and we never saw it again; it must have been killed and eaten. But for Tobosh's courageous action we might have found ourselves without transport and in a very serious situation.

The following night I was dozing off when Nevil suddenly remarked: 'Instead of walking two hundred weary miles around the end of the lake, what about going across it?' I thought, 'Poor Nevil, at last the hardships have proved too much for him, he has gone off his head'; indeed, I felt quite alarmed. Go across the lake—in what? But after Nevil had explained his idea in detail and knowing that he had been an amateur boat builder, I became infected by his enthusiasm. We talked far into the night, discussing ways and means of building a boat. Two days later we reached the narrowest point of the lake where we judged the distance across to be only about twelve miles. Indeed the opposite shore looked absurdly close and through our glasses we could even see small bushes growing on sandbanks.

The camp we chose for building the boat was at the mouth of a large sandy river-bed called the Serr el Tommia. This means the River of the Elephants. Here there was a certain amount of acacia timber but it was impossible to find a straight piece of wood, so we had to take small pieces and bind them together with a thong; fortunately there was shade under which to work. Meanwhile, after patching them up, I sewed a couple of canvas ground sheets together with the stout thread we used for repairing pack saddles—I was the sewing expert and Nevil the designer of the hull of the boat. Then came the most difficult task: binding the sticks together into the semblance of a boat frame. We used strips of raw hide for this purpose.

At last, on the 9th of June, the hull was ready. We made oars from acacia poles bound to boards taken from donkey boxes. A mast was stepped and a sail fashioned from our canvas bed-rolls. Nevil even contrived a most ingenious rudder and lee-board out of pieces of donkey boxes. All we now had to do was to wait for a favourable wind, launch the boat, set the sail and loll back in comfort while being wafted gently across the lake. How we pitied our staff and donkeys having to trudge through the heat and across the lava.

Next morning we took the boat down to the water and launched it. It proved somewhat unmanageable but at least it floated and we felt confident that with a few modifications it would serve our purpose. As it stood too high in the water we put in some ballast and we lowered the gunwales a little.

So full of confidence were we that we sent off the donkeys and staff laden with all the remaining supply of dried meat. We gave them instructions to make their way as best they could around the south end of the lake, and to meet us in about a fortnight's time at Egbert's village at the mouth of the Kerio. We told them that in case of dire necessity they could kill and eat one of the donkeys. Yusuf, always stout-hearted, volunteered to sail with us. Perhaps in his breast there were subconscious stirrings derived from his slave-trading forebears who had crossed the oceans in dhows laden with black ivory.

That evening we foolishly left the boat on the beach, loaded down with stones to prevent it from blowing away, and retired to our camp under the acacias. Next morning we found it a wreck; jackals had eaten all the thongs binding the frame. At first we were very depressed; the outlook was bleak indeed, since we now had no transport, and also no food. But the way the thing had happened was so funny that in the end we roared with laughter. We set-to and rebuilt the boat, using the inner bark of acacia trees for binding. This entailed considerable labour as all the suitable bark trees were over a mile inland and, besides this, since we had sent off our remaining provisions of dried meat with the foot party, we had to look for food which was not easy to find, for at this point of the lake game was scarce and fish almost non-existent. Fortunately, along the river bed there were thickets of *mswaki* or toothbrush scrub (*Salvadora persica*), which carried bunches of fruit, not unlike the English blackcurrant in appearance and flavour, but with a tang of nasturtium. However, *mswaki* berries alone were not sufficient to keep us going, and we had to spend a great deal of time foraging for more solid fare.

On one occasion I came on a goose sitting on its nest up in a thorny acacia tree. If I fired from below, undoubtedly I should hit it, but at the same time smash any eggs it might be sitting on; painfully and cautiously I climbed another thorny tree a few yards away until I was on the same level as the goose. Very carefully I took aim and blew its head off. That night we had three lovely fresh eggs and a tender goose. Next day Nevil returned to camp beaming—he had collected a dozen goose eggs. We told

On the march to Lake Rudolf, 1934
Beside our boat after crossing Lake Rudolf

Drop-spear trap

Mohamed the great elephant at Marsabit

Tusks of elephant who charged tent after I was mauled by lioness

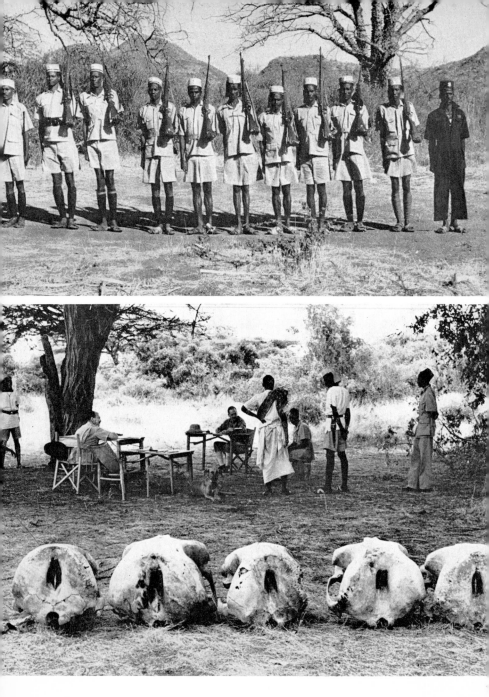

Some of my game scouts

Trial of Boran elephant killers with skulls of their victims

Yusuf to boil the lot and sat down in happy anticipation at having four eggs apiece. Unfortunately they were in a rather advanced state of development, but beggars can't be choosers, so we ate the lot.

When at last we once again had a boat, violent gales were blowing from the south and there could be no question of our sailing across. We built our hopes on the fact that at noon the wind usually dropped and a few hours later there was flat calm which lasted until about nine or ten p.m. We decided therefore to row across during the period of calm, hoping we could make the opposite shore before the gale got up again. As the sun set about six thirty p.m. we should have to make part of the crossing in the dark. We had no option.

At three p.m., ten days after the donkeys had left, we launched the boat and set off. Nevil and I rowed like mad and Yusuf bailed with an old cooking pot. As we progressed he was kept increasingly busy. By dark we judged ourselves to be half-way across. As there was no moon it was not possible to see the western shore but we could faintly discern the outline of the Loriu Hills which gave us a guide. Rowing doggedly, our hands raw and bleeding from the chafing of the rough wood of the oars, we had lost count of time when, suddenly, I heard a distant sound. We stopped rowing and listened, thinking it was the wind and meant the end of our chances. Then I recognised the noise as the croaking of multitudes of frogs. This meant that we must be near land. We redoubled our efforts and half an hour later hit the western shore. In the darkness it was impossible to tell where we had landed; all we knew was that it was on a pebbly beach.

My thoughtful mother had again provided a half-bottle of brandy with her usual instruction as to conditions in which we might open it. Nevil agreed with me that the appropriate emergency had arisen, so we shared it between us, pitying poor Yusuf who, being a devout follower of the Prophet, could not join in. Half an hour after we had landed the gale started, and blew like fury for the remainder of the night and till late into the morning. Had it caught us out at sea the boat could not have lived for more than a few minutes.

Dawn revealed that we had gone a good deal farther south than we had intended. We estimated that it had taken us about six to seven hours to make the crossing, the first ever recorded.

We tried to breakfast off the remains of the goose but it was so high that none of us could face it. About two p.m., the wind having abated, we set the sail and ran north before a gentle breeze and landed on a sandbank among a school of hippo. On the way Nevil had tried trolling with a large spoon, but a huge Nile perch struck and snapped the line and with it went our chance of dinner. We landed on a pebbly beach; there was not a bird in sight, so we went supperless to bed. By morning the wind was still blowing too strongly for us to venture out but we *had* to find something to eat for all we had had so far was one small cup of milk which Yusuf had managed to get from a poor Turkana. Luckily, just over the sandbank was an isolated pool covered with duck and geese. Nevil managed to bag four duck and a goose. We put the lot into a large pot and boiled them. They turned out to be very fat and tender and we enjoyed the best meal we had had for many a day. We felt sorry for the Turkana who have no bows and arrows and armed only with clubs and spears have little chance of ever having a feast of this sort.

We got going by about three-thirty p.m. but soon afterwards the wind dropped and we had to row until about eight o'clock, and landed on a muddy shore. Next morning, after an uncomfortable night due to mosquitoes and hippos, we threw caution to the winds and set sail in a moderate gale. We flew before the wind, keeping close inshore in case of an upset. By noon we reached Egbert's village, much to the astonishment of the inhabitants who had never seen a boat like ours. Unfortunately Egbert was away but his second-in-command produced a fat sheep and plenty of milk for which the three of us were very grateful. He was most anxious to have the wood of our boat, as there is absolutely no timber in the area. We took the craft to pieces, gave him the wood and kept the tarpaulin. The following day our men and donkeys arrived safe and sound and looking little the worse for their hard march.

We gave them a day's rest and the animals a chance to feed, then set off across the desert for Lodwar, the administrative headquarters, reaching it on the third day. Wearing my carefully preserved trousers, and Nevil trying to hide the holes in his, we called on Morgan, the District Commissioner, and William Hale, who were surprised to see us. They had last heard of us disappearing around the south end of the lake. They were even more astonished to learn that we had returned across the lake; at first they thought we were pulling their leg.

In those days the administrative offices and officers' houses consisted of no more than a collection of mud huts. The water system was camel-borne from the river below, and sanitation of the long-drop variety. We were given a very generous welcome and enjoyed our first civilised dinner. Next morning we said goodbye to our kind hosts and after making a few purchases at the local Indian shops set off on the long journey back.

For sixteen days we followed the Turkwel River, which was at this time of year fast-flowing and exceedingly muddy, to the top of the Turkwel Gorge. As we went along we prospected and at several points along the river got traces of gold in our pans, but nothing worthy of closer investigation. I used to get up at four in the morning, for at this time, even in a comparatively dull area, there is always something interesting to see: the spoor of the various animals which have been over the ground at night and the local bird life. At one point, when Nevil and I had gone ahead to look for a way through dense bush, our donkeys were put to flight by elephant and their loads, including a bag containing all my spare rifle ammunition, scattered. We never found the bag but it was discovered three years later by a Turkana and handed intact to the District Commissioner at Lodwar.

At the foot of the Turkwel Gorge a rhino came blundering into the safari and created a panic among the donkeys, who took off in all directions, shedding their loads as they went. It took us the whole day to recover our gear, so we had to camp on the spot. During the night there was a violent thunderstorm and between

the flashes of lightning and the crashes of thunder we could see
and hear the swollen Turkwel River rushing by. To add to the
wildness of the scene a herd of elephant came unexpectedly into
our camp. There were piercing trumpetings and the brilliant
flashes showed up huge shapes crashing away through the bush.
We were thankful that that night the donkeys had been secured
inside a particularly strong thorn enclosure.

There was a lot of game near our camp and the local Turkana
pestered us to shoot a buffalo for them. Since they live in a state
of semi-starvation, in a weak moment, we agreed, and set out to
hunt followed by many men, women and children. Soon we came
on the fresh tracks of a large lone bull. Ordering the crowd to
remain behind we went forward cautiously following the spoor;
then, suddenly, without warning, the buffalo appeared and came
straight at us. Nevil fired, hitting one of the beast's great horns;
this probably dazed it, but it came on. When it was almost
upon us I shot it in the point of the shoulder, causing it to swerve.
It rushed past us and collapsed a hundred yards away. Without
waiting to be called, or even ascertaining whether the buffalo
was dead, the hungry Turkana rushed up and settled on the carcase like a swarm of vultures.

The following morning we climbed a very steep and narrow
trail leading up to the top of the Turkwel Gorge. We skirted a
terrifying precipice, at one point a large boulder almost blocked
our path. The four leading donkeys managed to squeeze past,
their off-side loads literally overhanging the abyss, but the donkey
ahead of me which was carrying our bulky bed-rolls barged into
the boulder and its hind quarters swung round over the edge.
Just in time I grabbed it by the ears and shouted for help. Fortunately Nevil was close behind, and between us we managed to
haul it back on to the path.

We had intended continuing along the Turkwel as it looked
interesting from the prospecting point of view, that is to say we
saw quartz and granite, often an indication that gold may be
present, but the river was in high flood, making it impossible for
us to take samples from its bed. We might have had to wait
ten days for the water level to drop and we were at the end of our

resources. We therefore turned aside, descended once more into the Rift Valley and made for the Marich Pass. This had been the starting point of our safari; we returned to it on the 20th of July; though we had been away for nearly four months we found the truck was just as we had left it. We were disappointed at our lack of success as gold prospectors, but the trip had been so interesting that we felt it had been well worth while.

We asked our four Turkana, including Tobosh and the older man we had picked up at Egbert's village, whether they would like their wages in full or whether they would rather take over the nine remaining donkeys. Without hesitation they voted for the donkeys. It was a happy solution. We had become very attached to our animals and hated the thought of having to sell them to some trader who, in all probability, would have overworked and overloaded them. With the Turkana they would have an easy life, being called upon only occasionally to carry a few light loads. Besides the donkeys, we gave each man sufficient money to buy enough tobacco to keep him happy for a long time to come.

A few days after our return we heard that Vivian Fuchs (now Sir Vivian of Antarctica fame) had recently led an expedition to Lake Rudolf, the objective of which was to try to discover the geological formation of the Rift Valley lakes and in particular Lake Rudolf and to study the animals and the fish in the area. We also learned that two of his scientists, Dyson and Martin, had been lost. They had remained on the island while Fuchs returned to the mainland and then went down to the southern end of the lake. They had arranged to give fire signals, so long as one fire was seen every night all was well, if two were lit it meant that they were in trouble; but a night came when no fire was seen, nor was one lit on any of the succeeding nights.

When Fuchs rejoined the rest of the party and heard this he was alarmed and sent a message to the District Commissioner at Marsabit asking for an aircraft to be sent. It overflew the island and all the coastline of the lake without seeing a trace of the men. Later, an oar was found and identified as belonging to the expedition's Hudson boat, a craft made of canvas and about seven foot long, such as were used by the R.A.F. in the First World War. No doubt it had foundered in a sudden wind. A helmet belonging to Dyson or Martin was also found.

Soon after our return to Nairobi Nevil got engaged; his marriage brought our partnership to an end.

4: *Professional hunter, hotel manager, miner and dealer in beeswax*

EARLY IN 1935, having gained quite a lot of experience in the hunting field, I was offered my first assignment as a professional hunter. In those days there was no question of needing a licence to hunt. A man of experience would be taken on by a hotel or agency and would be responsible for transport, tents, supplies and stock and, of course, for the safety of his clients. It was his job to see that they didn't get into difficulties. Sometimes they nevertheless did, but if there were no risks involved in a big game safari they would have much less appeal. If a professional hunter made a few successful safaris then plenty of such assignments would come his way. The term 'White Hunter' was then in common use, as most of the professional hunters were Europeans.

On my first safari I had the good fortune to conduct two very charming people. They were a brother and sister called Ofenheim. Their father had been a surgeon, first in Vienna and then in London; Miss Ofenheim, who was about my age, was also a dedicated surgeon. Luck was with us and during a most enjoyable, though strenuous, three weeks of hunting in the Masai country near the Kenya-Tanganyika border, we succeeded in obtaining a lion, a buffalo and a rhino, apart from lesser game. What was even more valuable was that I established a life-long friendship with Miss Ofenheim, a remarkable woman who, in spite of possessing the means of independence, has sacrified her whole existence to her vocation.

Gethin and Hewlett, the firm which employed me as a hunter, owned, among other interests, a small hotel on the Kenya-Tanganyika border; after my safari they asked me to run it temporarily, during a period when a change of managers was taking place. This was something quite outside my experience but I agreed to help. Fortunately for everyone concerned there was an efficient resident housekeeper, so I did not have to experiment with the domestic side and was able to restrict my activities to keeping the staff and the mechanical gear in running order and, on occasion, taking my turn as barman.

Late one night one of our better-known politicians arrived, pale, shaking, clutching a revolver and gasping for a drink. After he had been supplied with a double I asked him what was amiss. He told me that a few miles back he had come on an enormous lion seated in the middle of the road. At first the king of beasts had refused to get up to allow the traveller to pass but after some time, yawning prodigiously, he had risen and slowly sauntered along the crown of the road. Every time the impatient motorist tried to pass, the lion turned around, and with rumblings in his throat, gave him a baleful glare. This performance continued right up to the gates of the hotel at which point the lion condescendingly went away. When I suggested that the lion was merely taking advantage of the illumination provided by the car's headlights, the motorist was not amused.

There were many slack periods when there was little for me to do. I availed myself of these opportunities to do some prospecting and exploring of the surrounding country. After two months a new manager named Ray Mayers arrived with his wife Helen; he and his family became great friends of mine. Soon afterwards Budge Gethin, director of the firm, agreed that I should continue my prospecting on a share basis; he would pay for my food and transport and we would share fifty-fifty in any returns.

The country near the hotel was a Game Reserve and gave me ample opportunity of observing animals, both large and small, while prospecting. Perhaps at this point I should make clear the difference between Game Reserves and National Parks, which may confuse some readers. So long as they cause no trouble, it is forbidden to kill animals in Game Reserves; but they are not the only inhabitants for Africans, and sometimes European farmers, also live in the Reserves. National Parks, on the other hand, have no inhabitants except for those who administer the Park for the benefit of the animals and that of the tourists who come to watch them. These may motor through the Park or, where such facilities are available, stay in approved sites. Having said this, I should add that in the days I am writing about only Game Reserves existed, for National Parks had not yet been created in Kenya.

It is probably about this time that I discovered that I much preferred watching animals to shooting them.

After prospecting a large area and finding only slight traces of gold I discovered a vein of pegmatite, a mixture of white quartz and pink felspar, containing sheet mica which looked promising. Samples were favourably reported on, so I started to work it. The market value of mica depends on its size and quality; the larger the sheet, the more valuable it is. To start with, the coarse grained pegmatite contained big sheets of mica but unfortunately at the end of four months the reef deteriorated into fine grained pegmatite which meant that the size of the mica became smaller, and was no longer a worth-while proposition so I abandoned the claim.

While I was working the mica I camped about a mile from the workings under some fine umbrella acacias which were laden with seed pods. The pods fell on my tent, slid down the sloping canvas and collected in heaps under the eaves. One bright moonlight night I became conscious of a curious sound around the tent. At first I could not place it, then it dawned on me that it was the noise of munching. Silently I got out of bed and looked out. The tent was surrounded by a large herd of impala busily picking up the pods; an unbelievably beautiful sight. Normally, antelopes are timid creatures but, like a lot of other animals, by night they appear to lose their fear of man. These impala became increasingly tame and every morning I watched a party of young males having a game of follow-my-leader; with heads and tails erect they would prance along in a line weaving in and out of the bushes, snorting and grunting. At certain times of the year these young males congregate, then there comes a day when one of them feels strong enough to challenge an older male, probably over a herd of females. They fight, and if the newcomer wins he takes over the harem which may number as many as sixty.

Suddenly one day the charming play of the young antelopes turned into tragedy. A pack of wild dogs 'came down like a wolf on the fold' and in a few minutes had torn one of the impala to pieces. This is literally their method of killing. Lions and leopards kill cleanly, always going for the throat of their prey, but each dog seizes a hold anywhere it can and tears out a mouthful of flesh while its quarry is still running. After this the impala dispersed, never to return.

Not very much is known about wild dogs. They are often associated with hyena, but there is no doubt that they are of the dog family though not closely related to the domestic dog. Ruthless killers, they will attack almost any animal but seem to have an instinctive fear of human beings, and though, if you come upon them suddenly, they may rush up in an alarming fashion, this will be out of curiosity and they will not attack. From what I have observed they seem to have quite a complicated family set-up and go in for a lot of ritual.

One day I climbed a hill called Lemeboti a few miles from my camp and came on a herd of over fifty Chanler's reedbuck or mountain reedbuck. A most unusual sight, for these beautiful animals, named after the famous explorer, are seldom seen in parties of more than six to eight.

While I was at this camp I was much bedevilled by a spotted hyena which used to come every few nights and steal from my tent. By some uncanny instinct it seemed to know when I was asleep. Among the things it stole were my boots from alongside my bed, a heavy iron kettle which was found a hundred yards away, and a cooking pot containing fat which I found a month later on the top of a hill three miles from camp.

Once, when I was walking along with my thoughts elsewhere, I almost collided with a rhino lying asleep. I do not know which of us was the more startled. I made for the nearest tree and swung behind it just in time as the rhino thundered past. I do not think it had any aggressive intentions—rhinos rarely do—probably it was simply trying to get away but, as the behaviour of rhinos is unaccountable, it is best to remove oneself from their path as quickly as possible.

An unusual scene I saw was that of a bat-eared fox sitting within a few feet of a hyena, both apparently completely at their ease. A more unlikely association it is difficult to imagine, for the hyena was a good hundred pounds in weight and these animals are at all times ready to eat anything, dead or alive, while the bat-eared fox was a dainty little creature scaling perhaps five pounds.

One day, while I was at the mica workings, a party of twelve Masai warriors appeared, dressed in their finery complete with spears and shields. They told me they were going on a lion-hunt. I would have liked to go with them but, the area being a Game Reserve, I thought this might be a little tactless. Also, an old Masai who was sitting nearby assured me it would be a waste of time because though the modern young *moran* warriors always made a great show of going off lion-hunting, as soon as they were out of sight they were apt to lie down under trees and then come back in the evening, hold a dance and boast of how they had chased a lion for hours on end but lost it. In *his* day the old man said that the *moran* made no fuss until *after* they had killed the lion, and he waxed indignant about the shortcomings and softness of modern youth.

Every two or three weeks I went into Kajiado, the nearest township, to replenish stores at the other hotel owned by the firm I was working for. It was now managed by a very charming Mrs Lindsay, and I was always invited to stay for a meal. I greatly looked forward to her pleasant and friendly company. Often we talked into the night and when I took my leave I was invariably the richer by some quite unlooked-for luxury which would make my solitary camp life easier. The District Commissioner and his wife were equally hospitable and I spent many an agreeable evening in their company. In fact, the nicest feature of life in Kenya in those days was the genuine kindness one met with wherever one travelled.

The mica venture having ended in disappointment, I began to look around for some new occupation. By now, having become a confirmed wanderer, I could not, in spite of being chronically hard up, bring myself to seek a settled job. Early in 1936 I conceived the idea of making my fortune by trading in the native reserves along new lines; beeswax was to be my main commodity. Certain tribes are great honey hunters. In order to encourage the bees, they fix the honey-barrels, made out of a hollowed log, in tall trees that can be seen all over the tribal area. They also make use of the honey-guide, as I have often done, to find bees' nests. This curious bird, a little smaller than a thrush, is known in most parts of Africa where there are bees. It has a very distinctive chattering call and if you whistle to it it takes in that you intend to follow it and flies from tree to tree or from shrub to shrub till it leads you to the bees' nest. African tradition insists that some honey must be left for the bird, if not, the next person who comes along will be led to a snake or to some other dangerous beast. In fact it is the grubs contained in the comb which the honey-guide is really interested in. This is surely one of the most curious symbiotic (mutually beneficial) associations between a bird and a human being.

Unfortunately, the Africans have not learned the first principle of bee-keeping which consists in seeing that each hive has a queen bee excluder—a partition inside the hive with an entrance large enough to admit a worker bee but too small for the queen with the result that the excluder curtains her off. I often tried to explain this to them but without success. They eat some grubs but it is the honey they are really keen on; most of it is made into mead. The residue of the comb, which contains valuable beeswax, is regarded as rubbish and thrown away, so I thought it would be an easy matter to persuade the tribesmen to save up their honey combs once they realised that these were of value. I succeeded in firing the enthusiasm of two of my farming friends who agreed to finance my new venture on a share basis. I knew too that, apart from beeswax, there were other products only waiting to be exploited, such as gums and leopard skins.

Once more I set off to the Kiero Valley, whose inhabitants I knew to be great bee-keepers and connoisseurs of mead.

First I made for Kabarnet, the headquarters of the Baringo

district, and then I called on Murphy, the District Commissioner, to whom I outlined my idea for helping to bring prosperity to the inhabitants of his district— He was most co-operative and promised to explain the virtues of collecting beeswax to his people.

In the meantime I planned to buy fifteen donkeys and set off on a safari embracing all the principal honey areas of the Baringo and Elgeyo districts, buying all waste comb and, as an object lesson, processing it in front of the local people. This was a very simple matter since all that was involved was boiling the comb in water, straining it and allowing it to cool, by which time the wax would form a solid crust on top of the water. I also intended to buy any leopard skins that were available.

I went to Karpeddo because it was the best place to buy donkeys, obtainable here from the Turkana tribesmen at twelve shillings apiece. I also hoped to get samples of gum. At Karpeddo I met the District Commissioner from Lodwar who had come on a tour with a camel safari and was holding a *baraza* (meeting), of the local Turkana worthies. They had assembled in large numbers for the occasion dressed in all their barbaric splendour. Many wore full-length leopard skins draped over their backs. Their heads were adorned with ostrich plumes and they held glittering, polished spears in their hands. But a Turkana's chief glory is his hair-do. His own hair and often that of departed relations is woven together into a mat which hangs down the back of the neck. This is smeared with blue clay until rigid. At various points dried cows' teats are let into the head-dress forming sockets for ostrich feathers. From the base of the *chignon* a long thin sliver of oryx horn curls up on a level with the head, the end adorned with a pom-pom of black ostrich feathers. Some of the older men who had outlasted numbers of their kin possessed *chignons* reaching down to their waistline. As can be imagined, a hair-do takes several days to perform. In order to protect its shape the owner, when sleeping, uses the head-rest; I have already mentioned it is eight to ten inches high and during waking hours does duty as a stool. Since the hair-dos once set are not interfered with for a long time, unwelcome guests are apt to take up lodgings in them and in order to discourage these a long thin iron skewer is carried thrust under the mat.

Another striking feature of male adornment is a leaf-shaped metal plate about three inches in length which, hooked into a perforation in the bridge of the nose, hangs down over the mouth. It muffles their speech and is only used on ceremonial occasions. The lower lip is also perforated, and an ivory ball, with a collar-stud shaped stem, is thrust into the perforation and hangs down on the chin. This last bauble when not in use naturally leaves a hole in the lower lip—a convenient outlet for jets of unwanted tobacco juice.

With the help of Gregory Smith, the District Commissioner, I soon collected fifteen first-class donkeys and a quantity of gum. This was a kind of frankincense obtained from a small bush tree (*Boswellia hildebrandtii*). Unfortunately it proved to be of little market value.

After my past experiences, I now used proper pack-saddles for the donkeys; these made a great difference to their comfort and saved much time and trouble on the march. On this occasion I followed a new route over the Kamasia Range. A steep ascent led to a high plateau. At one point, while traversing a narrow path skirting a ravine, one of the donkeys went over the edge and fell about twenty-five feet, landing with a thud on the sandy river-bed. I scrambled down expecting to find it dead, or at least badly injured, but it got up quite unhurt except for a slight graze on its rump. On the top of the Ribco Plateau I found quantities of ripe fruit growing on a thorny shrub (*Carissia edulis*). I ate a great amount of them as an antiscorbutic.

I visited all the likely centres of bee-keeping tribesmen. All appeared to be interested and promised to keep their honey-comb for me to buy the next time I came round. One evening I happened to make my camp not far from a mission station. While I was busy off-loading my weary donkeys a European stepped out of the bush and without introduction remarked 'Do you know Jesus?' I was somewhat taken aback and fumbling for words replied that I had not met him recently. This of course was just what he expected to hear from a trader—a notoriously immoral and godless fellow—and it fired his missionary zeal to 'pluck a brand from the burning'. I was subjected to a sermon and presented with a handful of tracts and asked up to supper at the station, where I knew there were several more of his friends. Feeling a little apprehensive I fortified myself with a couple of stiff tots of rum before announcing myself at the mission. Evidently I must have acquitted myself with credit as I enjoyed a pleasant evening without any attempts being made to induce me to mend my ways.

For the next four months I continued my wanderings, stopping a few days here and there, whenever there seemed to be a chance of buying beeswax. I seldom met anyone of my own kind to talk to, and being young and vigorous there were times when I was assailed by the urge for the fair sex. I was sorely tempted to acquire a native girl, particularly at a camp on the banks of a little river where the women used to come to draw water and to bathe. Two girls made a habit of displaying themselves, with the obvious intention of attracting my interest. In other places the girls certainly had the original mini-skirts and if they liked one these became mini-er and mini-er. On such occasions the only cure was to seize my rifle and go off, hunting in the hills, and stay out until I was bone-weary (though sometimes, I must admit, I left it a little late). Contrary to general belief, in the eyes of Africans, there is no stigma attached to a white man consorting with a native woman. In fact, I was asked by my men whether some physical impediment precluded me from satisfying a natural urge.

On one trip along the Kerio River I came on the camp of a Game Warden. He had arrived a few days previously to carry out a poisoning campaign against hyena and baboon which had become pests, the former attacking and killing livestock and the latter stealing crops. The camp was unlike any I had seen before. I found the warden seated in a bower of freshly-cut green branches, and for a distance of twenty feet around the ground was strewn with green leaves. At his invitation I pitched my camp close by. Tom Oulton was a character. He had come to Kenya at the turn of the century and was now in his sixties. He was an enthusiastic British Israelite and believed implicitly in the 'pyramid prophecies'. He explained to me how certain experts, after making careful and complicated measurements of the Egyptian pyramids, had reached the theory that these represent a map of the past and the future of the world. Oulton also had odd dietary fancies, one of which precluded him from eating any form of immature food, such as lamb, unfertilised eggs. Another of his fads was that the head of his bed must always point to the north, regardless of the shape or situation of the room, or tent, he might be sleeping in. We used to have long talks together and he kept me enthralled with stories of his early days in Kenya. He strongly advised me to apply for a job in the Game Department; indeed we talked for three or four days on this subject. But even after this I took no action, though all my life I had wanted to be a Game Warden.

Having done all I could to persuade the tribesmen to store their honeycombs I returned home, intending to revisit the area in three months' time, when I hoped there would be plenty of beeswax waiting for me to collect.

In the meantime I took several parties of tourists on photographic expeditions after big game; we travelled in a saloon car and a box-bodied Chevrolet safari car. The first of these tours was to the great Serengeti Plains in Tanganyika Territory. This, as I have explained, was before the days of National Parks and it was permissible to shoot most animals except lion. Crossing the plains with their teeming herds of wildebeest, zebra, eland and Thomson's gazelle, we made our camp under a large granite *kopje* called Seronera where today the National Park lodge stands. In the three days we were there we saw thirty-six lions. They had become so used to being fed that it was scarcely necessary to go out to look for them, for as soon as a car was heard, they would appear.

One morning, having located a pride of seven lion, I went out into the plains and shot a zebra and started to tow the carcase back to the trees where we had seen the pride. When still four hundred yards away two lionesses and six cubs of about a year old appeared, coming as fast as they could. I had barely time to jump out of the truck, unfasten the tow rope and get aboard again before they were on the carcase. In the distance we noticed a fine black-maned lion, the father of the pride, making his leisurely way towards us. By the time he reached the kill it was half eaten. With a rush and a mighty growl he scattered the others and got down to the feast alone. In prides, etiquette is very strict. The lioness kills; then, as a rule, the lion alone has his fill and only when he is satisfied may the lioness and the cubs have their meal. On this occasion one of the cubs, more daring than his fellows, came too close and received a buffet from its father which sent him sprawling. But once having asserted his authority the lion good-naturedly permitted his family to join in. Later one of the cubs, having had his fill, came and sat under the shade of the truck and looked up at us with mild curiosity.

One evening we came on a magnificent lioness on a rock, gazing out across the plains. She was sculptured by the setting sun, as though she were part of the granite on which she lay. I wondered how many lions had lain on the self-same rock during countless centuries while the human race was still in its cradle. It was a thought which made me reflect that though civilised man has spent untold treasure on preserving ancient buildings and works of art fashioned by the hand of man, yet he destroys these creatures which typify the perfection of ageless beauty and grace. And he does so for no better reason than to boast of a prowess achieved by means of a weapon designed by man to destroy man, or to use its skin to grace some graceless abode.

In my mind's eye I could see the vast herds of wild creatures on these great plains swept away by progress, as they have been swept away in other lands and, in their stead, herds of degenerate livestock; it was a depressing vision.

My two clients, Mr and Mrs Pflieger from Belgium, were the kind who had no desire to kill. Their rewards were the excellent photographs and unforgettable days spent in the midst of nature at its proudest.

On the journey back to Kenya we came on a rare creature, a pangolin or scaly ant-eater (*Manis temmincki*), a quaint armadillo-like mammal, covered with horny brown, overlapping scales or plates, about three feet in length. At our approach it curled itself into a tight ball which, such was its strength, it was quite impossible to unwind.

My next clients were an elderly couple from the States. I took them to the now famous Lake Amboseli which, in those days, was little known. After a successful morning photographing rhino and elephant, I suggested to them that they might like to rest until the afternoon. They agreed and retired to their tent. About two hours later I saw the man come out of his tent in full marching order, complete with camera, tripod, binoculars and knee-boots. (He had told me he was 'scared of snakes' and therefore took off his boots only on going to bed.) Thus accoutred he set off purposefully. I grabbed my rifle and hurried after him. When I caught him up I asked where he was bound for. He replied that he was 'off for a hike in the woods'. As we walked up a glade a bull buffalo galloped out of the bush straight towards us. I was fully occupied in watching it approach. It rushed past without, I think, any aggressive intent. I then looked around expecting to see my client busy with his camera but he was nowhere to be seen. Then, hearing a slight disturbance in a nearby thicket I tactfully turned my back and called. Presently he appeared, rather dishevelled, and gasped 'Boy, that was the meanest-looking animal I ever saw in all my life'. I complimented him on his presence of mind and off we went again. A little way on, we were passing a clump of bushes when, with loud snortings, a rhino burst forth. This was too much for my client. We headed for camp, all thought of a hike in the woods forgotten.

Towards the end of March I returned to my beeswax trading and revisited the areas where I expected to find the tribesmen waiting with sackfuls of wax. I was disappointed, for few had taken the trouble to save up their comb. After devoting nearly two-and-a-half years to trying to persuade the tribesmen to save wax I decided it was a hopeless task.

Some friends of mine, the Browns, consisting of a mother, daughter and two sons, owned a hunting lodge near Isiolo on the borders of the Northern Frontier District. They asked me to run it and to try to develop it into a centre for hunting and photographic safaris. These hunting lodges, copied from India, are small camp-style hotels consisting of thatched buildings. Visitors usually bring their own food. Here the climate was about the nicest in Kenya; never very hot or very cold. I agreed to try my hand.

Early in June I set off with my donkeys to walk the two hundred miles to Isiolo. I was accompanied by a Mr and Mrs G, who had come along for the sake of the adventure, and by John Brown. Mrs G was a small, slight woman who, in spite of her delicate appearance, was completely fearless; hard as nails she never for a moment faltered on our long march.

She had had a tragic past. While out on a foot safari with her first husband in a remote part of Northern Rhodesia, he had been taken ill with black-water fever and had died. To find herself in the wilds with no European man to help her must have been a terrible situation, but undaunted she took charge of the porters and walked back to civilisation.

In about three weeks we reached the hunting lodge at Isiolo where I was, so I thought, to start my career as a hôtelier.

PART TWO

I find my Vocation as a Game Warden

5: *Putting down poaching*

THE DAY AFTER MY ARRIVAL at Isiolo, I received a telegram from the Game Department offering me the job of Game Warden in charge of the Northern Frontier District; evidently Oulton had put in a good word for me. I wired back my acceptance. It was then arranged that the Acting Chief Game Warden, Frank Clark, should come to Isiolo to interview me. He was a tremendous character who, years earlier, had poached ivory in the French and Belgian Congo.

A few days later he appeared. Our interview was mutually satisfactory, and in July 1938 I was enrolled as Temporary Assistant Game Warden at a salary of thirty pounds a month.

After a few days at my home I collected equipment at the Nairobi headquarters of the Game Department and received my orders: they were to carry out extensive foot safaris throughout the Northern Game Reserve, as it was known at that time. I then returned to Isiolo where, owing to the kindness of the Brown family, I was able to use the hunting lodge as my base—there was then no official residence for a Game Warden.

I was eager to get off on safari as soon as possible, but first I had to mend all my donkey saddlery and engage a few men as Game Scouts. At the end of a fortnight all was ready and I set off on my first safari as a Game Warden. It lasted three and a half months, during which time I crossed the Northern Game Reserve from south to north. I intended this safari to be a general reconnaissance of my area with the intention of getting to know the country, the amount of game and the incidence of poaching.

Although I had not planned the expedition as an anti-poaching patrol, I in fact caught twenty-five poachers, most of whom were

79

later convicted and punished for various offences against the game laws. The majority of the poachers were Turkana tribesmen.

The Turkana hunt with the aid of dogs. A couple of Turkana will leave their *manyatta* (village) with half a dozen mongrel dogs trained to bay up such animals as oryx which, after a short chase, invariably turn on the dogs and stand to fight (and woe betide any dog which comes within the sweep of the oryx's long rapier-like horns). While thus engaged it is an easy matter for the poacher to run up and spear the animal. Larger animals such as giraffe, elephant, rhino and buffalo are stalked and also speared from close quarters.

One of the Turkana I arrested was found to be in possession of traps which consisted of raw-hide nooses. These nooses are laid on the ground along well-used game paths. The loop of the noose is placed on a circular frame about twelve inches in diameter, resembling a hubless wheel with innumerable spokes. The inner ends of the spokes converging on the centre are sharpened. The contrivance is placed over a hole about six inches in depth and carefully covered over with grass and earth; the free end of the noose is fastened to the middle of a heavily notched stick several inches thick and about four feet in length. The unsuspecting victim coming along the path steps on the wheel and its foot goes through. In sudden panic it dashes away with the wheel firmly attached to its foot by means of the sharp spokes. The noose gradually tightens with the weight of the stick being dragged along; in time the wheel may be kicked off but by then the noose is firmly fast. Finally the animal is followed up by the poacher and found in an exhausted condition. It is then either speared on the spot or driven back to the poacher's camp and despatched.

I came on a Grevy's zebra with one of these nooses around a fore foot. The attached stick had been banging against the creature's hind legs which were raw and bleeding. In fact it was in such a state that I deemed it kindest to put it out of its suffering. The Turkana poacher swore it was not his work, but I felt like tying one of his own nooses around his neck and dragging him along for a day's march. This is undoubtedly an exceedingly cruel form of trap but is the 'civilised' steel gin trap any less cruel? How many hundreds of thousands, perhaps millions, of animals have suffered nights of unspeakable agony, held fast in the toothed jaws of gin traps, to provide furs for fashionable and 'civilised' women and civic dignitaries during the past century? Even to this day steel traps are used on farms in Kenya against leopards, hyena and other predators.

When I was at Wamba, a small village at the south end of the Mathews Range, the local Samburu headman came to my camp and told me about a rhino which had killed a woman while she was out gathering firewood in a valley some fourteen miles to the north. Besides killing the woman it had chased a number of people who had had narrow escapes. As it was part of my duty to deal with dangerous animals, I instructed my servant, Benua Jawali, to pack up some food and my bed roll, in case I had to spend the night out, and to put them in my car which had been brought to Wamba from Isiolo by a friend. Accompanied by a young missionary who had come to see the fun (I am always rather shocked when missionaries show pleasure in hunting and I think St Francis would share my view) I set off for Ngeng. When I arrived in the valley I was met by a Samburu who told me that that very morning he had been chased by the rhino and that it was now lying up in a thicket on the hillside. Numbers of spectators had gathered on the opposite slope to view the proceedings. Cautiously we entered the thicket. The wind was variable and without warning the rhino appeared, rushing upon us with distinctly hostile intent. Luckily my shot turned it and it careered down the valley where eventually we found it dead. It had an old and festering wound in one shoulder, caused in all probability by a spear, which no doubt accounted for its aggressive nature.

Late in the afternoon, on our way back to Wamba, we met Benua Jawali walking along the track carrying my bed roll on his head. At the last moment he had forgotten to put it in my car and without a second thought had set off on foot to bring it to me. He had covered twelve miles through country strange to him and abounding with elephant and rhino. I was much touched by his loyalty and devotion. He was a man in his sixties, and I certainly would not have expected him to do what few younger men would have undertaken in the circumstances.

At one of my camping places in a narrow valley in the Ndoto Mountains called Lodwar (this means the place of cattle-sickness or rinderpest), I had shot half a dozen chestnut-bellied sandgrouse. Benua Jawali hung them up for the night in a tree under which he was sleeping. He woke up to see the hind legs of a leopard beside his face; it was reaching up to take the sandgrouse. The following night I woke to find the same leopard in my tent standing by the foot of my bed. The flash of my torch caused it to make off. Although there were a lot of leopard in the area under my control I seldom had much trouble with these beautiful and intelligent animals. I know it is said that the leopard is a killer and kills for the love of killing. I do not believe this; certainly, a hungry leopard will take a goat but it is only when he gets into a goat enclosure and the animals mill around in a confined space that he kills wantonly; occasionally also, a young leopard, like any other young predator, may lose its head and kill for the pleasure of it, but as a rule an adult leopard only kills for food, so, where there is plenty of game about, they don't give much trouble. I never came across a man-eating leopard though they are perhaps the most courageous of all animals and in ninety-nine cases out of a hundred a wounded leopard will charge whereas quite often a lion will try to get away.

The next morning I took a walk up the dry Lodwar river-bed and came on two huge old bull elephants. The larger carried tusks of at least one hundred and thirty pounds each. The local Samburu told me that the two elephants had been in the valley for many years and that they never molested anybody. Cattle could graze alongside them without fear. I wondered how old the big one was, perhaps eighty or ninety or even a hundred years old? Such patriarchs are often found accompanied by one or two younger bulls. Probably with increasing age an elephant likes peace and quiet, away from the bickering and nagging cows and calves; his companion or companions are no doubt his bodyguard, perhaps detailed off by the herd to look after Grandpa?

A few marches to the north, in the South Horr Valley, I camped under a giant acacia tree; its bark smooth and polished by countless years of rubbing by elephant. The Samburu told me that it was the favourite tree of a big elephant which was in the habit of carrying a large stick with which he gently moved goats and sheep out of the way. I scoffed at the story but subsequent knowledge of the ways of elephant has made me wary of dismissing unlikely tales about them.

Continuing my safari, I rounded Mount Nyiro which was the northern boundary of the Game Reserve. It is an impressive mountain rising to a height of over nine thousand feet. One of my camps was at a little spring called Lararok which issued out from underneath a large rock at the western base of the mountain. Here the Samburu complained bitterly about the depredations of hyenas. One man showed me recently healed scars on his legs and said that one evening while returning to his *manyatta* he had been attacked by three hyenas and had only just managed to escape by climbing a small tree. He said that even then the hyenas had tried to get at him by jumping up. It is fairly unusual for hyena to attack people, but if one is very hungry and the victim runs away the hyena takes advantage of the situation.

The only efficient method of dealing with hyena is to poison them with strychnine. The Samburu agreed to provide a moribund ox as bait. It was killed and the meat cut up into pieces about the size of a tennis ball, in each of which I made an incision and inserted a dose of strychnine. The poison bait was then distributed among the Samburu who were told to place it along paths and around their *manyattas* in the late evening. Next morning more than twenty hyena were found dead, and unfortunately also one leopard and four jackals. Jackals are very harmless animals which only occasionally take a stray lamb or goat and perform a useful task in de-stocking the country, which in most parts is grossly over-stocked; the hyena, for that matter, is also extremely valuable in this respect. But on this occasion I had to act on complaints and do away with them.

On my return journey I arrived late one evening at Barsaloi, an old abandoned government post situated on high ground overlooking a broad sandy river-bed of the same name. Just below the camp in the river-bed was a small pool of water. Soon after sundown many elephant began to appear till finally the river-bed was one heaving mass of animals struggling to get at the water. The noise was deafening and continued until near dawn. I set off early to follow them up along the river-bed. Eventually their tracks led past a small hill which I climbed. There below me was a great herd spread out feeding; it was a stirring sight. I counted in the region of three hundred animals. Among the many bulls were four carrying tusks of a hundred pounds and over. I saw two pairs mating, a very rare sight which I had not witnessed before. The act was performed in the manner common to most animals. The only unusual feature was that a number of cows and calves gathered in a circle round the pair and appeared to be greatly excited. I spent the whole morning sitting on the hilltop with my glasses, fascinated by the scene.

On my return to camp I found that my Game Scouts had arrested two Turkana tribesmen who looked to them suspicious characters because they carried spears which had been bent and rather carelessly straightened, and to all appearances seemed to have been used recently. I had the men up for questioning. Suddenly they took fright and bolted; the whole camp set off in pursuit. One was caught almost immediately, the other took a headlong leap off the bank on to the sand twenty feet below where he found a Game Scout with spear poised waiting for him. This scout was followed by another who landed on the fugitive from the top of the bank. It was not the poacher's lucky day. Once more they brought them along for questioning, this time in irons. When the two men were asked to explain their strange behaviour they readily admitted that they had speared a giraffe and had been carrying some of the meat and a portion of skin when they unexpectedly blundered into my camp. Hurriedly they had hidden the meat and skin in a hollow tree and had then walked brazenly in, saying that they were on their way to Isiolo to look for work. They found work, hard work, in one of His Majesty's prisons.

Giraffe in the Serengeti

A few days later, at the end of a day's march in hilly country, I had gone ahead to choose a suitable camping place near water. The only level piece of ground I could see was in a grove of trees which unfortunately was already occupied by a large bull elephant. He was asleep, leaning up against one of the trees. As it was getting late and I was disinclined to go further I decided to evict him. Lodogia, my Game Scout, and I went up to within fifty yards and shouted, but the elephant was dead to the world. I told Lodogia to bang on a dead tree trunk but still there was no response. Going closer I produced a police whistle and blew with all my might. The elephant woke up, swung round and came straight for us. We had to fly for our lives. After seeing us off, he returned to his retreat to continue his interrupted slumbers. I had to halt the donkey column some way back and make an uncomfortable camp. It is a common belief that a whistle will move elephants; mine certainly moved this one!

Lodogia was one of my best men and one of the first I seconded as a scout. I did so because he came from the Mathews Range, which I wanted to explore. Tall, slight and very quiet, he was always polite and never rowdy, even when he had had more than enough drink; besides this he was a first class tracker, knew every inch of the country and the hide-outs of the leading poachers and was therefore very useful to me.

The later stages of my safari took me along the northern borders of European farms. These were known as T.O.L.s (Temporary Occupation Licences) and lay within the Game Reserve. The ranches in this region were enormous and ran to ten and twenty thousand acres. They were leased from the Government by people who had smaller ranches further south but who hoped that by getting this land on a temporary basis they might be able to hold on to it—in fact, it was really a semi-legalised form of land grab. I soon discovered that the Africans employed by the occupiers were engaged in large-scale poaching, apparently without any restraint from the farmers. I arrested a number of offenders and sent them off to the nearest magistrate for trial. As no Game Warden had ever before taken such a step my zeal met with considerable opposition from the farmers. Allowing farms within a Game Reserve was an unsatisfactory situation from every point of view.

A day's march short of my headquarters at Isiolo I camped on a small stream called the Ngare Ndare. While having breakfast two Rangers arrived from patrol, and close behind was a baby giraffe. They said it had followed them a long way. Quite fearlessly it came up and, leaning over the table, licked my face. Obviously it had lost its mother. There was little I could do. It was out of the question to take it along with the safari and I had no means of feeding it. I therefore decided to take it back to where it had been found. At first it followed obediently, later it became weary and I had to push it along. Finally, when both of us were nearing exhaustion, a small herd of giraffe appeared ahead. Much to my relief the youngster spotted them and at once set off at a gallop to join them.

Soon after my return to Isiolo I went to Nairobi to meet the Chief Game Warden[1] who had just returned from Malaya after being seconded to that country for one year to advise the government on game conservation. Archie Ritchie was a man of outstanding personality and presence and all of us who served under him came to respect and love him. At the outbreak of the First World War, impatient to see action, he joined the French Foreign Legion, then, after being invalided out, at the end of a year, he joined the Third Battalion of the Grenadier Guards. He was wounded at the battle of Loos and awarded the Military Cross in 1915. He was wounded again on the Somme in 1916 and a third time near Ypres in 1917 and made Chevalier of the Legion of Honour. He had a brilliant brain and a superlative command of the English language. With his abilities he might have gone far, but he was devoid of ambition and was happiest indulging his hobbies: natural history, botany and photography. In a sur-

---

[1] Some of the terms used by the Game Department are a little confusing. The use of ranger or scout for the rank and file was interchangeable and I myself was at one time described as a Game Ranger and another as a Game Warden.

prisingly short space of time he would master his subject and turn to something new. In appearance he was striking, being over six feet tall and broad in proportion, with a shock of white hair and a voice to match his size. With such a chief one was bound to give of one's best.

I was equally fortunate in working under Gerald Reece (later Sir Gerald Reece, Governor of British Somaliland), the administrative officer in charge of the Northern Province. Like Archie Ritchie, he was a born leader with a fine record in the First World War. He was devoted to the Northern Province and to its nomadic peoples and took a keen interest in the wild life of the country. To his juniors he was always known as 'Uncle'. We were at first a little in awe of him but he had the happy gift of putting people at their ease—even after reprimands. In our early acquaintance, being very much my senior in age and office, I always, as was proper, addressed him as Mr Reece. One day, in reply to a letter, he sent me a note ending 'Please do not call me "Mister", either "Reece" or "Gerald," whichever you prefer.' Naturally, from then on, it had to be 'Gerald.'

As I mentioned earlier there was no official residence at Isiolo for a Game Warden and it was only through the kindness of the Browns that I was able to continue using the lodge. Later it was decided to sell the place which was bought for a ridiculously small sum by the Government and became my headquarters. The buildings were of temporary construction, consisting of a group of *rondavels* (round thatched huts) and a large central thatched cottage. It was picturesque in its romantic setting, overlooking the plains and hills of the Northern Province.

I was thirty-two years of age and, having at last obtained a more or less settled job with prospects of a future, I began to have notions about acquiring a wife but, having little or no experience in this field, I was rather at a loss as how to set about the project. My dilemma was nearly solved for me by a very charming French girl who was a guest of the Browns and who seemed to take a fancy to me. But this was not to be. The collapse of the budding romance led to near heartbreak, on my side at least. But ultimately I came to the conclusion that all was for the best, for the

life I was going to lead for the next few years would be a hard one
and far from settled. I have lost touch with Juliette but, if she
ever reads these lines, I wish her well and hope she is as happy as
she deserves to be.

About this time I often met Brian Abbay, a most colourful
character who was also a guest of my host. Abbay was a retired
Indian Army Colonel of the old school. He had served in the
Boer War, the First World War and in various campaigns on the
frontiers of India. If his ghost will forgive me for saying so, he was
as tough as an old boot, both physically and mentally, and scared of
nothing. He had a great passion for the bush and for big game
hunting, and even tried, unsuccessfully, to tame a wild dog puppy.
Later he became my guest on several safaris, during which, with
his reminiscences of his many, and often lurid, experiences, he
was a most entertaining companion. On one occasion, while
staying with me, he went off on a buffalo hunt. He succeeded in
shooting a buffalo but it got away wounded; following up the
tracks Abbay was charged at close quarters and knocked over.
He told me how he avoided the sweep of the buffalo's horns by
clinging to a fore-leg until finally the buffalo caught him in the
head with the edge of a horn and he was knocked out. He was
brought back to consciousness by an over-powering odour and
found himself looking up into the face of a Turkana girl who had
his head pillowed in her lap and was bathing his face with cold
water. Although badly bruised, the tough Colonel was little the
worse for his experience.

A few years later he came to an untimely, but not inappropriate,
end off Lamu Island on the Kenya coast. The boat he was
sailing capsized and he was drowned. He had often told me that
he hoped to die with his boots on. From all accounts his funeral
was in keeping with his way of life. At that time the European
residents of Lamu consisted of the District Commissioner, a retired
civil servant, a pessimistic hotel keeper, Coconut Charlie, and
one or two temporary residents. The chief mourners were two
companions of the Colonel, one of whom had been in the same
boat and narrowly escaped an identical fate. By some miraculous
chance his feet had found the top of the boat's mast under water

and he had managed to cling to it with his nose above surface until help arrived. For the occasion the mourners repaired to the hotel and were appropriately primed for the ceremony which was conducted by the District Commissioner. As was meet, the coffin was draped with a Union Jack. But just as it was being lowered into the grave the District Commissioner suddenly remembered that it was the only flag on the island and hurriedly whipped it away. Of the Colonel's two friends, one was an enormous man of vast girth, and the other (the one who was nearly drowned) was very small, scarcely five feet tall. Every time the District Commissioner paused for breath during the reading of the service the two would chorus a loud 'Amen'.

Early in 1939 I had planned to carry out a long foot safari through the Mathews Range and Ndoto Mountains and north to Lake Rudolf, but I contracted a very persistent bout of malaria which kept me more or less inactive for nearly two months. Luckily there was a doctor at Isiolo in charge of a large camp of refugees who had fled from Ethiopia during the Italian invasion. He gave me a course of injections which finally overcame the fever, but it was not until early in March that I was fit enough to start the safari.

My party consisted of Chorono, a Kamasia who had accompanied me from Baringo and whom I had appointed Head Ranger, Kipkemei, another Kamasia from Baringo, (he was in charge of the fifteen donkeys and the mule which made up my transport), Lodogia and Lenyambete, both Dorobos from the Mathews Range, Tiwai, a young giant of a Turkana whom I had recently engaged as a Ranger and Lembirdan, a middle-aged and well-to-do Samburu. Lembirdan was an interesting character, intelligent and absolutely trustworthy; one day he turned up in camp and said he wanted a job, though there was no need for him to work as he had inherited plenty of stock, goats, donkeys and cattle, from his father. I liked the look of him and the fact that he wanted to join us out of a spirit of adventure. He turned out to be one of the staunchest of my men. Also with me was

Awalan, a Samburu of excellent character who came to a tragic end many years later when his *manyatta* was attacked by a band of Somali and Boran raiders who stabbed him to death, but not before, single-handed, he had speared two of his assailants. Benua Jawali, my old personal servant, was also of the party.

My previous safari had revealed that a good deal of poaching was being carried on by Dorobos living in their mountain fast-nesses in the Mathews Range. In particular I wanted to catch Lowakoop, a notorious poacher who had hitherto eluded all efforts by the Administration to effect his arrest.

Five days' easy march brought me to the southern end of the Mathews Range, where we camped at the mouth of a steep valley running down the eastern slopes of Warrgues Mountain, the highest in the range which reaches a height of nearly nine thousand feet. Lodogia and Lenyambete suggested we should search the top end of the valley where they knew of a cave which was often used by a well-known poacher. Next morning the three of us set off up the valley and after an hour's hard climb came on a well-used game path on which we saw fresh human foot-prints. Cautiously we followed the track. Suddenly Lodogia, who was ahead, stopped and with a grin pointed up into the trees. There, almost concealed in the foliage, was a poisoned drop-spear poised over the path. It was obvious from the signs, such as bruised leaves, that the trap had just been set. The Dorobo drop-spear trap consists of a log about three feet in length and three inches in diameter. A hard wood shaft some ten inches long tipped with an iron barb and liberally smeared with poison is fitted into a socket made in one end of the log. The contrivance is suspended over a game path. Any large animal passing below touches a trip cord and down comes the spear into its back. We decided not to disturb the trap but to return very early the next morning and hide in ambush. The plan worked perfectly. After about an hour's wait a naked Dorobo appeared sauntering down the path carrying a bow and poisoned arrows. He hadn't a care in the world. We pounced on him. The prisoner was middle-aged; he was well-known to Lodogia and Lenyambete who said that he had never paid any taxes in his life and was wanted by the authorities. Back at camp when he had calmed down, I talked to him, pointing out the serious nature of his crimes. Not only had he never paid tax, but he had set a very deadly trap which might easily have killed one of us. I said that if tried he would certainly go to gaol for a very long time, but suggested that if he cared to help me find Lowakoop I might let him go free and possibly even give him a small reward. I told him to think the matter over carefully and report to me after the next day's march.

The day's march was a long one skirting the eastern base of the range, through waterless thorn bush country, made penetrable by elephant paths. Without these paths it would not have been possible to cover the distance in the day. At length we arrived at the mouth of a big valley called Morit. There was a particularly large elephant path going up this valley which I knew led to water. Everywhere there were fresh signs of elephant and rhino and at one point the pug marks of four lions. To avoid a surprise collision with these animals which might lead to a general stampede of my transport I went ahead of the safari. The bush became denser and the trail steeper until late in the afternoon we came to a water pool in the bed of the river; this reeked of elephant but, as it was getting late, there was no time to go higher since it was essential to make a strong enclosure for the donkeys before it was dark. We all set to and cut thorn bush for the *boma*, a tedious but necessary task in lion country and one which has to be repeated at the end of every march. After the camp had settled down and all the men had fed, I sent for the prisoner. Lodogia acted as interpreter. He said that the man was willing to co-operate and had told him that Lowakoop had a honey store on the side of a cliff not far from camp. Further questioning revealed that Lowakoop had a Samburu woman with him whom he had recently abducted from a *manyatta* in the plains. The prisoner could not say where Lowakoop was at the moment, but thought he might be further to the north where he had a cave high up near the top of the range. He said he knew the cave well and would take us there but suggested that we should first look at the honey store. I agreed, indeed I was keen to go there for I had never seen such a store and had visions of some sort of cave containing honey barrels.

The night was not peaceful. Soon after dark elephant arrived in large numbers at the pool below, and their ear-splitting trumpetings, screams and roars, made sleep impossible. No sooner had one lot satisfied their thirst and gone on their way than another equally noisy herd arrived. In the early hours of the morning there was a tremendous uproar from the donkeys. I jumped out of bed and by the light of my torch saw a lion not more than twenty feet away from the *boma*. The torch frightened him and he disappeared into the darkness. It was fortunate that the donkeys gave tongue when they did, otherwise the lion might have been among them before I knew what was happening. None of my men woke up, and when I roused them and told them that a hungry lion was prowling about, they were much surprised.

Soon after dawn we set off to look for Lowakoop's honey store. Our guide took us to the top of the range, then along it northwards for an hour until we came to a cliff about two hundred feet in height. He said the honey-store was half way up. Even through my glasses I could not see any cave nor any means of climbing the cliff but our guide ran nimbly up the rocks on to a narrow ledge, grinning and beckoning. Lenyambete and Lodogia, being Dorobo and familiar with honey stores and their positioning, followed suit. Tiwai, my Turkana plainsman, refused to budge, saying that he was not a baboon. Wishing that I were a baboon, but loath to let the side down, I followed gingerly after our guide. Fifteen minutes of nerve-racking clutching and sidling brought us under an overhang where the ledge broadened out. Under the overhang were suspended two large barrels attached to stout stakes driven into a crack in the rock. The barrels were made of hollowed logs capped at either end with buffalo hide; they had a capacity of about eighteen gallons apiece. I was unable to imagine how, from such a precarious situation, Lowakoop managed to take down a barrel, refill it and replace it. Judging by the number of bees buzzing around, the store was not empty, but we could find no signs of recent disturbance. Much to the disappointment of my men I would not

Wildebeest having mud bath

Jackals

allow them to tamper with the barrels and, after taking a photograph, we retraced our steps.

Three days later, at the end of a tedious march across valleys
and ridges, we arrived at a little stream called Setim, which ran
off the mountains. Our guide assured us that Lowakoop's cave
lay near its source. I chose a camp site well hidden from prying
eyes up in the hills by trees and a ridge. At dawn we set off, the
prisoner in the lead followed by myself, Lodogia, Lembirdan and
Awalan. I insisted on our guide walking a few yards ahead as I
was not at all anxious to get a drop-spear in the back of my neck
and knew he would spot the traps far quicker than any of my
party. This soon proved to be a wise precaution, for as we followed
the game paths through the thick forest which clothes the upper
slopes of the range we came on no less than eleven traps. Near
the top we found a trap which had been sprung. And thirty
yards on was the victim, a big buffalo. It had been killed the
previous day and a good portion of the meat had been removed,
doubtless by Lowakoop and his woman.

Our guide said the cave was not far off. We climbed cautiously
and presently smelt wood smoke and shortly afterwards saw a thin
spiral of smoke rising from the foot of a small cliff. Silently we
moved forward and saw Lowakoop sitting by a fire at the mouth
of a cave, roasting great steaks of buffalo meat. We could hear
him speaking to someone inside the cave. Suddenly, as though
warned by a primitive instinct, he looked up. We rushed him but
his reaction was instantaneous, like a wild creature he was up and
away in a flash. Lodogia and Awalan gave chase, firing a couple
of shots over Lowakoop's head, but he quickly outdistanced them
and vanished into the forest. His girl-friend, trapped inside the
cave, proved to be a youngish and remarkably handsome and
self-possessed woman. She did not seem in the least frightened
by our sudden appearance and calmly showed us around the cave
which was about thirty feet in length by about ten in width, with
a low roof. Lowakoop's bow and poisoned arrows were hanging
from a peg, there were antelope horns containing magic powders
used for casting spells on the animals he intended to hunt; there
were a couple of crude iron knives, two earthenware cooking

pots, a leather bag containing a quantity of excellent honey, drop-spear traps in process of manufacture, a small blackened pot used for concocting poison and a little, neatly tied bundle of short sticks—but there was literally nothing to connect the abode with twentieth century man. It might easily have been the home of one of our prehistoric ancestors, indeed there was even a pair of friction sticks for producing fire. I asked the woman why she wasn't frightened. She replied that she was pleased to see us as she had become weary of the lonely life in the forest and wanted to get back among her own people, down in the plains. She added that we would never catch Lowakoop as, among other accomplishments, he was a noted witch doctor and had medicine to protect himself.

The bundle of sticks I have mentioned were Lowakoop's 'visiting cards'. They were the size of an ordinary lead pencil and on each was carved its owner's private mark, a series of diagonal cuts and notches. It was then customary for a Dorobo wishing to visit his neighbour's territory to carry some of these sticks and, as soon as he entered the area, to place them at intervals along the path. The point of the custom was that if the owner of the ground came on footprints and saw the sticks they conveyed to him that the visitor was on legitimate business and ready to disclose his identity. On the other hand, if he saw human footprints but no sticks, he would suspect that someone had come to steal his honey and would follow up the tracks, probably prepared to put a poisoned arrow into the intruder.

Poison for arrows and traps is made by boiling the wood of a tree (*Acokanthera friesiorum*), for several days until a dark pitch-like substance is formed. This is smeared over the arrow-heads and the drop-spears. When fresh the poison is deadly but it deteriorates with age.

By the time we started back for camp it was late in the afternoon and foolishly, against the advice of my men, I decided to take a short cut. As often happens with short cuts, we were brought to an abrupt halt by an impassable gorge; there was no means of getting around it. We had therefore to retrace our steps and when dark fell we were only a quarter of the way down the mountain. At this moment, a heavy thunderstorm reduced visibility to nil, so we just had to sit down where we were and wait for dawn. We were soaked through and it soon became bitterly cold. I tried every means I could think of to light a fire but the only fuel we could find in the darkness was sopping wet and all my attempts with paper and powder from rifle cartridges ended in failure. Presently, as we were sitting hunched up with our teeth chattering and rain pouring down our backs, there was a thunderous roar as a giant boulder came crashing down the hillside. All we could do was crouch lower and hope it would miss us. It went hurtling past fifty yards away. Suddenly I felt a clammy object pressed into my hands. It was a ranger's sandal made out of an old motor tyre. Thinking our predicament had proved too much for its owner, I was about to hurl it back with the injunction to pull himself together when he suggested trying to light the rubber. I cut the sandal into strips which ignited easily and soon we had a roaring fire going. The rain stopped and when we were warm and dry I tied strips of the rubber on to sticks and, using these as torches, we found our way down to camp just as dawn was breaking.

After breakfast and a rest I called the men together for a council of war. All agreed that it was futile trying to chase Lowakoop over the mountains; guile must be used. Lenyambete, the oldest of us, suggested that he and Awalan should take 'Mrs Lowakoop' to her home in the plains and there, with the connivance of her parents, who had no love for Lowakoop, lie in wait for him. Sooner or later, said Lenyambete, he was certain to come there to look for her. I had my doubts and wondered if the Rangers had not fallen for the charms of 'Mrs Lowakoop'. However, as I had no better suggestion to make, I agreed to the plan and sent them off. As there was no knowing when, or indeed whether, Lowakoop would turn up, I carried on with the safari. Two days later I camped in a little forest glade at the top of the range and, while I was having a late breakfast, noticed a wild-looking face peering at me from the undergrowth at the edge of the glade. I jumped up and gave chase, calling to my men to follow. Soon two Rangers appeared, leading a frail and ancient

Dorobo between them. He was unarmed and naked except for an old antelope skin draped over one shoulder. The first thing I noticed about him were his bright and childlike eyes, and then his hands which were screwed up like the claws of a dead bird and almost totally crippled. After giving him a good feed and a handful of tobacco to chew, he told me his story.

As a young man he had been a notorious honey thief and had spent his time robbing the hives of the Dorobo in the hills. Finally he was caught and, according to Dorobo custom, a terrible punishment was inflicted upon him: his hands were tightly knotted and tied back on to his arms with bow-string sinew and then he was cast adrift to fend for himself; the idea being that even if the victim survived he would be permanently crippled and unable in future to climb trees to get at honey. Assuming that the man was at least fifty years old when I caught him he must have spent something like thirty years wandering alone about the forests, existing on the remains of lion and leopard kills and the few roots and berries he could secure with his almost useless hands. Perhaps mercifully, he was now partially insane. How he had managed to survive for so long in country teeming with dangerous animals such as elephant, rhino, buffalo, lion and leopard was a miracle. I tried to get him to understand that I would send him to the government station at Maralal where he would be fed and looked after for the rest of his days but he would not hear of such a plan; indeed he seemed quite upset at the idea. He asked for some more tobacco, which I gave him, then he walked over to the camp fire, picked up a smouldering brand and quietly disappeared into the forest. That was the last ever seen of him.

I continued my safari northwards, descending into the semi-desert plains where there was very little in the way of fodder for my pack animals; in the circumstances it was possible to do only a half day's march at a time, so as to give the animals a chance to feed. At night they had to be put into a *boma* for fear of attacks by lion, thus further reducing their feeding time. I usually placed the *boma* between my sleeping place and the men's and I often hung a hurricane lamp from a pole on the most exposed side of the *boma*. But I relied chiefly on the donkeys themselves to give the alarm if lions approached. In particular my biggest and oldest donkey, Korofi (the Wild One) was invariably vigilant. I could afford to ignore the unlovely voices of all the other donkeys, but as soon as Korofi started to bray I was on the alert and would get out of bed with torch and rifle to foil an attack. I lost a few donkeys from lion in the course of years but not nearly as many as would have been killed but for Korofi's vigilance. He was possessed of an exceedingly independent spirit and in spite of carrying the heaviest load would never fail on the most exhausting march. But he would not be driven and would choose his own time and pace. On the march he would trot ahead of the others until he came to a tempting patch of grass, then he would stop and start feeding, paying no attention to the rest of the caravan as it went past. When satisfied he would trot along, catch up and forge ahead until he saw the next inviting piece of vegetation. My men, knowing his habits, never interfered with him. Poor old Korofi, he carried my loads for sixteen years with never a breakdown, but at the last, when I was not there to help him, he was killed by a lion.

It was now over a month since I had left Isiolo. During this time I had explored the Mathews Range, the greater part of which had never before been visited by a white man. I had harried the poachers, arrested a number and confiscated a quantity of ivory and rhino horns. From time to time it had been necessary to send prisoners and trophies off under escort and obtain fresh food supplies by donkey. I now planned to concentrate on the Ndoto Mountains further to the north where there was every reason to believe that a lot of poaching was taking place.

After descending from the northern end of the Mathews Range we camped in the El Gerre valley which divides the range from the Ndoto Mountains. There was plenty of game in the valley, elephant, rhino, buffalo, giraffe, Grevy's zebra, (*Oryx beisa*), lesser kudu, Grant's gazelle, long-necked gerenuk and up in the hills to the north and south, greater kudu, besides many lesser creatures and a great variety of bird life, including large flocks of the beautiful vulturine guinea-fowl. My camp was rather closer to a

big game path than I liked, but there was no other suitable site
in the vicinity. After putting the donkeys into a strong *boma*
for the night, I placed a hurricane lamp on the path so as to give
timely warning to animals using it and thereby prevent them from
blundering unexpectedly into camp and stampeding the donkeys.
Late that night when the whole camp except myself was asleep I
heard a curious clicking sound which appeared to be coming
nearer. A few moments later a rhino sauntered along the path
straight towards the lamp. He came nearer and nearer until I
could not believe that even a rhino could fail to see the light. But
it was not until he was six feet away that he stopped. I expected
to hear a loud snort and to see the lamp go up in the air in pieces.
But rhino are unaccountable creatures and, after inspecting the
light for a few seconds, he calmly walked around it and carried
on his way. As soon as day broke I went to look at the path,
superimposed on the tracks of the rhino were the fresh pug marks
of four lions. They had passed within twenty feet of the donkey
boma and gone on without a pause. This in itself was surprising
but what astonished me still more was that none of the donkeys,
not even Korofi, had given the alarm. I feel sure they must
somehow have known the lions had fed well and were not
interested in them.

Having sent all the men out on an investigation, I had to spend
the day in camp, so I decided to follow up the lion spoor. It led
along the path for about a mile and then turned down towards the
El Gerre river-bed where there was good cover. This should have
satisfied my curiosity since obviously the lions had gone to lie up
for the day. But humans being almost as unaccountable as
rhino, I carried on, advancing very cautiously, making no sound
over the soft ground. Suddenly, as I came round a bush I saw
the four lions asleep, the nearest lying on his back with his legs
in the air; he was not more than eight feet from me. To put it
mildly, I was frightened. Had the lions seen me suddenly at
such close quarters the chances are that one or more would have
attacked. Holding my breath I slowly backed away and I do not
think the lions ever knew they had been spied on.

The following day my men returned with a motley collection of prisoners and suspects and, as exhibits, four rhino horns and a number of bows and poisoned arrows. One of the suspects I questioned gave his name as Nyama Yangu; Nyama Yangu means 'my animals' or 'my meat' in Swahili. Now this was the native name given to Arthur Neumann, one of the best known and respected old-time elephant hunters; he had hunted in this area somewhere about the turn of the century. I asked my suspect how he came by his name and he told me that he had been born the day Nyama Yangu had camped in El Gerre, not far from my present camp, and that was why his parents had given him the name. Neumann was one of the very few Europeans who left a lasting impression on the Samburu, and at the time of which I am writing many still remembered him and spoke about him with respect and affection. Some twenty-five years later a luxury lodge was built on the Uaso Nyiro River, for the benefit of tourists and others interested in the wild life, on the site where Neumann had his base camp and which ever since his day had been known by the Samburu and other tribes living in the vicinity as 'Kampi ya Nyama Yangu', or 'Nyama Yangu' for short. I did my best to plead for the retention of the old name as a memorial to a very fine man, and in keeping with local tradition. But today it is unimaginatively called 'Uaso Nyiro Game Lodge', and so it will remain for everyone except the older Samburu and myself who will continue to call it Nyama Yangu.

The following day I crossed the El Gerre valley into the Ndotos. For the next three weeks I was busy collecting illegally obtained ivory and rhino horns and arresting poachers. Never before had the local Dorobo met anyone who took such a close and inconvenient interest in the welfare of wild animals. In a little valley called Keno where I camped for a few days, one of my prisoners offered to show me a cave where he believed some ivory was hidden. Like many of the Dorobo hide-outs it was in an exceedingly inaccessible place, being on the flank of a rocky and precipitous hill. As usual, the guide sped ahead, disdaining to use hand-holds, while I laboured behind clutching at any protuberance which offered a grip. While doing so, I put my hand on something soft and, looking down, nearly fell off the cliff, for it was an enormous puff-adder coiled up in slumber; we killed it, and it measured over six feet, the largest I had ever seen or heard of.

At length, having stirred up the Dorobo poachers sufficiently for one season, I carried on northwards along the eastern slopes of the Ndoto Mountains, arriving in the Ngoorinit Valley, a very attractive and spectacular valley bounded by gigantic domes of granite rock, with a little stream coming off the mountain; all around is bush vegetation. We camped in the shade of a tree and watched the elephant and rhino. Near here the Martin Johnsons had camped some fifteen years earlier; they were among the first to show to the world the wild life of Kenya on the screen.

6: *I come to grips with a lion*

ALTHOUGH IT WAS a place of great interest I did not stay long at Ngoorinit for I was anxious to get on to Lake Rudolf. Two days later I pitched camp on a pleasant little stream in the long Arsim Valley at the northern end of the Ndotos. Here I was met by a deputation of local Samburu tribesmen who complained bitterly about lions. They said that a pride of three had become exceedingly bold and raided their cattle *boma* almost nightly. Recently they had started man-eating. A youth had been killed and eaten a few weeks ago and another man seized by the shoulder and dragged out of his hut. Fortunately he had been rescued by his companions. I saw the unfortunate victim: his wounds had healed but one arm was permanently crippled. I told the deputation that I was willing to spend a week hunting the lions, provided all the young and able-bodied men turned out to locate them. I would wait in camp and as soon as there was any definite news of the lions I would go out after them. They agreed that this was a sound plan and that parties of *moran* would be sent out immediately. However, knowing the Samburu, I was certain nothing would be done for a day at least, while they argued among themselves as to who was to do the dirty work. For two days I sat in camp waiting for news. On the third morning, while I was having breakfast, I heard a tremendous uproar behind the camp which resolved itself into the frightened braying of a donkey mingled with the angry trumpeting of an elephant. A moment later one of my donkeys passed the tent with an enormous bull elephant in pursuit. They disappeared out of sight up the valley. I returned to my interrupted breakfast. Presently I noticed a lone Samburu some distance away; he was following the path taken by the elephant, and before I could shout a warning I again heard the trumpeting of an elephant and the Samburu reappeared running for his life with the bull, evidently a thoroughly bad-tempered old beast, after him; fortunately he reached safety.

Becoming weary of waiting in camp for news I went for a solitary walk down the valley. After I had covered about six miles the sun was high in the heavens, and it was getting uncomfortably hot, so I started for camp. When still about two miles short of it I saw a lioness crossing my path about a hundred yards ahead. As there was only a limited number of lion in the area I thought she was bound to be connected with the marauders; I had a shot at her and she rolled over, but was up again in an instant, and made off into a patch of long grass before I could get in another shot. I had seen blood on her shoulder, but rather low down. Cautiously I walked around the cover which was not more than thirty by forty yards square. There were no tracks leading out. Again I walked around, looking carefully for any signs of movement. Then I climbed a tree, but could see nothing, so, finally, I went up close to the grass and hurled stones in, still there was neither sound nor movement. At length I found myself standing about fifty yards away from the cover, thinking that in all probability the lioness was dead and how hot it was, and that the best plan would be to go back to camp and return in the afternoon with some of my men when we would surely find the lioness dead or alive.

I had just turned my back to set off when there was a low growl behind me; spinning round I saw the lioness starting to charge. I took a quick shot but still she came on. At that moment I was not unduly worried because I felt confident of stopping her with my next shot at close quarters. I worked the bolt of my heavy magazine rifle to eject the spent round and put in a fresh one. It jammed! The empty case had not been extracted properly and became buckled by my frantic endeavours to reload the rifle. I realised that I was helpless. As the lioness reached me I tried to ram the muzzle of the rifle down her throat. She bit it savagely and tore it out of my grasp. Then she reared up and seized me by the right forearm which I had put up to protect my throat. She hurled me backwards to the ground. I can remember getting to my feet and seeing the lioness standing a few feet away and myself trying to draw the hunting knife which I wore on my right side, but my arm was numb and powerless. The lioness came at me again and caught me by the left thigh, again bowling me over.

The next thing I can remember clearly was sitting on the ground, with my rifle lying a few feet in front of me. I could not see the lioness and thought she might be behind me, watching, and that the slightest movement on my part might bring her on me again. For a long time I sat motionless, not daring to stir. At length the tension became unbearable; I was sure that the lioness was somewhere behind me; meanwhile I was losing a lot of blood. Slowly, I inched forward and recovered my rifle and with difficulty managed to get it working again and reloaded. Then I struggled to my feet and looked around for the lioness, but she had vanished. I started to hobble towards camp but after a few yards felt so faint that I had to sit down with my back against a tree. I then fired off shots at intervals. After about an hour one of my Dorobo prisoners appeared. He tried to help me to get up but by that time I was feeling very groggy, my wounds had begun to hurt and I had a raging thirst. I sent the Dorobo off to tell my men to bring water and a bed to carry me to camp. At last, late in the afternoon, I was brought into camp. Immediately I scribbled a note to the District Commissioner at Maralal, a good hundred and twenty miles away, and sent Lodogia off with it.

I knew that my greatest danger was gangrene and that it was vital to keep the wounds clean, so I instructed my men to wash my injuries with a strong solution of epsom salts every four hours, regardless of any protests on my part. By chance I happened to have some sulphanilamide tablets in my medicine chest, a drug that had only recently become available in Kenya. Shortly before setting off on my safari I had been to a chemist's shop to get something for a poisoned finger and had been recommended the sulphanilamide and had bought myself a small bottle of the tablets.

Together with the frequent cleaning with the salts these undoubtedly saved me.

Lion mauls seldom look serious externally, as they show up only as round punctures from the canine teeth, but deep inside the tissues are mangled and bruised and, owing to the lion's habit of eating putrid meat, they are apt to turn septic very quickly, so, unless medical attention is available without delay, there is the gravest danger of gangrene.

That night I developed a bad attack of malaria, no doubt brought on by the shock of the mauling. Owing to high fever and the pain of my wounds I could not sleep and, during the early hours of the morning, I heard my riding mule snort in alarm and start straining at the chain with which she was tied to a tree in front of my tent. Next I heard her break the chain and go off; shortly afterwards came the scream of a furious elephant, a moment later I saw its dark shape coming straight for my tent. Benua Jawali, who was lying on the ground beside my bed, quickly helped me up and handed me a light rifle which fortunately was already loaded. I steadied myself against the front pole of the tent and fired into the middle of the advancing mass. The elephant swerved and swept past the tent. At daybreak he was found dead eighty yards away. My bullet must have taken him in the heart. It was the same beast which had chased the donkey and the Samburu the previous morning.

Hearing of my mishap, a number of Samburu came to camp, bringing a fat sheep as a present. They examined my wounds, gravely shook their heads and urged me to drink hot mutton fat. I knew that the drinking of sheep's fat among the Samburu is reserved for those in extremis and almost akin to the last rites. So, as can be imagined, this did nothing to cheer me up.

The next five days were like a bad dream. I can remember hearing lions close to camp, tearing at the dead elephant and shall never forget the terrible stench of the decaying carcase or the repeated agony of having my wounds dressed.

While I was still in this state Lenyambete and Awalan arrived back with Lowakoop. Their plan had worked to perfection.

On the sixth day after I had been mauled, Mullins, the District Commissioner from Maralal, arrived in a truck. He had started off as soon as he got my note and had driven all night over the most shocking bush tracks and across country. I think he was quite surprised to find me still alive. He told me that the R.A.F. unit stationed in Nairobi had very generously agreed to send an aircraft to Maralal to pick me up. The journey to Maralal took twelve hours and was a nightmare, but when I got there I found that the R.A.F. had sent two light bombers, complete with a doctor, his assistant, a blood transfusion apparatus and various instruments for removing limbs. The doctor was amazed, and perhaps a little disappointed, at the healthy state of my wounds for he had expected to find me in the last stages of gangrene. Getting me into the bomber was quite a performance. I felt that, given a little assistance, I could manage to climb in through the cockpit. But no, there was a regulation drill for evacuating casualties, so, not wishing to cause any further disappointment, I allowed myself to be strapped up in a kind of strait-jacket and was pushed like a parcel through the bomb hatch and flown to Nairobi. This was my first experience of flying.

At the end of three weeks I was fit enough to leave hospital with a stiff right arm, which a month's massage put more or less right. By mid-August I was back again on duty and shortly afterwards the World War started. I was anxious to join the forces immediately but Archie Ritchie persuaded me to carry on, saying that as the entry of Italy into the war seemed imminent, and invasion of Kenya a likelihood, there was every possibility that my knowledge and experience of the Northern Province would soon be put to good use.

On 5th of September, two days after the declaration of war with Germany, I happened to be camped on the Uaso Nyiro River, near a little-used motor road which connected with outposts on the Ethiopian border some two hundred miles to the north. Late in the night we were woken by the sound of heavy motor vehicles passing in the direction of Isiolo. There were many of them and we wondered whether the Italians had started to invade Kenya. Later we learnt that the District Commissioner at Moyale, which lies on the border, had received orders from Nairobi by radio to evacuate Moyale immediately. He had no choice but to obey this order, although at the time no shot had been fired along the border in anger. Knowing the District Commissioner in question, I can imagine how much it must have gone against his grain to pull out in evident flight. To make matters worse a standing military patrol at Merti, a point where the road from the north reaches the river, had not been warned about the evacuation. So, when he saw a long string of vehicle headlights coming down from the north, the officer in charge of the patrol concluded that the invasion had started and carried out a precipitate evacuation without a shot being fired. To add insult to injury, a few days later a message was received from the officer in charge of Italian Moyale, saying that he could no longer keep order in British Moyale and please would the British return and re-occupy the station. Among the tribesmen along the border our prestige received a sorry blow, but one which was later to some extent redeemed, by the very gallant defence of Moyale after re-occupation, when the shooting had started in earnest.

When I got back to headquarters I was allotted the extremely distasteful task of eliminating game on the T.O.L. farms along the Samburu border—principally zebra and oryx. The decision to take this drastic step was due to incessant complaints from the farmers that at a time when it was necessary to increase production to help the war effort the game was seriously competing with livestock for grazing. Perhaps the decision was a right one, but to add to the tragedy thousands of the animals I was obliged to kill were wasted. Neither meat nor hide were taken and the carcases were allowed to rot where they fell. (A thousand oryx and zebra represented over a hundred and fifty tons of perfectly wholesome meat.) I suggested that the poorer members of the Turkana tribe, who live in a chronic state of under-nourishment some eighty miles to the north, should be permitted to camp in the area, dry the meat and take it back to their homes. But it was thought the scheme would create too many administrative problems, and, more particularly, that it would be difficult to get the Turkana off the farms when the shooting ended. Daily I went out in my car over the plains and would return in the evening weary and sick at heart having killed anything up to a hundred animals. A dreadful aspect of the slaughter was that while engaged in the actual shooting I observed that I unconsciously developed a ruthless blood lust. This gave me pause for thought and some inkling into the mentality which perpetrates massacres.

During the remaining few months which preceded the entry of Italy into the war I carried out another long foot safari through the Mathews Range and on to Lake Rudolf and Mount Marsabit. On the way, near the north-eastern end of the range, I arrived in a locality known as Kitonongop, where the local Samburu were being terrorised by a pride of about five lions; so terrified were they that they were on the point of evacuating the area. Evidently the lions had become exceedingly cunning and bold. Late in the afternoon on the day of my arrival, as the donkeys were being off-saddled, there was a tremendous commotion at a nearby *manyatta* and I learnt that a lion had just taken a sheep and was eating it inside a thicket close by. The Samburu told me this lion was a big animal and very aggressive and would attack anyone who approached while he was feeding. I abandoned caution and walked up to the thicket, expecting to hear at least a warning growl, but all was silent. On entering the thicket I found the half-eaten remains of the sheep and the pug marks of a big lion leading away. Together with Lodogia and Lembirdan I followed up the spoor until it was too dark to distinguish tracks on the ground; all we saw was a glimpse of a large animal as it disappeared into the thick thorn bush.

All night lions roared not more than a mile from camp. One of them in particular had a deep, gruff roar; I had no doubt that this belonged to the one I had followed. At dawn, when I was about to set off, a Samburu came running in to say one of his cows had been killed during the night. With the man leading, we went to investigate and came on the kill in thick cover with the lion still on it. Unfortunately the Samburu had failed to warn

me that we were getting close and he was in the direct line of
fire when I first caught sight of the lion. By the time I had
pushed him aside the animal had moved out of sight; it was a fine
big lion with a dark tawny mane. We continued hot on his trail
which led in a circle, until once again we heard crunching of
bones at the kill. But the lion had heard us and dashed away
and I never even caught a glimpse of him. Again, we took up his
tracks and followed for a further two hours. Although we several
times heard him just ahead of us it was impossible to get close
enough to see him in the thick bush. Eventually we stopped for a
rest, and I was having some cold tea when I heard yells and cries
from a *manyatta* some distance away. When we reached it we were
told that another goat had just been taken, this time by a lioness.
It was too late in the day to attempt to follow.

During the night I was woken up by an odd sound which at
first I could not identify, then I realised it was made by lions
drinking from a small rain pool not more than a hundred yards
away; when they lap water they make a sound like a dog
lapping, only much louder and with longer pauses between each
lap. Cautiously, I got out of bed and went to the door of the tent
with a torch and my rifle ready. I saw five pairs of eyes reflected
in the beam. I had a shot, but must have missed.

In the morning I again visited the remains of the cow but no
lions had been there. After making a wide circle through the bush
we returned to camp. I was sitting, having tea rather late in the
afternoon, when suddenly there was a great uproar, the terrified
braying of a donkey and the growls of lions. I raced over to find
two young lions on top of one of my donkeys. I was breathless
from running, my aim unsteady, my shot missed and the lions
made off. I followed up until nearly dusk when the lions apparently went through a small herd of elephant, causing great alarm
and excitement, with loud trumpetings from the cow elephants
who were milling around in the bush looking for the lions. We
had to get out very hurriedly. Lion sometimes attack the young
of elephant and therefore a herd containing cows and calves will
not tolerate the near presence of lion although adult bulls are
usually quite indifferent to them.

The poor donkey was so badly injured that I had to shoot him. In desperation I poisoned the carcase with strychnine, the first and only time I have deliberately used poison against a lion. During the night I heard them at the carcase. At first light I found two hyenas dead near the remains and the tracks of two lions leading away. We followed the spoor and soon came to a place where they had vomited up their meal, and further on put them up in thick cover. I never got a sight of them but as they had gone straight up a twelve foot river bank it was evident they had fully recovered from the effects of the poison. On my return to camp, Chepkemei, my donkey *syce*, informed me that soon after I left another lion had come and dragged the donkey remains away. Once again I set off, but the lion must have heard us coming for he kept just ahead of us, working round back towards the donkey remains. This time I concealed myself behind a termite mound and told my men to talk loudly and leave me alone. I hoped the lions, hearing the voices recede, would think we had given up the chase and come back to the kill. This stratagem often proves successful but the lions of Kitonongop were possessed of diabolical cunning and no doubt laughed. I lay in wait for two hours without result.

That night, as if in derision, the lions came close to our camp and roared until the early hours of the morning. At first light we set off. The spoor led westwards along a big game path for about six miles. On the way our hunt was interrupted by a truculent bull elephant who would not give us way and later we were held up by a herd of cow elephant with calves; we had to give them a wide berth as they were already incensed by the passing of the lions. Again we got back on to the lion spoor and came to a place where they had made an unsuccessful attack on a giraffe; shortly afterwards the tracks turned off the path into particularly dense bush. I felt certain they had gone to lie up for the day. With infinite caution we followed, and after a few minutes heard the familiar low growl and the sound of the lions breaking away. Already a week had been spent on the hunt and the safari was well behind schedule, so I was obliged to admit defeat and advise the Samburu to vacate the territory of the Kitonongop lions for a time. I told them I hoped to return.

While engaged in hunting these lions, my old friend Lowakoop turned up, having served his sentence in prison. He was beaming and wanted a job. I liked the look of him and promptly engaged him as a Game Scout. He proved to be a delightful character. When I left the Game Department to join the forces he was turning out well and would undoubtedly have become invaluable. But when I joined the army all my Game Scouts were temporarily transferred to the Samburu Tribal Police, and Lowakoop found the discipline and duties of a policeman irksome to his untamed nature and returned to his old haunts in the forests of the Mathews Range. He was never heard of again and it was rumoured that he had been killed when the roof of his cave collapsed. Some years afterwards I visited the cave and certainly, if he had been inside at the time, he could not have survived.

Shortly before leaving Isiolo I had acquired a new riding mule, quite a smart-looking young mare. Unfortunately, one of my more amorous natured donkeys, Punda Milia, fell violently in love with her and his feelings were reciprocated. This led to many embarrassing situations while on the march, and meant that I had to keep a wary eye behind in case the love-lorn Punda Milia sneaked up unaware, in spite of being given the heaviest load to discourage his ardour. At night in order to ensure peace in the donkey *boma*, it was necessary to isolate Aphrodite, the mule. Although this step prevented actual violence in the *boma*, it did not prevent Punda Milia from giving vent to his feelings in night-long braying which at times nearly drove me crazy, indeed I was often tempted to take a gun to him. One of my Game Scouts suggested tying his tail down, the theory being that a donkey has to raise its tail in order to bray. The first trial proved this idea to be a fallacy, for having his tail secured made not the slightest difference to either the tone or volume of Punda Milia's unlovely voice. In the end I traded him off to the Samburu for a gelding.

The next place of interest on the line of march was the Horr

Valley which divides the towering nine thousand feet Mount Nyiro from the lesser range of Donio Mara. The scenery is spectacular and at this time of year there were remarkable cloud effects. The morning would dawn with a heavy cloud bank over Donio Mara, which, driven by the prevailing east wind, would pour off the hills, rushing down the steep slopes like a gigantic water-fall to be dispersed abruptly by the warm air rising up from the valley. There were many greater kudu in the surrounding hills and their smaller and even handsomer cousins, the lesser kudu, were in strength along the valley floor. A beautiful little stream tumbled down the precipitous east flank losing itself in the deep sand at the bottom. This stream was a favourite watering place for elephant and buffalo and a few rhino and lion, besides lesser game.

The local Samburu elders arrived in a deputation, bringing me a fat sheep and quantities of milk as a present. (This pleasing and hospitable custom has now died out.) They complained bitterly about the depredations of hyenas and of one in particular which had taken to attacking stock in broad daylight and also of a leopard which had developed the same habit. As complaints of this nature were common and not infrequently frivolous, I made it a practice to tell the Samburu that I was quite prepared to poison the hyenas provided they supplied the meat for bait. This was a sure test of whether or not a complaint were genuine. If there was an argument about producing a beast I would pack up and move on, knowing that if they were in real trouble, they would have no hesitation in complying with my proposal. In this instance, as it turned out, there was no necessity to kill a beast for bait, for the morning after my arrival a youth came running to report that a calf had just been killed by the hyena. I went along and found a big calf lying beside a little dry stream-bed. It had been almost completely disembowelled and was breathing its last. A hyena's normal method of attack is to tear open the flank. Using the same strategy I had employed unsuccessfully on the Kitonongop lions, I sent the men away talking loudly and posted myself behind a convenient rock. I had not long to wait before the hyena appeared, making for the calf.

I killed it with a bullet through the shoulders. It was an unusually large female.

In the evening, using the calf's meat, I put out thirty poisoned baits for hyenas along the valley. At first light next morning I went out to inspect them. Most had been taken by hyena but much to my dismay I found that two lions had eaten several of the baits. I followed up their pug marks and came to a place where the lions had lain down and rolled, evidently feeling the effects of the strychnine. Further on they had stopped again and vomited copiously. In the vomit were large numbers of red berries of the bush *Cordia gharaf* which have a sickly-sweet flavour. I had never heard of lions eating these berries, or for that matter any berries, so I could but conclude that these had deliberately eaten the fruit as an emetic. Not long afterwards, I put them up in thick cover; they left me in no doubt that they had recovered from the effects of the poison of which I was very glad, as I had no wish to injure them.

No sooner had I returned to camp than another report was brought in by a Samburu to say that the leopard had killed a calf. I went out to see the calf which had been barely touched apart from claw marks on its face and deep punctures in its throat. Again I waited hidden behind a rock for nearly four hours. Just when I was on the point of giving up I heard vervet monkeys chattering in excitement from the tree tops a short way down the dry watercourse, a sure indication that they had seen the leopard. The sound came nearer as the monkeys ran along the branches overlooking the leopard. At length, after twenty tense minutes, the leopard emerged and very cautiously approached the kill. I kept absolutely motionless until it had reached its prey, waited for it to put its head down, then slowly brought my rifle up and pressed the trigger. The leopard was an adult male but small, scaling not more than sixty pounds.

Leaving the Horr Valley, the safari struck across very broken lava country in the direction of the south end of Lake Rudolf. We camped for the night at a spring called Laisamis, situated in a deep gorge. Along the paths leading to the water I noticed

several boulders covered with a thick chalky deposit which at
first I could not account for, then I remembered that I had seen
the same sort of thing near water in rhino country, and that this
deposit is the result of rhino urinating against rocks over long
periods—possibly for centuries. In fact, there were no longer any
rhino in this area; they had long since been exterminated by
Turkana poachers.

Our next stop was on the lake shore at the mouth of a dry
river-bed called Surrima, where six years earlier Nevil Baxendale
and I had camped. I was eagerly looking forward to catching fish
as a change from mutton and venison and hurried down to the
water with my fishing tackle. By dusk I had not had much luck,
securing only two small tiger fish which are almost inedible owing
to the multitude of their small bones. I could see giant tilapia
swimming about in the clear water but, as a rule, these fish, which
eat micro-organisms, will not take bait. As it grew dark I noticed
that the tilapia were coming close inshore. Thinking it might be
possible to shoot some of them I went to camp and collected a
rifle and torch and returned. Holding the torch under the barrel
of the rifle, my first shot bagged a huge tilapia of about twelve
pounds. Soon, I found that it was unnecessary to hit the fish as a
bullet striking the water a few inches away was sufficient to stun
it. It did not take me long to get enough fine fish to feed the whole
camp. This is not a sporting method of fishing and I have only
employed it when in want of food.

In the morning I sent men out on patrol to hunt for Turkana
poachers. They returned in the late evening with a prisoner
whose face seemed familiar. It turned out that he had been one of
our guides when Baxendale and I had been on the prospecting
safari. As he had not committed any very heinous crime I gave
him some tobacco and let him go.

Our next stop was at Loingalane Spring. The mud and thatch
buildings of the old military post had completely disappeared.
Only the earth works and neat rows of white stones marking the
paths within the perimeter were left. Such orderly rows of stones
are often the only enduring relics of British military occupation
in the remoter parts of Africa. I like to think that some archaeo-

logists of the future will be puzzled by the stones and ascribe
their geometrical patterns to an unknown prehistoric cult.

Leaving Loingalane we turned east and climbed the seven
thousand foot Mount Kulal which had beckoned Nevil and
myself from across the lake. Kulal is a huge ancient volcano
which eruptions have split into three parts. The three peaks are
separated from one another by terrifying gorges and chasms.
It is not possible to travel with pack animals from one peak to
another without first descending to the foot of the mountain and
making one's way around and up again. I chose the southern
massif which is the largest and is covered at the top by dense
forest. This is the home of the regal greater kudu and while
exploring the massif I came on several small herds. I had never
shot one of these animals and for a long time it had been my
ambition to secure a record trophy. One morning when out
alone, I saw a magnificent bull kudu who was standing still on
the ridge's summit. I stalked to within sixty yards of him without being seen. The kudu was grazing slowly in my direction. I
watched fascinated until he was no more than thirty feet away.
I thought how easy it would be to shoot him and possibly collect
a record head—but also what a despicable act it would be to put
an end to the life of so noble a creature; at length he passed
fifteen feet from the place where I was sitting.

My next objective was Mount Marsabit which loomed eighty
miles across the desert towards the east. The only water on the
way was a small water-hole at the foot of Kulal and another at the
foot of Marsabit with an intervening stretch of forty miles of
arid desert which was going to be trying for the pack-animals. A
short morning's march brought us to the first water-hole and there
I rested the donkeys until late afternoon, when we set off and
walked until past midnight. After we had rested for two hours
we went on again and by two a.m. reached the Kargi waterhole
at the base of Marsabit. The remainder of the journey, which
occupied two days, was along barren ridges of broken lava
country, a mass of loose stones that one kept tripping over, terrible
stuff to walk across. This stretch proved more fatiguing to both
man and beast than the desert. A few miles away from the

administrative centre of Marsabit we encountered a heavily armed police patrol who appeared to regard us with the utmost suspicion. Nothing I or my men could say would convince the African policemen that we were harmless and had no intention of attacking the Marsabit headquarters. I soon learnt the cause of their suspicion: Italy had just declared war. With two policemen trailing us with rifles at the ready we marched into Marsabit.

7: *Military interlude*

I WAS MOST ANXIOUS to get back as soon as possible in order to join the forces so, after resting the animals for a few days, I set off and in twelve days' marching reached Maralal, the administrative centre of the Samburu district. Here I learnt, much to my disgust, that my orders were to stay in Samburu for the present. I was to patrol the northern borders of the district, and by my presence and that of my six Scouts and eight policemen, allay panic among the tribesmen—the area was four thousand square miles. It was thought that the tribesmen might take fright at rumours and migrate southwards into the European settled areas. I was also to endeavour to repel any invaders, such as armed raiders from across the Ethiopian border, who might take advantage of the situation to carry out forays. I made my headquarters at Baragoi, a small village about sixty miles north of Maralal. I had no radio nor were there any other means of communication, apart from the traditional runner with a cleft stick; for transport I had my animals and a light pick-up truck.

The following two months were a time of dreary waiting for news. I had Scouts out to the north as far as Loingalane to give warning of raiders and, as I thought it possible that enemy reconnaissance aircraft might fly over, I tried to camouflage my car by plastering mud over the brighter parts, but as this created a near-panic among the Samburu I hurriedly washed the mud off and thereafter kept the chromium parts brightly polished.

One morning I went out to supply the camp with meat but it was one of my off-days, my shooting was atrocious and I fired a number of shots before getting enough meat. The sound of firing convinced the Samburu that the Italians had arrived, they started to bolt and it took a lot of persuasion to reassure them. As I was anxious to get news of what was happening in other parts of the Northern Province I made a quick trip by car to Marsabit, arriving there just after the station had been bombed by Italian aircraft. The police officer with whom I stayed gave an amusing description of the raid and informed me that there had been no casualties apart from a few sprained ankles sustained in the rush for the cover of the nearby forest. Soon after my return to Baragoi I received permission to join the forces.

At the start of the war we had very few troops in Kenya, only three or four battalions to stop a possible invasion of eighty thousand troops coming in from Ethiopia, and we had no armoured cars till some weird armoured vehicles were produced in the railway workshops, but the settlers formed a hastily trained East African reconnaissance unit which operated with guns mounted on trucks. Later troops came from West and South Africa.

After a short spell of leave, spent at my home, I was enrolled in Military Intelligence and was ordered to report to Wajir which was one of the forward bases for operations against the Italian forces. Arriving there I was directed to the intelligence officers' camp which was some eight miles out of the station near a group of wells called Arbo; there I found two of my old friends, Andrew Fowle and Roy Leny. I use the word camp, but in fact there was no such thing, we slept in the open under bushes and during the day used the shade of a small tree as our mess room. Our task was to obtain information about enemy dispositions and troop movements. For this purpose we employed a number of Somali secret agents recruited from local tribesmen. They were sent out to mingle with people living in the areas occupied by the enemy, and to glean what facts they could. Although the men had no training they frequently brought back valuable and accurate information; while it was difficult for them to tell the differences between a tractor and a tank, or an armoured car and a truck, they were very accurate about the position of enemy forces and the number of men involved. Usually one of us would take an agent out by car along camel tracks as far as we dared to go in the direction of the enemy, dump him, and bury a can of water in the sand for him to drink on his way back. The agents received no regular wages but were paid by results and given a little cash for expenses. The fact that a Kenya Somali could wander about in Italian territory without raising comment is accounted for by the nomadic life of the people and the fact that the international boundary was a mere line on the map and took no account of tribal grazing grounds; as a result, comings and goings across the border were frequent and a normal part of life.

We were often called upon to send out search parties for men who had got lost; most of our agents were good trackers and seldom failed in their task. The country around Wajir is for the most part dead flat and covered in thorn bush which grows to a uniform height of about twelve feet. There are no land marks, every way one turns one sees only the same thorn bush. A man lost in such country is in a terrible predicament with his visibility reduced to less than a hundred yards and, unless he is rescued within twenty-four hours, he will almost certainly die of thirst.

One of our reconnaissance aircraft failed to return after a patrol to the north of Wajir. About a fortnight later an agent reported that it had come down in the bush and that the pilot and observer had been found by some Somalis who were prepared to help them (most of the Somalis were pro-British and anti-Italian). They would have taken them to their *manyatta* and after giving them food and drink have guided them back to Wajir. Unfortunately, the airmen, probably imagining that the Somalis were enemies, drove them away at gun point and set off on their own. They were never seen again and almost certainly must have perished from thirst.

Our camp had been deliberately situated well away from that of the brigade occupying Wajir, for we wished it to be readily accessible to tribesmen bringing in information. Not far from us was Ali Sagara's 'shop'. He was an enterprising trader, the only one who had remained behind when the bombs began to fall. His shop, set up in the bush, did a roaring trade with the troops and tribesmen. Ali Sagara never failed to keep us supplied with canned goods, beer and spirits, and this in spite of the fact that the nearest source of supplies was at Isiolo, more than two hundred miles away. In those days there was no NAAFI, we were supposed to draw rations of fresh vegetables and bread, but by the time they reached us the bread was fit to build a bomb shelter and a goat would not deign even to sniff the vegetables. I remember a particularly revolting ration item called 'Soya Link', though it looked like sausages it tasted of sawdust but, as during the 14-18 War, there was always a surfeit of bully beef and jam and the last could at least be relied upon for establishing friendly relations with Somali children.

One morning a young Somali, whom we had not seen before, appeared and reported that there was a large Banda (irregular Italian native infantry) hide-out at some wells called Guguxa some eighty miles to the north-east and that it was being used as a base from which to ambush our motorised patrols. It was decided to attack the position with a company of the Gold Coast Regiment. As no one, apart from the Somali, knew the whereabouts of the wells he had to come as guide, dressed for the occasion in military uniform. We em-bussed in the early hours of the morning and drove without lights along the road to El Wak until a point was reached at which the guide indicated we should leave the transport and walk. Our Somali said the wells were at about two hours' march. In the event they turned out to be nearer five hours away and it was well on in the heat of the day when we arrived in an area of particularly thick bush.

There was not a breath of wind and the heat from the blazing sun was like a furnace. Our guide told us the hide-out was close by. The commander of the company to which we were attached had decided upon a somewhat complicated manoeuvre and a good deal of time was required to get the men into position. To add to the delay one of the British N.C.O.s fainted from heat-stroke and a party had to be left to guard him. Cautiously we edged forward. I was in the centre with one of the platoon commanders. Presently we heard voices issuing from a series of depressions in the ground some twenty yards ahead. An African soldier next to me was carrying a rifle with a discharger cup on its end loaded with a bomb. Instead of holding the muzzle up he had it pointed down and I expected any moment to see the bomb drop out. My attention was so much distracted by this sight that I failed to notice the platoon commander hurl a grenade into one of the depressions—unfortunately the wrong one. After the explosion half a dozen Banda shot out of a neighbouring depression and disappeared into the bush followed by a fusillade of shots. The platoon commander turned to me and apologised for throwing his bomb into the wrong hole. Suddenly I recognised him as an old schoolmate, Hughes, whom I had not seen for over sixteen years. At that moment we all rushed forward and I never had the chance of meeting him again. In spite of much firing no one was hit but I was greatly relieved to see that the soldier had shot off his bomb. Evidently we had surprised a water party for there was a small well in the bottom of the 'right' depression with water bottles and half-filled cans lying around. As the whole countryside had been alerted it was pointless to go on. We started back in the heat of the afternoon. An hour later firing broke out in our rear; the Banda had rallied and come after us, they stayed on our heels for the next two hours in spite of heavy counter fire from automatic weapons and rifles. Most of the men were pretty well exhausted by the time we reached our transport.

On another occasion, with a different company of West Africans, I happened to be with the company commander, a fiery Irishman: as we approached an alleged ambush, where the enemy were said to have machine guns concealed in trees, he turned to his orderly and said 'Give me the bombs.' The orderly, with a sheepish grin, replied 'Sah, I forget them.' 'You b....
Wa-wa!' the commander roared. I never discovered what Wa-wa meant, doubtless something impolite in West African dialect. Fortunately the enemy were not at hand.

Out with a Nigerian company on patrol I noticed a soldier pick up an elephant dropping and, carefully wrapping it in a handkerchief, stow it in his haversack. At the next halt I mentioned the incident to the C.O. He had the man up and made him turn out his haversack and out came the elephant ball. When asked why he was carrying elephant manure round the country he replied that he intended to take it back to his home where elephant balls were considered to be a rare and powerful medicine. The country where these elephant signs were seen was completely waterless and for months on end between the rainy seasons the animals living in the area can have had no surface water to drink.

The District Commissioner, or civil administrator, at Wajir, was my old friend Hugh Grant, who had been one of my partners in the goat trading venture at Lake Baringo. He asked me whether I would be prepared to join him in raising an irregular force of Somali and Boran tribesmen to counter the Italian Banda. I readily agreed. Soon afterwards we started to recruit the men, and the wilder and woollier they were the better we liked them. Our base camp was on a dry river-bed called Lake Dima, about seventy miles south of Wajir. In a short time we were joined by five more officers and started intensive training with emphasis on rifle shooting, water drill and long and hard patrols with camels. In spite of being born and brought up in desert country the men were surprisingly improvident with their water ration; unless closely checked most of their water bottles would be dry by noon. But once having exhausted their supply they would carry on without apparent distress much longer than we Europeans could, though we had carefully husbanded our water. Our Somalis told us that it was their custom when going on a long march through waterless country to chew quantities of the tender leaves and shoots of miraar (*Catha edulis*); this small, twisted tree grows in parts of the Highlands at an altitude of about six thousand feet. It is claimed that the leaves contain a drug which stimulates wakefulness and deadens fatigue and thirst. I once tried it, but the taste was very bitter and I thought the cure worse than the complaint.

Hugh Grant was a born leader and was in his element with such a force as ours. His enthusiasm and energy made us all keen to finish training and take the field, and after two and a half months we felt ready to tackle anything. We had hoped to work as a single unit but higher authority decided to split us up among the regular forces to act as scouts. My platoon was detailed to join the South Africans who had recently taken over the Wajir sector.

For the next month we accompanied motorised fighting patrols which sallied out of Wajir two or three times a week. Usually two trucks were allotted to carry my platoon.

Coming back from a patrol we passed a pride of lions sitting close beside the road. They gazed at us in mild curiosity and showed no nervousness as the eighteen heavy vehicles of the patrol rumbled past; lions, in fact have no fear of anything on earth except man. Some way further on there were excited signals from the truck behind us which was carrying the rest of my men. We stopped and discovered a free fight going on in the back of the second vehicle. It took the united efforts of the South African drivers and myself to part the contestants. Evidently motorised soldiering did not agree with my irregulars.

A few days later we were ordered to go to Dif, which is on the border. Here the South Africans had established a perimeter camp. We arrived just in time for quite a sharp air-raid. Bombs fell close and machine-gun bullets whistled around; luckily no one was hit. Just as the Italian aircraft, five Caproni bombers and four Fiat fighters, had finished their attack and were turning back, a lone Hurricane fighter appeared, skimming low over the bush, the first we had seen: it went straight into the Italian formation and in a few minutes it had brought down three bombers and one fighter. Hitherto the Italians had had it very much their own way in the air as we had little with which to oppose them apart from a few antiquated biplanes.

The long awaited advance into Italian territory had started, and so small was the opposition that we went along much faster than was expected. My task for the next few days was to take patrols ahead as soon as the troops halted for the night, to guard against surprise attack during the hours of darkness. Consequently we had little chance to sleep.

During a patrol we picked up a Banda who had lost touch with his comrades and blundered into us. There was little of value he could tell us and in the ordinary course of events he would have been sent back as a prisoner of war, but I liked the look of him and prevailed upon authority to allow him to remain with me; eventually I engaged him as an irregular soldier. I called him Ali

Banda and he proved himself a most faithful and loyal member of my little force.

At length we reached the town of Kismayu on the coast. Here we rejoined Hugh Grant and the rest of the Irregulars. Because the advance had progressed so fast there had been no time to organise the administration of the conquered territory; Grant's Irregulars were therefore given this unwelcome task. All of us were bitterly disappointed. We had joined the Irregulars expecting to be in the thick of the fighting, now we were to become policemen and administrators. It was a depressing outlook.

There were a number of Italian farms on the Juba River which it was reported were being looted by the riverine tribesmen. The few occupiers who had remained behind were said to be in grave danger of being murdered, so we set off to try to restore law and order. Each platoon was allotted an area. Mine was along the south bank of the river. Most of the farm-houses I visited were deserted and had already been ransacked but at length I arrived at a small house which appeared to be undamaged. The door was thrown open and an elderly Italian greeted me and ushered me inside. He was alone, all his servants having fled. He gave me to understand that he had expected to be attacked at any moment. I asked him what he would have done had I not arrived. He led me into his bedroom and pulled open a drawer. It was crammed full of hand grenades. Just at that moment one of my men came in to report that a large mob was approaching, indeed we could already hear the shouting. Quickly I concealed the men around the premises with strict orders not to move until I gave the signal and then to go into the mob with rifle butts. On they came, shouting and yelling, brandishing all manner of weapons, but I did not see any firearms. When they were almost within stone-throwing distance I gave a blast on my whistle. My men came out of hiding like terriers and charged the mob with wild Somali war cries. Without hesitating the crowd broke and fled in all directions, hotly pursued by the Irregulars. It was nearly dark by the time the last of my men returned, hugely pleased with themselves. It was too late to think about moving on, so I decided to spend the night and was very hospitably entertained by the farmer. He gave me the best dinner I had tasted for a long time, washed down with plenty of wine. As the evening wore on he became more voluble and confiding. With the help of his limited English and my few words of Italian I gathered that he was a rabid anti-Fascist. Indeed, every time the name of Mussolini was mentioned he spat violently and shouted *porco*.

Next morning, leaving a guard, I set off to look for a suitable headquarters and at length came on a fine new house in a large banana plantation. It had been thoroughly looted, all the furniture was gone and the rooms had been defiled with human excrement. I sent off a strong patrol to arrest the headman of the local village. In due course he was marched in and I gave him a lengthy harangue, telling him that the British were now in occupation and that all property looted from Italian farmers must be returned immediately and moreover, that, as I wished to occupy the house, he must collect his people and give the place a thorough clean-out and restore the stolen furniture. As I had expected, he denied all knowledge of what had gone on. I led him to the front of the house and pointed to a large tree with many spreading branches and said, 'At dawn tomorrow you will hang from one of those unless I sleep on a comfortable bed in a clean house tonight!' Then I sent the headman back under escort to his village to think things over. In a very short time a long procession of villagers appeared, carrying almost the entire furnishings of the house on their heads. I set them to washing the rooms, and saw to it that the headman removed some of the filth with his own hands. It was obvious that the plantation had been well cared for and that machinery had been used to cultivate the land, but there was no sign of any tractors, so again I sent for the headman and told him that I was seriously thinking of using the tree as he had not obeyed my orders, for 'Where are the tractors?' Swallowing hard he said that he had been meaning to tell me about the tractors but he was so frightened that it had slipped his memory, they were quite safe as he had carefully hidden them in the forest by the river to await the return of the farmer. Presently there was the roar of heavy engines starting up in the distance and out came two caterpillar tractors. One of my men who was on sentry duty, knowing nothing about the tractors, jumped to the conclusion that we were being invaded by enemy tanks. Hastily he took cover in a ditch and opened fire, fortunately his aim was poor.

A couple of days later the farmer arrived together with his wife; they were pleasantly surprised to find most of their property intact. It was the policy of the military government to get the farms re-occupied and back under production as soon as possible. I then moved my headquarters to another house a few miles up the Juba River opposite a small town called Margarita or Jamama. The house and plantation turned out to have been the property of General Graziani, the Commander-in-Chief of the Italian forces in North Africa. Here again I had to use pressure to get the contents returned.

The Juba contained many crocodile which had an extremely sinister reputation. They were particularly dangerous in times of flood and the local people when drawing water used a gourd fastened on the end of a long pole in order to remain out of their reach. An Italian farmer told me that one night he had a dog taken off the veranda of his house by a crocodile. On one occasion when I was watching a herd of goats being taken to water at a shallow place on the river where the people had built a small stockade in a half-circle protecting the drinking place I could see the poles jerking violently as crocodiles tried to get at the goats. One lot of goats had drunk and were standing on the bank six feet above the water but outside the protection of the stockade. Suddenly a huge crocodile shot out of the water and snapped at a goat missing it by a fraction. The next time it tried the same manoeuvre I was ready and shot it through the head.

A measure of peace and quiet having been restored along the Juba, I was posted to Afmadu, a small station in the desert between the river and the Kenya border. The only prominent feature of the place was a fine, large, white concrete house, the residence of the former Italian Administrator; on the outside it was rather battered by our shell fire and pockmarked by bullets but the inside was little damaged. A few hundred yards away there was a big dump containing hundreds of wooden land mines and a dozen cases of hand grenades; all were standing out in the blazing sun. Vainly I tried to get engineers to remove the dump until finally I decided to destroy it myself. As a preliminary measure I had the cases of grenades removed and buried in a hole over which fire-wood was stacked and set alight. At the end of twenty minutes there was a shattering explosion and an enormous column of black smoke. That had gone off all right, but now I had to deal with the land mines: I was chary of moving them for fear of setting one off and decided to destroy them *in situ*. A fire was made and this time I took the precaution of evacuating the house as it was a little too close for comfort. The wooden mine containers crackled merrily but at the end of half an hour nothing else had happened. In fact they were empty which, on reflection, was perhaps just as well as I would have had a lot of explaining to do if the house had been flattened by the blast. Even my destruction of the grenades was a highly irregular procedure contrary to all military manuals, and one for which I was later severely censured.

Half a mile from the house were the remains of an Afmadu village. There was little left of the mud and thatch houses, and the place was infested with rats, which sought sustenance at my house. While sitting on the veranda sipping my sundowner it was one of my evening amusements to take pot shots at rats with a heavy Italian machine gun mounted on a tripod beside my chair. Apart from the rats, this procedure discouraged human night prowlers and even during the day tended to keep the front of the house clear of importunate tribesmen.

I was now entirely alone and during the next two months seldom saw a visitor, but my life was full of interest and I came to know and like the local Somali tribesmen who would bring their problems to me to settle. One morning a young Somali appeared and dumped a white cotton bag in front of me. He said he had found it in the bush on the line of the Italian retreat. The bag was stuffed full of Italian lire notes amounting to about three hundred thousand. There had been a rumour of the murder of an Italian pay-master, perhaps this was part of the haul.

The country was by no means quiet and there were frequent reports of banditry by disbanded native soldiery, all of which had to be investigated. On one patrol, following such a report, I was leading along a path when I almost stepped on the largest Egyptian cobra I had ever seen. It reared itself up with hood extended almost on a level with my breast; it was of a brownish grey colour and at a guess I would say that it was not less than nine feet in length.

On a visit to an outpost, and while I was inspecting the men's rifles, I was astonished to see one with its muzzle bulged out like the mouth of a blunderbuss. On enquiry it appeared that a pull-through had stuck in the barrel and the members of the outpost had held a committee meeting on how best to remove the obstruction. Finally it was agreed that the best mode of proceeding was to place another rifle muzzle to muzzle with the blocked one and fire a bullet down it. Why no one was hurt I never discovered.

The Afmadu area, although semi-desert, contained a variety of wild life such as giraffe, oryx, Grevy zebra, ostrich, Grant's gazelle, gerenuk (Waller's gazelle) and Hunter's antelope, besides a fair number of lion which could be heard roaring most nights. The Italians had left a tame ostrich behind which had been wounded in the fighting and walked with a slight limp. Every morning while I was having breakfast, its long neck would reach in through the window for scraps from the table.

After nearly eleven months of active service I was granted leave. As there was no means of transport from Afmadu I went to Kismayu on the coast, hoping to get a boat there to take me to Mombasa and then go on by train to Nairobi. When I reached Kismayu I found that there were no boats. At length I got in touch with an Arab trader who was anxious to visit Kenya in order to stock up with trade goods and was awaiting permission to leave with a couple of ancient trucks. In return for the promise of a lift I was able to help him secure the necessary permit. While arranging about the transport I was hospitably entertained by the local Administrator and stayed in his house. During the night I was awakened by what I took to be an explosion. As many unexploded bombs and shells had been left lying about by the Italians, explosions were fairly common; I turned over and went back to sleep. In the morning I found that an enormous chandelier had fallen from the ceiling and crashed in splinters on the bedside table. A few inches to one side and it would have landed on my head which would have been an odd way of ending my career as a soldier.

Later in the day I went to the Arab's shop and learnt that all was ready for our take-off but that we must wait for the cool of the evening because, so he assured me, the trucks could not travel in the hot part of the day for fear of over-heating the engines and bursting the tyres. On inspecting the vehicles I appreciated the need for the precaution. Never had I seen such scrap iron on wheels, obviously the trucks had been resurrected from some refuse dump. This was borne out by the Arab who told me that all his sound vehicles had been commandeered by the Italians for the war effort or rather for their flight from Kismayu. Eventually we set off and for some hours, apart from frequent stops to fill the radiators, we travelled in a fairly normal manner. Then suddenly, without any apparent cause, the truck in which I was a passenger together with the Arab, shot off the road and was brought to a standstill by a tree. Our best headlamp was shattered. The Arab staggered out and lay on the ground groaning and the whole company gathered around to commiserate. After a brief survey I assured him that he was not fatally injured and insisted on going ahead. At length we arrived at the border cut and there was a prolonged dispute as to which way to go. I was drowsy at the time and paid little attention but presently, as we jolted on our way, I noticed the Southern Cross away over to our right. Plainly we were travelling due east, straight towards the sea. We must have taken the cut instead of the road. I halted the caravan and tried to explain the mistake. The drivers and the Arab were obdurate and said they knew the route well. Finally I lost patience and forced them to turn back. On returning to the place where the doubt had arisen I recognised it as being close to our camp site where the lone Hurricane had downed the Italian aircraft. After this I had no difficulty in finding the right road. It was indeed fortunate that I had discovered the error as there was barely sufficient petrol to reach Wajir.

Back in Nairobi, after a long talk with Archie Ritchie, it was decided that he would apply for my release from the military forces on the grounds that initially I had been given leave to join up to fight in the war and had not undertaken to become an administrator-cum-policeman in occupied territory. My release was sanctioned and I returned to my duties as Game Warden.

8: *Man-eating lions and elephant control*

THERE WAS A GREAT DEAL of work awaiting me. It had not been possible to provide a replacement during my absence and poachers and illegal traders in ivory, rhino horn and leopard skins had taken full advantage. Also, there were many complaints of marauding lion and elephant from various parts of the Northern Province. My first task was to try to clean up some of the poaching on the T.O.L. farms on the southern border of Samburu District. Once again I made myself thoroughly unpopular with the European farmers by arresting their employees who had been killing game on a large scale, but on this occasion the full weight of the law was behind me in the form of Pete Jay, the Police officer in charge of the Rumuruti District, who accompanied me on the safari. He was a good companion, a very cheerful character, full of excellent stories. Jay was anxious to round up trespassers, principally unemployed and lawless Turkana who had infiltrated on to the big ranches and were living by poaching and thieving livestock. The combination of my Game Scouts and his Police Scouts made a very tough force.

During a patrol we came on a spring in a depression, known as Loito Gito. Here, out of the bare earth, rises a heavily grassed mound, about six feet in height and forty feet in diameter, its shape is that of an inverted saucer. In the centre of the mound is a miry pool which is said to be bottomless. As the edges are perpendicular any animal which takes one step too far is caught in the morass and slowly disappears out of sight. It is a matter for conjecture what strange creatures may lie hidden in the depths of the bog. The local Dorobo told us that it had always been there and that in times of drought it swallowed up many animals but that they often retrieved the beasts before they finally disappeared. In fact it was a natural trap which kept the Dorobo supplied with fresh meat.

While I was doing my best to stop poaching and preserve the wild life of the country, legalised slaughter of game was taking place on a vast scale in the European ranching areas. Thousands of animals were being shot to feed the Italian prisoners of war. This massacre was not carried out by Game Department employees but by private persons who sold the carcases at a handsome profit to the prison camps, regardless of whether the animals killed were pregnant females or with young. The slaughter on the ranches of such animals as eland, oryx and zebra meant that irreparable damage to wild life was not confined to these areas alone. From time immemorial the animals had made their regular migrations, from the highlands to the plains in the low country to the north in the rainy seasons, and back again in the dry and even today some animals, particularly the oryx, have not recovered from this wartime slaughter. Another which has almost reached the point of no return is the Kenya hartebeest. The claim that there was no other means of feeding the prisoners was without foundation for even in the war years many parts of the country were grossly over-stocked with domestic animals. So, let it be faced, that it was the easy way out for the Government, by accepting it they solved the problems of feeding the prisoners on cheap meat, mollified the European farmers, who were continually complaining about game on their land, and avoided the thorny issue of de-stocking in the over-stocked native areas.

I next turned my attention to the northern part of the Samburu District where I had received information about a Turkana poaching gang. A new Police officer, Alan Peverett, had just taken up duties in Samburu, and as he was anxious to get to know his area, it suited us well to join forces. He was a man with twelve years' experience in the Police and had been all over the country. He, with eight constables and baggage camels, and I with an equal number of Game Scouts and my mules and donkeys, left Maralal and headed for the Ndoto Mountains where I wished to investigate the shooting of an elephant by a Police patrol which claimed that it had been done in self-defence.

Before long we had ample evidence to show that it had been a wanton act of killing for which there was no excuse. A police constable with a tribal policeman and some local Samburu had seen a party of three bull elephants over three hundred yards away across a little valley, feeding on the steep slope opposite. The tribal policeman bet the constable that he could not kill the elephant. The latter knelt down and, taking careful aim with his old World War I 303 rifle, fired and hit the elephant in the brain; it then crashed down the hillside. Certainly a record for a brain shot. The elephant carried tusks of over a hundred pounds a side. The shooting of animals by patrols in 'self-defence' was all too common, so it was with much satisfaction that I saw the man convicted and punished. I hoped this case would have a salutary effect.

Our next camp at Arsim was of painful memory. From here we planned to carry out a raid on a small water-hole about a day's march to the north into the desert where the Turkana poaching gang was said to have its lair. The leader was a Turkana named Adukan whose name was constantly associated with the killing of giraffe and rhino in the country between the Ndoto Mountains and Mount Kulal. We set off before dawn, leaving the transport to follow later and made for a small hill called Aberin at the foot of which lay the water-hole. Our sudden arrival took the poachers by surprise and we captured four men but not Adukan. They told us that he had gone out that morning to inspect traps (Turkana wheel traps as described in Chapter 5); they added that on the previous evening he had been 'throwing his sandals' and had said that he felt uneasy and that there was danger in the air. The throwing of sandals is practised by some of the older Turkana who claim to be able to foretell the future by watching which way they fall. There was a quantity of dried giraffe meat, pieces of skin and tail in the hide-out, sufficient evidence to charge the prisoners. We learnt that all giraffe and rhino skin was fashioned into sandals and when there were sufficient for two donkey loads they were taken into Turkana country south of Lake Rudolf and sold, the price being a fair-sized goat for two pairs. The tail was sold to Samburu women who used the long tough hairs to thread beads. When asked what they did with rhino horns they told us that they were useful for pounding sandals but otherwise valueless! They explained that giraffe and rhino skin make the most durable sandals and that the hide is cut into the required shape and then pounded for several hours until soft and pliable; the uppers consisted of thongs made from the skins of such animals as oryx, eland or water buck; and they added that sandals were at a premium in Turkana country as most of the giraffe and rhino had long since been exterminated in that region.

Leaving Aberin we turned eastwards, crossing the main Isiolo to Marsabit road, and after a week reached the border between the Samburu and Boran tribes at some wells called Kom where the fast-diminishing water was shared by the two tribes. We were just in time to prevent a battle between them which would certainly have ended in bloodshed had we not appeared on the scene. We convened a *baraza*, or meeting, of the elders from both sides and after a lengthy and heated discussion, divided the water-bearing sands equally between the two parties. The trouble had arisen when, being themselves too idle to dig their own wells, the Boran used wells dug by the Samburu. The dispute was settled, at least, until the rains covered the wells with sand—in the following dry season they would have to be re-dug and then there would be more trouble—but that was a future headache for the Administration.

My cook Kanyari had acquired a young black-headed ram. This creature became his shadow and would not leave him for an instant. It slept alongside him at night and when Kanyari brought my early morning tea the ram was there to greet me. On the march it was always six inches behind the old man. When I went out hunting for meat for the camp, Kanyari usually accompanied me. Being the only Moslem in the camp he had to 'hallal' the meat. The ram came too. I made Kanyari swear a solemn oath that he would never kill the ram for eating. He kept the vow and in the end the animal survived him. Unfortunately with advancing years the ram became bemused by the fair sex and lost most of his touching loyalty.

The last part of our safari was along the palm-fringed banks of

the Uaso Nyiro River, a welcome change from the desert and full
of interest. Wild animals and tribesmen with their stock from
many miles away watered at the river and throughout the day
and night there were constant comings and goings. In two days'
march we crossed the spoor of more than sixty rhino. These
animals usually spent the day four or five miles away but at dusk
they would start making their way towards the river, reaching
their favourite watering place after dark. Rhino on the whole are
solitary and silent creatures but, at the water, they seemed to
forgather with their neighbours; there were bathing parties,
flirtations and fights accompanied by weird high-pitched screams
and long drawn-out groans, not the sort of sounds one would
expect from such massive beasts. Buffalo herds also came by
night to drink. Oryx and zebra preferred the heat of the day to
slake their thirst. Elephant drank at any hour of the day or
night, depending on the distance from their feeding grounds.
Sometimes a herd would spend the heat of the day under the
shade of the palms or bathing in the river. Almost on the minute
at eight a.m. great flocks of sand grouse would appear to drink
and after about an hour the flight would cease almost as suddenly
as it had started. Crocodile were fairly numerous and had a bad
reputation. One of the Game Scouts, an old soldier, said that
some years ago he had been a member of a patrol of the King's
African Rifles which had arrived at the river and found it in high
flood. Since it was necessary to cross, the officer in charge asked
for a volunteer to take a rope over and fasten it to a tree on the
opposite bank. One of the men, a native from Lake Victoria,
volunteered and swam across but on his way back, as he was
showing off his prowess, he suddenly gave a cry, was pulled under
by a crocodile and never seen again. Many years later a Dutchman camped close to the water's edge. He slept on the ground
surrounded by strips of meat hung up to dry into biltong, which
was of course asking for trouble. During the night a crocodile
crawled up the bank and, not discriminating between dead and
live meat, seized the Dutchman by a foot and started to drag him
towards the water. Fortunately the man had a rifle beside him
which he was able to fire off, scaring the crocodile away.

Alan Peverett and myself had become quite attached to the four prisoners captured at Aberin and we decided it would be a shame to send them to gaol where they would be obliged to associate with the scum of the towns and leave at the end of their terms saturated in the atmosphere of common criminals. Far better, we thought to get them jobs. I engaged two, Gobus and Ebono, who served me loyally for many years. The other two were placed with another Game Warden; one was killed by a buffalo some years later while carrying out his duties as a Game Scout. Alan was an experienced police officer and through his help we caught twenty poachers most of whom were convicted and sent to prison.

My next task was to deal with man-eating lions in Samburu country at a place called Lalelei, two days' march north of Maralal. In the course of the last twelve months nine tribesmen had been killed and eaten. The area for the most part was open grassland interspersed with big tracts of very dense thorn scrub. On my arrival the Samburu told me that on the previous day a youth had been killed while herding cattle. I went to the scene and found that three lions had gone through the herd of cattle and chased the youth round a bush, killing and eating him on the spot; probably hyenas had finished up what the lions had left. All that remained were a few blood stains on the hard ground. The occurrence was unusual for the lions had deliberately chosen to attack a human being when cattle were available, and, as it turned out, had no injuries, which is usually the case with man-eaters.

I made camp on a bare ridge near by and planned to start the hunt on the following morning. A particularly strong thorn *boma* was constructed for the donkeys and mules; it was placed between my tent and the men's camp. The two exposed sides were protected by hurricane lamps on poles. Late at night there was an uproar in the donkey *boma*; I leapt out of bed, grabbing my rifle and a torch, and was just in time to see a lioness forcing her way through the thorns of the *boma*. Luckily my shot killed her outright and the men were in time to stop the animals from breaking out. I felt sure there were other lions around so I went back to bed intending to keep awake, but it had been a long and tiring day and I soon fell asleep. Some two hours later I was again woken up by the donkeys and dashed out, this time with only a revolver and the torch. Another lioness was about to force her way in. I emptied the revolver at her as she made off but apparently without effect. Again I retired to bed and, try as I might, could not keep awake. In the morning when Kanyari appeared with my tea, complete with his young ram, he said 'Wake up *bwana* (sir), and come look outside.' There were the pug marks of a lion all around the tent. At one moment it had been within eighteen inches of my head with not even the canvas between us, as I had only the outer fly of the tent pitched and the marks were actually under the eaves. I was badly shaken at the thought of a man-eater almost within eating distance while I slept.

We set off, four armed Game Scouts and myself, to follow up the spoor of the lions of which there were four. After three hours of following the tracks, losing them and finding them again, they led us into an area of dense bush. I spread the scouts out in a line at about twenty yard intervals with myself in the centre, and we beat through it. We had transversed the bush and were just emerging into the open when there were loud yells and low growls on my left. I saw Game Scout Tiwai on the ground with a lioness on top of him. Game Scout Awalan being next in the line ran up without hesitation and, putting the muzzle of his rifle almost into the lioness's ear, shot her dead. We pulled her off expecting to find Tiwai seriously mauled, but there was not a mark on him. He had managed to hold the lioness off as he lay on the ground by kicking her in the chest. I found that one of my revolver bullets of last night had grazed her across the chest, which doubtless accounted for her bad temper. The unfortunate Tiwai had obviously had a bad fright but he was chaffed unmercifully by the rest of the men for making such a noise.

For the next month I continued the hunt and finally shot six more lions, two exceptionally big males. One of these we hunted for three days. On each occasion when we put him up, we found that he had been lying in bush close to a rhino. If it had happened on one occasion, I would have said that it was a coincidence but, when it occurred three times I was convinced that the lion had deliberately sought the company of the rhino, perhaps he believed he would give him warning of our approach. Rhino themselves are not particularly alert creatures, but invariably they have a following of tick birds, or oxpeckers, which give instant warning to their host of the approach of danger by making a loud hissing sound. It is odd that these same birds, when associating with domestic cattle, will ignore the presence of human beings. On the last day we followed the lion for nearly ten hours until finally he lost patience and took the offensive, enabling me to stop him with my heavy rifle. I might here mention that after my unpleasant experience at Arsim (described in Chapter 6), I had disposed of my heavy magazine rifle and bought myself a double barrelled 470 which never let me down, and in thick bush and at close quarters was far superior to any magazine rifle.

Experience has taught me that when following up lions, particularly a wounded one, the female is far more tricky and dangerous than the male. A lion when cornered will usually start to growl and give away his position before attacking. Not so a lioness, she will stay hidden in complete silence until the enemy is within easy distance and only then will she utter a low growl as simultaneously she makes her lightning charge.

When moving camp a couple of days after the donkey *boma* had been attacked, all the donkeys had been saddled and loaded. The last objects to be tied on were the two dry lioness skins. The donkey selected to carry them protested vigorously and had to be held by two men. As soon as he was let go, he started to buck and kick and dashed in among the others who, scenting lion, at once stampeded in a headlong gallop, shedding their loads as they went and disappeared over the horizon in a cloud of dust. It was two days before all the gear and animals had been recovered. Thereafter the skins were carried by a man well in the rear.

At this time Game Scout Lembirdan, who had been sent to the Mathews Range to investigate a report, had a very close call with a bull elephant. He was walking along a path through thick forest high up in the hills when he unexpectedly came face to face with an elephant, which promptly charged. Lembirdan turned and ran with the elephant following and rapidly gaining on him. As he ran, he fired his rifle over his shoulder without effect. Then he swerved off the path and found himself on the edge of a sheer river bank with no means of further retreat. The elephant was almost on him when he fired again. Luckily the bullet penetrated its brain and as it fell Lembirdan was drenched by its blood, which gives some indication of its closeness. The elephant was a notorious killer and in the course of years had accounted for a number of Samburu. It carried one large tusk of over a hundred pounds in weight. The other was broken off short at the root and much decayed, no doubt causing a chronic, gargantuan toothache giving rise to a jaundiced view of life.

One of my camps, while hunting the man-eating lions, was close to the base of a range of small hills. While having breakfast I heard the call of wild dogs in the hills. It is a clear bell-like note 'Hoo-hoo-hoo' repeated five or six times with a second's pause between each 'hoo'. As we were having a day off, I went to investigate. I was walking along the edge of a deep gully and suddenly came on some eight dogs baying a magnificent greater kudu bull. At my abrupt appearance, the dogs slunk away into the bush. The kudu and I stood motionless staring at each other for several minutes, not more than fifteen yards apart. He was breathing heavily and looked exhausted with foam at his mouth. Evidently it had been a long chase and I had arrived on the scene in the nick of time to save him from being torn to pieces. At length, having recovered his breath, the kudu decided it was time to move. He went down to the edge of the gully but, finding the descent almost perpendicular, hesitated and came back and again stood looking at me and into the bush where the dogs had gone. He seemed to be weighing up the chances of escape; finally he made up his mind that the gully was the lesser of three evils, plunged over the edge, landed easily on the soft sand twenty feet below and then was away up the opposite hillside. Immediately the dogs took up the chase again, but now I could take a hand; luckily I was carrying a very accurate light rifle and was able to kill three of them on the slope opposite. I then followed as fast as I could and succeeded in shooting two more. The remainder, realising the odds were too great, sheered off the line taken by the kudu. He was saved—for that day at least.

Apart from man, these dogs are the most ruthless killers in creation. Once a pack goes after an animal there is little hope for it.

At the end of 1942 I was ordered to take over the Garissa District in addition to my normal beat. This meant a great deal of elephant control work as well as anti-poaching, mostly along the Tana River. In the dry season large numbers of elephant drank at the river and as at many points they had to cross cultivation in order to get to the water, there was endless trouble over damage to crops. Also, the Tana River was one of the most favoured hunting grounds of sportsmen from overseas as it carried some of the finest ivory to be found in Africa. The control of elephants is arduous and not infrequently dangerous work. My sympathies were almost entirely with the elephant. How were they to differentiate between unprotected cultivation and their natural food? The riverine tribesmen were far too idle to build fences and guard their crops at night. But it was my duty to protect the native cultivators however much it went against my inclinations to kill these noble creatures.

I shot a number of elephant, one was a big old bull which had done much damage to a banana plantation during the night. After having his fill and ignoring the protests of the owner, he had taken shelter in the depths of the riverine forest to pass the daylight hours in slumber; there I eventually tracked him. He was standing in a most awkward place and in order to get a clear shot at his head, I had to crawl through the branches of a fallen tree until I was almost too close for an effective brain shot. He fell like a log to my shot and I thought it was all over. But just to make sure I exchanged my heavy rifle for a light one and walked round the stern of the elephant with the idea of putting a bullet in the back of his head; one of my Scouts was in the act of cutting off its tail when suddenly the elephant heaved himself to his feet. Promptly the man carrying my heavy rifle took to his heels; I had to chase him to recover it; meanwhile the elephant had moved off. The Game Scout shot at him with his ineffective service rifle and before he disappeared I managed to give him another two shots, but at an awkward angle and from rather far away. We followed him for six hours without coming up to him, and it was not until late on the following day that we found him dead. Unfortunately, unlike the Turkana, the neighbouring tribesmen do not eat elephant, so the meat was wasted.

9: *I get married*

THE DISTRICT COMMISSIONER in charge of the Garissa District was William Hale, whom I had met on the Kerio River in 1934 while prospecting for gold. He and his wife Morna, short for Lamorna, invited me to a Christmas Eve party. It was a very cheery evening. Among the guests were George and Lois Low of the Veterinary Department, old friends of mine, and a married couple, Peter and Joy Bally. Peter Bally, a very keen botanist, was Swiss. At this time he was working for the Coryndon Museum and Joy was making paintings of flowers; they had come to Garissa to collect plants.

My recollections of the evening are vague, but I do remember waking up in the morning fully dressed with my feet on the pillow. I had planned to carry out a foot safari with camels to the Boni country near the coast, about a hundred and fifty miles to the south-east of Garissa. The Ballys asked if they might join the safari; I readily agreed. We set off following the north bank of the river. Any misgivings I may have had regarding the ability of Joy Bally to stand up to the hardships of a camel safari were soon put at rest. She was an indefatigable walker and possessed of boundless energy both physical and mental. Very soon it was apparent that there was a strong mutual attraction between us which grew with every day we spent in each other's company. I therefore determined to break up the safari as soon as possible before the situation went beyond my control. The opportunity offered itself at Ijara, a small trading centre about a hundred miles from Garissa. The Hales and Lows were due to pass through on their way to Lamu and it was arranged that the Ballys should go with them while I continued my safari into the Boni.

The Boni Forest, as it is sometimes called, is an area of park-like country with patches of dense forest and grassland of about fifteen hundred square miles containing a large amount of wild life such as elephant, buffalo, a few rhino, giraffe, oryx, Hunter's hartebeest, waterbuck, lesser kudu and the little oribi, leopards and a great number of lion. The area is sparsely inhabited by the Boni tribe who live in small isolated villages surrounded by half-hearted attempts at cultivation but their main interest is poaching by means of their powerful long bows and poisoned arrows. No Game Warden had ever made an anti-poaching safari in the country so my visit was a complete surprise to the people. I searched each village and in every one I found evidence of large scale poaching—such as game meat and skins. As it was not practicable to arrest whole villages, I picked out only the worst offenders to send to the magistrate at Lamu for trial. The remainder I let go after confiscating their bows and arrows, which I burnt.

Leopard and rhino were at one time numerous in this country, but had by now been almost exterminated, the former for their skins and the latter for their horns, which were sold to traders at the coast. Probably at least ninety per cent of leopard skin coats worn by fashionable women in the western world are made from skins illegally obtained. One wonders how many of the carefree wearers pause and give a thought to the unfortunate leopards which in many cases have endured hours of unspeakable agony held in the jaws of toothed steel traps to provide their coats. It is these ladies who are directly responsible for the near exter-mination of leopards in many parts of Africa. The market for rhino horn is the creation of Asiatic superstition encouraged by unscrupulous traders who endow it with miraculous aphrodisiac qualities.

In a short time news got around of my activities and the poachers began to conceal evidence of their crimes. A notorious poacher whom I was particularly anxious to arrest disappeared into the bush. A long time afterwards I learnt that he had been killed by a large python. The man it seems had stopped at a water-hole to have a drink and was suddenly seized by the python.

He succeeded in drawing his knife and stabbed frantically at the slowly constricting coils around his body. In doing so he accidentally stabbed himself; man and snake were both found dead. The only other case I know of in which a python deliberately attacked a human being occurred some ten years later in the Meru country. A party of prisoners under the charge of guards had been sent out to collect firewood in the forest. One of them wandered a little away from the rest. Suddenly, cries for help were heard and when the guards and prisoners ran to the scene they found the man held fast in the grip of a big python. In this case, the snake was soon chopped to pieces and the prisoner rescued, little the worse for his experience.

One of my Boran Game Scouts used to relate that when he was a boy, the stock returned to his *boma* one evening with a camel missing. Early next morning a search party went out and discovered the camel dead with a python attempting to swallow it. Not unnaturally, this was a tale I found even more difficult to swallow than the python his victim. But not long afterwards my brother Terence came across a giraffe lying dead with a python under it, also dead. One can only surmise that the python must have coiled itself around the giraffe's neck and strangled it, and that the great weight of the giraffe (one, which a friend weighed, scaled three thousand pounds) pinned the python to the ground. At this rate the camel story may not be altogether impossible. Why these two snakes should have tackled animals which they could not possibly swallow must be left to the imagination.

The Boni Forest was swarming with tse tse fly and fourteen days after entering the area one of my camels went sick with trypanosomiasis. The following day it could hardly move and I had to shoot it. The remaining camels looked none too fit and I was afraid that they too had contracted the disease. Camels go down very quickly with trypanosomiasis; most other animals just gradually lose condition, get thinner and thinner and finally die. Because of my doubts about the camels I decided to make for the coast at a little village called Makowe, which was the embarkation point for the island of Lamu where I intended to take the prisoners before the magistrate for trial. On the way I fell ill with a severe attack of malaria and could only manage half-day marches as by noon I had a high temperature. After three days of this routine I arrived at the Ijara-Lamu motor road and was lying under the shade of a tree when I heard the sound of motor vehicles approaching from the direction of Lamu. It was Hale's party, including the Ballys, returning to Garissa. I thought of stopping them as my quinine had run out and it might have been possible to borrow some. But it struck me that 'a young Game Warden lying ill in the bush far from aid' would certainly arouse womanly sympathies which might lead to complications, so I decided to let them go by.

Luckily the fever left me and three days later I was in Lamu with the prisoners attending court. The cases were tried with speed, and directly the last man had been dealt with the court adjourned and we set off for the District Commissioner's house where I was entertained to a very pleasant luncheon. It is related that this expeditious District Commissioner, after a short spell at Lamu, had had four rubber stamps struck for dealing with importunate petitioners. (1) 'Shauri ya Police' (it is the business of the Police. (2) 'Shauri ya Customs' (it is the business of the Customs). (3) 'Shauri yaku' (it is your own affair). (4) 'Shauri Mungu' (it is the will of God).

Lamu is an old Arab town dating back many hundreds of years containing some eight thousand inhabitants consisting of Hadra-maout and Muscat Arabs, Bajuns, Swahilis, Indians and a few Pokomo from the Tana River. It has a romantic atmosphere of decayed grandeur evidenced by the large dilapidated double-storied houses built of coral rag, divided by narrow winding streets where only two people can walk abreast in comfort. It used to be noted for the beauty of its women and the devoutness of citizens and at one time was a thriving port which carried on an extensive trade with Arabia but the abolition of slavery, the development of Mombasa and the building of the railway have left it a backwater slowly stagnating to death. While shopping I passed a coffee house bearing a sign in English: 'This is hygene house, no spitum or other dirty business permitted'.

In the District Commissioner's house were a magnificent pair of elephant tusks, weighing over a hundred and fifty pounds each, over nine feet in length and beautifully symmetrical in shape. They had been obtained near the Tana River during the reign of Queen Victoria. Another relic of the past displayed on the wall was an enormous war horn intricately carved from an elephant tusk, known as the Siwa, said to be over seven hundred years old and used to this day on certain ceremonial occasions.

After my brief visit to Lamu I returned to camp on the mainland near Makowe. It was clear that my camels were in no state to make the long march back to Garissa under loads. I therefore hired a trader's lorry to take my camp gear and myself to Garissa while the camels followed unladen. After spending another month in the Garissa District, I returned to Isiolo where I found a message from my chief telling me to go to headquarters at Nairobi.

I arrived in Nairobi fully intending at all costs to avoid meeting Joy. But fate decreed otherwise, as the first person I met on stepping out of my car to book a room at an hotel was Joy, and human nature being what it is that was the end of all my fine resolutions and inevitably I decided I could not live without her. There followed a period of much emotional stress in both our lives. We longed for the day when all the usual sordid formalities connected with the divorce proceedings would be over and we could face the world together as man and wife. I will always remember with gratitude the great help and guidance given me by Archie Ritchie. In difficult circumstances he was a true friend.

It was arranged that, while waiting for the divorce to go through, Joy would make a camp on the upper slopes of Mount Kenya and paint the mountain flowers. Her flower paintings were already considered outstanding and some years later, at an exhibition in London, she won the Grenfell Gold Medal. I felt anxious about the project as she would be camping alone at an altitude of about eleven thousand feet on the upper edge of the forest belt among elephant, buffalo and rhino and the nearest place from which she could get help in case of trouble was a good three hours walk away at the foot of the mountain. However, as she had set her heart on the plan I had to agree, though with misgivings.

As I had a few days' leave we set off together to establish the camp. The expedition was made possible by the generous help of a friend, Raymond Hook, who supplied the pack mules to carry tentage and food. The site for the camp was in a beautiful little forest glade close to the open moorlands leading up to the towering snow-clad peaks of the mountain. There was a convenient tree with a sloping trunk which would provide shelter in case the camp were invaded by elephant or buffalo. After fixing up the camp we went on with a couple of mules and a small tent with the idea of climbing to the foot of the main peaks and then going around them, at an altitude of about fifteen thousand feet. I had never been up so high before and was pleased to find that the altitude had little effect on me. Joy once again showed herself to be a tireless walker and we completed the round trip in about eight hours. After a most enjoyable few days, I had to return to Isiolo.

My last foot safari as a bachelor was to the Samburu country. At Maralal I was called on to deal with an elephant which had been terrorising the inhabitants of a small valley called Bawa. It had killed cattle and was in the habit of chasing people. Soon after pitching camp I sent out some local Samburu to look for it. They returned rather late in the evening and said they had found it near the top of the valley. By the time I reached the place, the elephant had moved and joined up with the others. In the gathering darkness it was difficult to pick him out so I decided to call off the hunt and try again the following morning. In the course of the morning a Samburu appeared and complained that he had just been chased and that the elephant was in thick bush about a mile away. I set off with Lembirdan and four Samburu. Soon we were on the fresh tracks and judging by a heap of steaming dung, the elephant was close ahead. At one point we lost the spoor and while we were casting around, the four Samburu, who were some little way in front, suddenly appeared and flashed past me running hard. Expecting the elephant to emerge from the same direction I stood ready to give battle but instead, without warning or sound, it appeared from my left, looming out of the dense cover almost over me. There was no time to aim and I fired blindly into its face and then, turning to get out of its way, tripped over a fallen branch and fell in a heap in front of it. Just as I was expecting to feel a massive trunk around me or a giant foot crushing the life out of me, Lembirdan, who had stood as firm as a rock, fired, and caused the elephant to turn away. It was a near thing and taught me a good lesson: never to turn one's back, however close an animal might be. After I had collected my wits we again followed up the spoor and came on the elephant in even denser bush. Two more shots from my heavy double-barrelled rifle brought him down. He was a very big bull with tusks of about seventy pounds a side. His front feet measured twenty-two and a half inches in diameter. There seemed to be no cause, such as old wounds or a broken and decayed tusk, to account for his aggressive nature.

On my way back to Isiolo I had occasion to search a small Somali village in which I had reason to believe that illegal ivory was hidden. The scouts and I turned the place inside out without success but, not far away, was a small rocky hill which looked as if it would afford ideal hiding places for ivory so I climbed it, but when nearing the top, I was set on by a swarm of bees. My descent was headlong with bees stinging me all over the back of my neck and arms, doubtless much to the delight of the Somali family who had a grandstand view from their huts. The East African bee is much more aggressive than its European counterpart and its sting is more virulent; I had heard of a farmer who had recently been killed by bees. Fortunately I am not allergic to bee stings and apart from the initial pain there were no ill effects.

As soon as I reached Isiolo I took the weekend off to go and visit Joy at her mountain camp, which was on the upper edge of the forest belt among masses of wild flowers, including giant lobelias which looked almost prehistoric. Beyond them grew huge heathers and still higher one came to snow and ice. There was an old track leading to the lower forest edge and here I left my car. There was only an hour and a half of daylight remaining and I was none too sure of being able to find my way up through the forest in darkness. But, being in love, such difficulties did not daunt me, nor did the prospect of meeting elephant and buffalo on the path. I had covered two-thirds of the way when night fell; after this I had to proceed more carefully so as not to miss the small game path and it was as well I did so, as a short way on two enormous black shapes emerged out of the gloom and with loud snorts crashed away. They were two bull buffalo which had been taking their ease in the path. I went on with redoubled caution, and it was eight p.m. by the time I reached Joy's camp. She was quite upset at the idea of my coming up through the forest in the dark and alone. But I pointed out that it was strong proof of my devotion.

She had been much troubled by a solitary bull buffalo which had taken up its abode in a patch of giant heath less than two hundred yards away and was in the habit of coming through the camp at night. Once it had blundered into the ropes of the tent in which she was sleeping. On another occasion she had met it on a path while out for a walk. Her cook was very frightened and talked of leaving. In the circumstances I thought it best to get rid of the buffalo before there was an accident. As a rule, buffalo in a herd are not dangerous, unless one is unlucky enough to get in the path of a stampede, but solitary bulls are often inclined to be bad-tempered and will sometimes attack without provocation.

It was easy to follow the tracks of the bull in the soft ground and after about an hour we saw him across a valley grazing on the opposite ridge above a cliff. It took another hour to get across and within suitable range. I had with me only a light rifle which would be good enough provided the animal was hit by the first shot in a vital place. Presently he turned, offering an easy shot at the shoulder, and I fired. Promptly he came straight towards us in what appeared to be a determined charge, then suddenly he crumpled and rolled over the cliff. The bullet had got him through the heart. He proved to be the fattest buffalo I had ever shot, his meat was remarkably tender and, owing to the coldness of the climate, it kept fresh for over ten days.

On our way back from the hunt I began to feel ill; I had, in fact, not fully recovered from a bout of fever. I just made the camp then I collapsed into a delirum and did not regain my senses until late at night. According to Joy I raved like a lunatic and had to be held down. This had never happened to me before and the only cause I could think of was a new anti-malarial drug called atebrin. The following day I was perfectly all right and was able to return to Isiolo. Afterwards I learnt that a few people are allergic to the drug and to its substitute mepacrin, and that there are cases on record of deaths and temporary insanity due to these drugs.

No sooner had I returned than there was an urgent summons from Marsabit to come and deal with marauding elephant. When I arrived there I found that a party of four bull elephants had formed the habit of raiding the police lines almost nightly. In the lines were some native-type maize cribs, small round huts made of grass, perched on stilts, two feet off the ground. Several had been knocked over and rifled by the elephants. One I noticed had a small hole in the side where an elephant had forced his trunk through and helped himself to almost the entire contents of maize cobs. It was a bright moonlit night when I took up my station slightly to leeward of the maize cribs. After a chilly wait of two hours the four elephants appeared out of the forest, which was close by, and advanced over a patch of open ground towards the cribs. I aimed at the shoulder of the leader and fired. He fell and immediately his comrades gathered round him and, supporting him, made for the forest and disappeared. It would have been futile, and also suicidal, to try to follow by night into the blackness of the forest. In the morning, as soon as it was light enough, Lembirdan and I took up the spoor, which was easy to follow as there were quantities of blood along the tracks; I felt sure the stricken elephant could not have gone far in spite of being helped by his fellows. Some two hundred yards inside the forest we came on him dead. I had heard about elephant helping a wounded comrade but this was the first time I had seen it.

A few nights later Lembirdan and I were sleeping in the open near the edge of a maize field which had been regularly raided by a solitary bull elephant. The field was about five acres in extent and carried a very fine crop, the maize stalks being seven feet in height and densely planted. This was a most unpleasant place in which to tackle an elephant at night, particularly as the owner told us that the elephant was very aggressive. Hoping we might get the beast before he entered the maize, I instructed the peasant to keep a sharp watch and wake us immediately he heard or saw it approaching. About two a.m. I was woken up and told that the elephant was already inside the field, and indeed we could hear him munching away at the maize. It was bitterly cold and low cloud obscured the moon. I did not like the situation one little bit but, not wishing to show fear in front of the peasant, I whispered to Lembirdan that we were going in. Very slowly we advanced towards the sounds of loud eating and breaking wind; evidently the elephant was enjoying himself. Among the maize there appeared to be a few small trees but as we were passing one of these, Lembirdan tapped me from behind. I looked around; the tree had gone. It was the elephant, he had been standing on a small mound and the steady rustling of the maize stalks indicated that he was coming straight at us. I switched on a torch held in my left hand alongside the barrel of the rifle, but the light reflecting off the maize merely dazzled me. I fired when the elephant was ten feet away. He swerved, leaving a broad swath of trampled maize as he headed for the forest. We were on his spoor as soon as it was light and followed him for eight hours, but never came up within sight or sound of him. The following day we searched again without success. Probably the shot had struck high in the head, missing the brain.

Whenever there was a weekend free I used to go up the mountain to see Joy. Once, when I had hoped to visit her, news was received of man-eating lions on the Kinna River about a hundred miles to the east of Isiolo on the border between Boran and Meru country. It was reported that a Meru and his two wives had set off to a Boran village in order to trade their loads of maize for goats. They had started back for their home in the hills rather late in the day with four goats. After walking for a time the man of the party complained of feeling ill and lay down under a tree. His women urged him to make for the nearest Boran village and there spend the night as the country was notorious for lion but he said he could go no farther and told the women to make a fire and build an enclosure for the goats. When it grew dark, the women became frightened and decided to pass the night in the branches of the tree. Some hours later three lions suddenly appeared out of the darkness and killed and ate the unfortunate Meru and his goats under the horrified eyes of the two women. A short time previously a Boran had also been taken out of his hut.

I set off in my light truck and after a journey of six hours over very rough tracks arrived at the Kinna stream where I pitched camp under a fine grove of palm trees close to a Boran village. I sent for the headman and told him to warn his people to keep a look-out for lion and report immediately when any were seen. Meanwhile, I engaged two local Boran who were reputed to be good trackers and had intimate knowledge of the habits of the lion in the area. That night lions roared continuously some way down the stream until the early hours. On the dark still air, which carried only an occasional ghostly rustle from the palm fronds, their voices expressed the very spirit of the wild and the free. While listening to their chorus I thought what a glorious theme it would make for some great composer. I also pictured some bygone ancestor crouching in his smoke-blackened cave, listening and reaching for an extra log to put on the fire and perhaps offering up a silent prayer to some strange god for the safety of himself and his sleeping family, as the self-same sounds I was hearing drew nearer; and above all I hoped that this link with the past would never be silenced.

At dawn, the two Boran, Lodogia carrying my heavy rifle, and I with the light 7 mm. Mauser started off down-river. After about a mile and a half we came on the fresh spoor of a big lion which had been down to the water to drink. The Boran proved to be first-class trackers over hard and stony ground; after following for a short distance away from the river they remarked that the lion was heading for a well-known lying-up place in dense thorn bush. An hour later the pug marks we were following led into the bush they had described and we put up the lion. He was very much wide awake and made off before I could get a shot. We followed through the thicket and over more open country until we reached another area of dense thorn. Then began a game of hide and seek which lasted for more than four hours. Again and again we heard the lion ahead. He crossed and recrossed the ground already covered but kept just out of view. At length, tired out, I thought we were going to have a repetition of the Kitonongop affair. It was stiflingly hot and we stopped for a rest and to make some tea. It seemed pointless going on, the lion had every advantage and could play with us in the same manner until dark. But one of the Boran suggested we try again for just half an hour. Once more, slowly and with great caution, we took up the trail. A Boran was in front keeping his eyes to the ground, closely followed by myself with my attention concentrated ahead. After a few hundred yards I saw the lion lying stretched out asleep with his back turned towards us. No doubt thinking we had given up the chase he too had decided to have a rest. He sat up and looked around but it was too late. I shot him through the neck killing him instantly at a range of no more than thirty feet. He was a fine big animal in perfect condition. When we skinned him, there was an iron arrow-head embedded in the wall of his stomach encased in a capsule of fat. As we marched back to the village there was much rejoicing. The women gathered around giving vent to their feelings with shrill ululations. Amidst all the excitement I could not help feeling sorry for the poor old lion. It was not his fault that he had taken to eating the Meru and their goats. Nature had designed him to look upon all animals as legitimate fare, including the two-legged species.

Lest it be imagined that I am a dead shot and always get my quarry in one, I have to admit, as almost every hunter must, that there have been more occasions than I care to remember of animals getting away wounded in spite of every effort on my part to end their suffering. But there is neither pleasure nor profit in recounting such incidents.

At last, the weary months of waiting were at an end and in

Drought in Lorian Swamp, camel cemented in dry mud, dead elephants in background

Start of the flood in Lorian Swamp

Joy beside our Landrover in the Sahara

Hogar Mountains in the Sahara

Elephants in Barsaloi Lugga

Elephants eating hedge near house at Isiolo

January 1944 Joy and I went to Nairobi and were quietly married.

A few weeks later we happened to visit Nairobi again and instead of staying in an hotel or with friends we made a camp a few miles outside the town in the Game Reserve near a place known as Lone Tree in the middle of what is now the Nairobi National Park. Our camp was a novel attraction to friends who, while sitting over a drink or meal, could watch many species of animals feeding a few yards away and in the evenings often see and hear lion close by. Unfortunately the lions had become too popular for their own good. Large numbers of people in cars would come out over the weekends and look at them. As was inevitable there were always certain types who either through ignorance or bravado or both would do the most stupid things, such as getting out of their cars close to the lions or picnicking with women and children in the shade of trees close to thick cover where lions might be lying-up. Sooner or later this state of affairs was bound to lead to a tragedy, particularly as the Game Department had neither the staff nor organisation to control the ever-increasing crowds. Already it was suspected that at least three African soldiers from a nearby military camp, absent without leave, had been killed and eaten. Finally, at a meeting at the departmental offices, it was decided with much regret that the lions had to go and another Game Warden, Eric Rundgren, and I were allotted the extremely distasteful task of shooting them. Owing to the crowds during the day, it was necessary to carry out the job secretly and at night and it was vital that no lion should get away wounded. Since it is an assignment I look back on with sorrow and disgust, suffice it to say that the operation was successful and the few remaining lions moved away. It is pleasing to add that a year later this area was established as the Nairobi National Park and it was not long before the lions were back and this time with a sufficiency of devoted staff to care for their interests and curb unruly sightseers.

It was Ritchie and Cowie, both extremely interested in conservation, who conceived the project of a National Park and, when it came into being, Mervyn Cowie became its first director.

10: *Joy and I make a foot safari*

BACK AT ISIOLO a few weeks later we started of on our first
foot safari together, to the Mathews Range and on to Lake
Rudolf; it lasted nearly two months. During this time Joy
collected hundreds of plants including several new species and
made many paintings of the more interesting specimens.

Soon after crossing the range, the safari nearly met with
disaster. One morning Joy, a Game Scout and I, mounted on
mules, were riding ahead of the pack animals along the banks
of the dry Seya river-bed, when suddenly a cow rhino with a
large calf appeared out of a thicket, snorting loudly and coming
straight at us. All three mules bolted. After a few yards I fought
my steed to a standstill, only to see the other two mules dash by
riderless. With my heart in my mouth I returned fearing to
find Joy at least badly injured. She was lying on the ground
groaning; the Game Scout bending over her, trying to help
her up; luckily the rhino had swept past, missing her by a
foot and although badly shaken by the fall, she was otherwise
unharmed.

Rhino are the bane of foot safaris. Many a time their sudden
and snorting appearance has stampeded my pack train with the
result that their precious loads were scattered and damage done
to their saddlery which it required many hours of work to mend.
On one such occasion, I was riding alone ahead of my safari in a
broad sandy river-bed when one of the creatures took it into its
foolish head to come down the river bank puffing like a steam
engine. My mule decided to seek safety up the opposite bank in
dense wait-a-bit thorn and went on until both rider and mount
were hooked up unable to move, large pieces of my clothing and
not a little of my skin being left on the bushes to mark our pro-

154

gress. Fortunately, the rhino showed better judgement and chose an easier route past us.

On yet another occasion, I was riding the same mule along the crest of a ridge when suddenly there were the usual snorts and up from the side came a rhino. By now, I had worked out a rhino drill and was ready to leap out of the saddle and take my chance on solid earth. I did so, but one of my feet caught in a stirrup iron and I came a cropper with one leg hung up as the rhino dashed past a few yards away. Astonishingly, Aphrodite, the mule, stood rooted to the ground and never moved while I disentangled myself. I like to think it was an unselfish act of sacrifice on her part—but more probably her well-developed instincts of self-preservation had temporarily deserted her.

Avoiding rhino has been the cause of many displays of agility. My old servant, Benua Jawali, once shinned up a thorny sapling to avoid the oncoming beast. When nearing the top, the sapling gracefully bent over and deposited him almost on top of the rhino.

The next place of interest was Barsaloi where my men had chased the poachers on an earlier safari. Here, a few days before our arrival, a Samburu tribesman had been killed by an elephant. It appeared that he had been walking along a path leading from the water when he came on a big bull elephant. The animal was feeding off an acacia tree which he had felled, and was completely hidden by the foliage. The elephant charged; the man tried to get away by crawling into the branches of the fallen tree but he was plucked out and literally dug into the ground. An area of about thirty feet square looked as if it had been ploughed. Here the elephant had repeatedly thrust his tusks through his hapless victim. The man who showed us the place declared that every afternoon since the tragedy the elephant returned to the scene and stood over the remains of the Samburu until evening. This story was borne out by the tracks which made it plain that the elephant had returned to the exact spot on more than one occasion. We waited until late in the afternoon for him to re-appear, then hearing that there was an elephant in the river-bed near by, went to investigate and found three bulls together. As it was impossible to tell which, if any, was the culprit, I decided that the best plan was to approach to about forty yards and then shout. If one of them showed signs of aggression, I would shoot. In the event, all three without hesitation made off as hard as they could go.

Many incidents within my own experience and within the experience of others, go to show that elephants have what can only be described as an abstract conception of death, and that this goes for both human and elephant deaths. There are well-authenticated instances of elephants burying persons they have killed under piles of brushwood and leaves. One such case occurred close to my headquarters at Isiolo. Late one evening Gobus, my Turkana ex-poacher, and his aged mother, were returning from a village where they had gone to visit friends. After walking some distance Gobus, answering a call of nature, told his mother to continue along the path and said that he would catch her up shortly. The old woman, being half blind, strayed off the path and after wandering until dark, lay down under a tree, prepared to spend the night out. Some hours later, she woke up to find an elephant standing over her, feeling up and down her body with its trunk. Paralysed by fear she lay still. Presently, more elephants appeared and trumpeting loudly broke off branches and covered the woman under a great pile and then left her. Meanwhile, Gobus hurried along the path expecting to find his mother already back at his quarters near my house. By the time he learned that she had not arrived it was already dark. In the morning, a man herding goats heard faint cries for help and found the old woman imprisoned under the pile of branches, quite unhurt. Perhaps the elephants thought she was dead.

Another strange incident occurred at Isiolo some years later. Elephants had been causing a good deal of damage to the gardens of government officials in the station. At length, not satisfied with nightly raids, one elephant took it upon itself to chase the District Commissioner off his own front lawn, nearly catching him as he gained his doorstep. This was going a bit too far. The following night I had a telephone call from Robert

Nimmo to say there were three elephants near his kitchen. They were still there when I arrived. Robert held a torch over my shoulder and I shot the largest through the brain and brought it down within a few feet of the kitchen. Personally, I dislike elephant meat, though the fat is excellent for cooking, but the Turkana regard roast elephant meat as a great treat, so the following morning I called upon them to dispose of the carcase. What was left was dragged a half mile away into the bush. That night elephants carried a shoulder blade and a leg bone of their dead comrade back to the exact spot where he had been killed. I can offer no explanation for this odd behaviour.

Another touching case of loyalty was reported to me by a Boran tribesman. The incident occurred near the Tana River about one hundred and fifty miles east of Isiolo. There were four old bull elephants, friends who always stayed together. The oldest died. His three companions kept watch over his body for over a week. They then drew out the tusks of their dead comrade and carried them away. Again it is difficult to think of an explanation.

We continued our safari crossing the El Bata plains to the South Horr valley. Here I received information that the notorious poacher Adukan, some of whose companions we had captured at Aberin, was in hiding at Langupenei (the place of caves) at the northern end of the Donio Mara range which bounds the east side of the valley. I sent six Game Scouts to try to surprise him and effect his capture. Two days later they returned bringing Adukan hand-cuffed. He had been found sitting alone in a cave and had offered no resistance nor made any attempt to escape. When I asked him why he had allowed himself to be taken so easily he replied that it was futile to fight against fate. He knew he would be captured that day. His sandals had told him so. He was a big muscular middle-aged man. I was much impressed by his forthright manner and independent spirit and took a liking to him but as he was a desperate character, I deemed it wise to keep him in irons at night. Two days later, he came up to me and asked to be relieved of the hand-cuffs, adding that two of his cronies, Gobus and Ebono, who were in my employment, had assured him it was a good life, not too much work, plenty to eat and sufficient tobacco to keep them happy. He said that he too would like to enter my service. Assuming a stern expression I replied that in view of the numbers of giraffe and rhino and other animals he had killed, he was due to go to gaol but that a lot would depend on his behaviour during the remainder of the safari and that, for the present, he was to take charge of the other prisoners, of which there were a dozen, and see that they did not escape. I agreed that he could sleep unfettered at night. He kept faith and at the end of the safari he entered my service. I used to call him my 'giraffe insurance', for his becoming a law-abiding citizen probably saved the lives of at least twenty giraffe a year besides many rhino and other animals.

Leaving the Horr valley, we made for the south-east corner of Lake Rudolf, crossing broken lava country which was hard on the pack animals, until we entered a gorge with towering basalt cliffs and followed the sandy bed of the dry river towards the lake. A mile and a half from the lake, the gorge opened out into a stony plain. At the mouth of the gorge, Joy discovered rock engravings on the smooth face of the cliffs. We examined them carefully and found hundreds scored into the stone, depicting animals and a few human figures. There were rhino, oryx, ostriches, crocodiles and what looked clearly like a mammoth with long up-curving tusks, small ears and a high forehead. There was also a file of twelve giraffe, apparently being led by a man. Obviously the engravings were of very ancient origin; they suggested that, at that time, man must have domesticated the giraffe. Joy took tracings and photographs which later she showed to leading London archaeologists who judged them to be of the Magdalenian period. They were the first prehistoric engravings recorded in Kenya. In spite of the interest they aroused in archaeological circles, no expert has, to my knowledge, yet visited the site.

Following the lake shore northwards our next objective was the top of Mount Kulal, two days' hard going for the donkeys. Camp was made on the top of the southern portion of the mountain in a little glade surrounded by dense forest. The local Samburu warned me that lion had been causing much trouble and advised me to construct a strong enclosure for the donkeys and mules.

This was not easy as there were no suitable thorn trees in the forest. I took the usual precaution of placing our tents on two sides of the enclosure and a hurricane lamp on the most exposed side; in spite of this, lions attacked that night. As usual, Korofi was the first to give the alarm and I was out of bed with rifle and torch within a few seconds and just in time to see a lioness trying to force her way into the enclosure, not more than twenty feet away from our tent. I managed to kill her with my first shot. As far as it was possible to tell in the darkness none of the animals had been injured, but in the morning it was found that one of the donkeys had been bitten in the hind leg. Although there were only two small punctures, in three days' time the leg went septic and a few days later I had to shoot the poor donkey as it was unable to continue the march.

Apart from the poacher Adukan, we had a dozen other prisoners with us, and their food was almost finished. I therefore went into the forest to hunt for meat. As there were only two species of animals in any quantity on the mountain, namely greater kudu and buffalo, the choice had to fall on the latter. After a morning of fruitless effort, I finally came on a cow buffalo which I shot. Unfortunately, I had not noticed that it had a small calf. I felt most upset and thought the kindest thing to do would be to put a bullet through its brain there and then. However, it was so friendly that I could not bring myself to do the deed. With little urging it followed me back to camp until we suddenly appeared in front of Joy who was busy painting a new plant. During the next three days Cigirria Egitok (Long Ears) became the darling of the camp. He took to the bottle without the slightest trouble and seemed to thrive on cow's milk, of which fortunately there was plenty obtainable from a near-by Samburu *manyatta*. One of his favourite tricks was to approach an unsuspecting person from behind, thrust his head between the legs and heave, sending the victim sprawling. Now arose the problem of what to do with Cigirria Egitok. Obviously he was too young to march, too heavy to ride on a donkey and, besides, required vast quantities of milk daily. Finally, at the suggestion of Lembirdan, we hired a camel as transport and two cows in milk as commissariat. For

over a week Egitok travelled without ill-effect strapped to the
side of the camel, counter-balanced by a load of elephant tusks.
We gave him to Raymond Hook who let him run with his cattle
until full-grown, on his farm on the slopes of Mount Kenya.

Having sent off Cigirria Egitok and the prisoners under the
escort of two Game Scouts, Joy and I, together with the remainder
of the safari team, including the poacher Adukan, descended the
east side of the mountain and made across a thirty mile stretch
of the Hedad desert to the foot of Mount Marsabit. Here, on the
edge of the ancient lava flows, we found hundreds of stone cairns
varying in height from about three feet to over fifteen. Some of
the larger were surrounded by one or two circles of stones. In the
midst of the cairns, there was a platform of loose stones about
thirty feet in length by about ten wide and some four feet in
height. Obviously the work of some bygone race. The local
tribesmen, Rendile and Gabbra, could tell us nothing about these
strange monuments. Presumably the cairns were placed over
graves but what the purpose of the platform could have been it is
difficult to imagine. Throughout the northern regions of Kenya,
groups of stone cairns are to be found, usually situated around
springs or near paths passing through defiles and in many cases
on the slopes of hills. They are scattered haphazard without any
sort of order, and they are not in the most accessible of places,
where one might expect burial grounds to be found. Giving rein
to my imagination, I see them as the graves of warriors killed in
battle. Tribal custom decreeing that the dead must be interred
where they fell. If my guess is anywhere near the truth, the
country must have contained a far larger population in those days
than it does today and there must have been many bloody battles
with heavy casualties. In the Wajir District in north-east Kenya
there are numerous ancient wells and dams, many of them still in
use today.

On a later safari to Lake Rudolf, Joy dug up some of the
smaller cairns. After much labour in clearing many tons of
stones, the sum total of our efforts was the disclosure of a large
number of scorpions, centipedes and a few snakes. But failure
seemed merely to stimulate Joy's determination until, at length,

Guss water hole at Lake Rudolf

Elephants at Uaso Nyiro

the scouts and prisoners were near mutiny, and I was obliged to keep a sharp look-out ahead for cairns and carefully steer the safari out of sight of them. Nevertheless, Joy's persistence was rewarded: two small cairns on a peninsula in the lake produced a couple of crumbling skeletons, lying on their right sides in a foetal position. El Molo tribesmen who had a small village on the end of the peninsula could tell us nothing about the graves; although there was no doubt that they were of much more recent origin than those found near Marsabit.

A day and a half's tiring march up the lava strewn slopes of the mountain brought us to the village of Marsabit and the head-quarters of the district. Here we were pleasantly entertained by the government officers for two days and then continued our safari along the forest edge on the eastern slopes of the mountain. In a little valley one of my Game Scouts showed us a cave under a small cliff of soft rock. It was about thirty feet in length by about twenty in width, with a ceiling of a uniform height of about five feet six inches. At first I thought it had been the dwelling of prehistoric man as the walls and ceiling showed the marks of what might have been blunt picks, but closer inspection revealed that the marks had been caused by the horns of rhino. In fact, the entire cave had been hollowed out of the rock by these animals in the course of centuries. Evidently the rock contained salt and the rhino were in the habit of prising off chunks to eat. There was fresh rhino spoor inside the cave.

On the south of the mountain we camped on the lip of a beauti-ful crater surrounded by forest. Its floor consisted of grassland and in its centre lay a small lake bordered by reeds and covered with water fowl. It was commonly known as Lake Paradise, so named by the Martin Johnsons who some fifteen years earlier had established a semi-permanent camp on the cliff overlooking the crater. It was a lovely scene. We made our camp at a place where the almost perpendicular walls of the crater had given way to a grassy slope leading down to the lake. During the night, which was brilliantly lit by the full moon, a herd of buffalo came slowly past on their way to the water. They were followed by three enormous bull elephants. The one leading was the largest and appeared to be tuskless, the second carried a very fair pair. The third—I rubbed my eyes in disbelief—it seemed to have the longest tusks I had ever seen on a living elephant and they gleamed in the moonlight as he walked past with unhurried tread. In the morning, the elephants were still in the crater so we went to have a closer look, thinking the moonlight might have played tricks. But there was no doubt about it, one of the elephants had an immensely long tusk. The second tusk had been broken and was considerably shorter. This elephant became known as Mohamed and in later years was seen and photographed by many people. Finally he disappeared, and long afterwards his remains were found intact. He had died of old age which, in the case of elephants, means the wearing out of the teeth. The ivory is now in the museum at Nairobi. One of the tusks weighs over a hundred and forty pounds and is nearly eleven feet in length. There is not much known about the age of African elephants but, in all probability Mohamed was little short of a hundred years old. He was a very peaceful animal and could easily be approached to within a few yards. He was often accompanied by one or two younger companions.

11: *African hunting methods*

FOR SEVEN YEARS I had been entirely dependent for motor transport on my own light pick-up truck which had given sterling service but was now almost falling to pieces. At last the Government felt obliged to provide me with a three-ton lorry, which made a great difference to my mobility and comfort on safari. It meant that I could travel entirely self-contained, with a full complement of eight to ten Game Scouts, food and water and a complete camping outfit. No longer was it necessary to rely solely on donkey transport, although this was still useful for the more mountainous parts of my area.

At this time I was the only Game Warden in charge of an area something over eighty thousand square miles in extent which included the districts of Samburu, Marsabit, Moyale, Mandera, Wajir, Garissa, Isiolo and parts of Meru and Nanyuki. These contained a variety of tribes, speaking different languages; the Samburu who are akin to the Masai, the Turkana, Rendile, Gabbra, Boran, Ajuran, Galla, Pokomo, Boni, Dorobo, Meru, Tharaka and Wakamba and some eight tribes of Somalis. As can be imagined, with only thirty-five Game Scouts, it was impossible to cover such a huge territory and therefore my efforts had to be concentrated on the areas containing the greatest amount of wild life and the most heavily poached.

Among the worst active offenders were the Boran. As I have already said custom decrees that no Boran may call himself a man before he has blooded his spear in some dangerous creature; before the advent of Pax Britannica it was usually a member of a neighbouring tribe. Even a woman counted but earned lower marks than a man, regardless of his age; but woman who was pregnant and carried a male child earned double marks. It was

163

when these practices were forbidden, that the young men turned their attention to animals such as lions, elephants, buffalo and rhino to prove their manhood.

Usually a spear-blooding party would be preceded by a *ngoma* (sing-song and dance) at a group of villages, both men and women taking part. The elders would boast in song of their former prowess, the number of enemies slain, the lions and elephants speared. Then the women and girls would join in, teasing the young men for their lack of courage and comparing them unfavourably with their fathers. When thoroughly roused, the youths would organise a hunt. A dozen or more, almost naked and armed with two spears apiece and accompanied by a pack of mongrels, would set forth. As soon as the quarry was sighted, the hunt would be on. Frequently, one or more of the party might be killed or seriously injured, particularly when lions were involved. The first man to draw blood would claim the trophy. Anyone who showed cowardice was liable to be severely beaten by his fellows and would be ostracised. On the return of the party to the villages, a great fuss was made of the victor. As a mark of distinction he would wear his hair long and in a fuzz and would anoint it with fat; in many ways a fine sporting tradition, and good for the morale of the tribe. Certainly much more sporting than going out to blast some unfortunate animal with a high-powered rifle while protected by a hairy-chested professional hunter with an even larger gun. What is regrettable is that the rules of the Boran game do not specify the age, size and sex of the animal concerned, therefore an elephant qualifies whether it is three feet high or ten, and a lion is equally acceptable whether it is only a few days old or a ferocious man-eater. Consequently, many of the hunts end in the massacre of babies and females.

I heard of a case where a gang of Boran speared sixteen elephants out of a herd, mostly little calves, and another which took place during a severe drought and resulted in the killing of upwards of thirty elephants which were weak from thirst and hunger. In these two cases, good work on the part of my Game Scouts resulted in the arrest and conviction of most of the offenders. In contrast to such savage and pitiless slaughter, it is

pleasing to record instances of real courage where the odds were
with the animal.

There was a young rather effeminate-looking Boran who was
constantly teased about his looks. At length he could stand the
banter no longer. So, picking up his two spears and calling to
his dogs, he set off alone and killed a lioness. I heard about the
incident and sent Game Scouts to arrest him. He was brought
before me and with naïve frankness told me the whole story, after
which I had not the heart to prosecute him, and let him go.
Another young Boran speared and killed a full-grown bull
elephant, entirely unaided. He claimed that the animal had
attacked a flock of sheep he was herding and that, being in sole
charge, he felt duty bound to protect the flock. This may or may
not have been true, but it was such a daring effort that I let him
go free.

Once, I had occasion to hunt a lion which had killed and eaten
a Somali tribesman about forty miles from Isiolo. The man had
been herding a flock of sheep and goats, and on his way back to his
home in the evening had found his pathway blocked by a flooded
river. He therefore made himself as comfortable as circumstances
would allow on the bank, and waited for the water to subside.
During the night a lion appeared, scattered the goats and sheep
and devoured the Somali on the spot. It was about a week later
when I heard of the killing. I made my camp close to the scene.
Hoping my fire would attract the lion's attention, I placed the
carcase of a zebra close by and sat over it for three nights, without
result. Next morning a Boran herdsman, employed by a Somali,
arrived at camp and told me that he had just seen the lion and that
it had attempted to stalk him. I set off at once, with Game Scouts
Lodogia and Olo, the latter a rather highly-strung Somali, and the
Boran. After an hour's walk we came to the place where the lion
had last been seen. The pug marks were visible in the soft ground
and it was an easy matter to follow them across a stony plain
dotted with low thorn bushes. We could see where the lion had
slunk from bush to bush in the wake of the herd of goats and of the
Boran. Suddenly we saw the lion, but he saw us and made off.
I took a running shot and heard the bullet hit, there followed

an angry grunt. Olo and the Boran raced after the lion. A wounded lion is a very dangerous proposition and must be followed with the utmost caution, so I shouted to them to stop but they were too excited to listen and disappeared out of my sight. The lion was in fact crouching under a small bush and as Olo and the Boran rushed wildly past him, he sprang on Olo bringing him to the ground. The Boran was armed with a light and rather blunt spear but, without hesitation, he went to Olo's help and hurled it at the lion. It bounced off the animal's ribs and fell to the ground. Seeing this, the Boran calmly walked up to the lion as it was savaging Olo, recovered his spear and endeavoured to ram it into the lion's shoulder. It bent double. Hearing the screams and growls, I came running up with Lodogia. The lion left Olo and came for me; I flattened it with a shot from my heavy rifle.

Olo had been bitten in both arms and a foot, luckily there were no broken bones. Undoubtedly the Boran's courageous action had saved him from serious injury. This was the more remarkable as the Boran was a complete stranger to us, and not even of the same tribe as Olo. No one could have blamed him if he had kept clear. We were a long way from camp, it was the heat of the day and we had no water to give Olo who was still under shock and complaining of thirst. I sent Lodogia off at a run to call up my driver, Ibrahim Ali, with the truck, while the Boran and I carried Olo for half a mile to a place accessible to the lorry. As soon as it arrived, he was taken to hospital at Meru, a distance of over a hundred miles. Thanks to modern drugs and the skill of the doctor, he was discharged from the hospital after a fortnight, little the worse, apart from some deep scars. The lion was a fine big animal in excellent condition, but almost maneless. I was so impressed by the bravery of the Boran, Godana Dima, that I engaged him as a Game Scout. He gave me many years of loyal service and more than once proved his courage in dangerous situations.

Another method of hunting employed by the Boran and their near relatives along the Ethiopian border, the Gabbra, was to hunt giraffe on horseback. Their ponies, mostly greys of about twelve hands, are fast, sure-footed and hardy. They are unshod and have been trained to do without water for up to four or five days. The saddle is a simple wooden frame covered by a blanket. Only the big toe goes into the stirrup, so they ride partly by balance and partly on the rein; unfortunately the local-made bits are cruel and do much damage to the ponies' mouths.

Wearing only a small turban and a piece of white calico around their middles, the tribesmen raid deep into Kenyan territory. They run the animal down and spear or shoot it at close quarters. Giraffe, apart from supplying vast quantities of meat, are valued for their thick hides, which make the most durable water buckets and sandals. These buckets, which hold about a gallon, are used for bailing water from the bottoms of deep wells. Six to eight men, depending on the depth of the well, stand one above the other on cross-beams or niches cut in the sides of the well and pass the filled buckets up in an endless chain, right hand to right hand, while the empties descend from left hand to left hand. The work goes on at great speed, the rhythm helped by a deep-throated chant. At the top the buckets are emptied into clay troughs. Here relays of livestock quench their thirst.

Part of the southern boundary of my beat was the Tana River. The Wakamba tribe lived on the opposite bank. During the dry weather the river is easily fordable in many points, so gangs of up to forty poachers cross over and set up their camps or hide-outs there, usually along the banks of water courses among doam palms. Soon after this, the brewing of palm toddy starts. It is done by stripping the heads off the palm stems and collecting the sap in gourds tied to the mutilated heads. (This is a destructive practice as it kills the tree.) Almost immediately, the sap starts to ferment and in two days there is a most potent drink.

Meanwhile hunting parties, armed with bows and poisoned arrows, go out. The method most favoured is to build platforms in trees overlooking game paths or watering places, and wait for some hapless animal to pass below. Poisoned drop-spear traps are set for the larger animals, such as rhino and hippo. The meat of the animals killed is dried in strips and then sold to agriculturalists living in the hills. Trophies such as rhino horn, ivory and leopard skins are sold to traders. Many such camps were raided by my Game Scouts and myself. Frequently we caught poachers, many too drunk to attempt to escape. I believe what hurt them even more than being arrested was to see their toddy filled gourds being shot out of the trees.

In order to try to check this large-scale poaching, I established an outpost on the Bisengurach River, a clear stream which flows into the Tana. It consisted of six Game Scouts under the charge of a M'Kamba corporal, named Munda, who had done nine years' service in the Police and then joined the Game Service; by this time he had been ten years in the Police.

Some months later, on one of my periodic visits to the outpost, I found him very sick. He was a lean wiry type, but was now terribly emaciated and too weak to get up. I told him he would be sent at once to hospital as I felt sure he was suffering from chronic malaria. He replied that his sickness could not be cured in a hospital; he had been bewitched and the only hope of saving his life was by sending for a notorious female witch doctor, who lived across the Tana River in Ukambani, to remove the spell. Unless she came, he would surely die. I laughed at his fears and assured him that a course of treatment in hospital would soon put him right. He was most reluctant to go. However, I insisted and sent him off in my truck to Wajir hospital with a note to the medical officer in charge whom I knew to be a very capable and clever doctor. About a month later, I heard that Munda was dead. Shortly afterwards, I met the doctor who said that he had treated Munda for malaria and that he had responded well to the treatment till suddenly, for no apparent reason, he had given up the will to live, and died. This taught me never to scoff when any of my men were taken ill and claimed to have been bewitched. In future I gave them an advance of pay and a fortnight's leave and told them to go off and get themselves de-bewitched. It always worked. After Munda's death, I had to burn the outpost, as it was said to be contaminated with bad 'medicine', and build a new one. In spite of a fresh start, Kinna Outpost, as it was called, seemed to have a 'hoodoo' on it. If it wasn't witchcraft, it was something else; for instance, a wife of one of my men was poisoned, it was thought, by her husband's girl friend. Undoubtedly, Kinna Outpost was a thoroughly demoralising place and I had to change the men around frequently.

Lodogia, in spite of my precautions, one day came to me with a long face and said that he and his family had been bewitched and asked for leave to go and consult a famous practitioner in the wilds of Samburu. After some weeks, he returned apparently well satisfied. The witch-doctor had charged a fee of a bottle of brandy, five pounds of tobacco and two goats.

I have never heard any satisfactory explanation of the powers of witchcraft, which, in spite of increasing education and enlightenment, is still strong in many parts of the country.

As another means of dealing with the poaching along the Tana, I cut a motor track, a distance of about thirty-five miles from the outpost to the river; part of it ran through dense thorn bush country. When making such tracks, I always took advantage of the main elephant paths, for these animals show good sense in choosing the easiest gradients and crossings of water courses and, where possible, they keep to the tops of the watersheds. It took a month's hard work to finish the track. At one point it passed a huge baobab tree with a hollow trunk which had been used as a hideout by poachers for countless years and could easily accommodate six men. Soon after the track was finished, I had occasion to drive down to the river. When nearing the banks, I heard loud singing and yelling. I left the car and with two men crept silently through the bush until we saw a party of six Wakamba poachers having a sing-song and dance on the water's edge. Obviously, they were happy and full of palm toddy. We rushed them and managed to grab one each, the remainder, regardless of crocodiles, leapt into the river and swam across.

Although most of the poaching was carried on by African tribesmen, it was also necessary to keep a sharp eye on European hunting parties. If conducted by reputable professional hunters, they usually behaved in an exemplary fashion and abided by the game laws written and unwritten; in fact, they were a great help to me, as many of the hunters were honorary Game Wardens and took a keen interest in conservation. But some of the private hunting parties were of a very different kind. A favourite dodge was for a whole family, including Pa, Ma, offspring, in-laws, uncles and aunts to take out licences to shoot elephant. Many of these people scarcely knew one end of a gun from the other and the party was simply a racket to make money out of ivory. Pa alone did the shooting which was, of course, quite illegal. The only way to obtain evidence in such cases was through the local African trackers and guides who had been employed by the party concerned. In other instances a party would observe the letter of the law but, through inexperience, only wound, say, an elephant. Anyone worth his salt would naturally do everything in his power to find the animal and put it out of its agony and indeed the law laid down that a person wounding an elephant (or any other beast) had to make 'every endeavour' to kill the animal, and that only if he failed to find the victim was he at liberty to shoot another. But, since it was almost impossible to give any legal definition of 'every endeavour', in many cases wounded elephants were not searched for as well as they might have been. A few years later the laws tightened up and the loss of a wounded elephant meant the loss of the licence.

In the course of my duties I constantly came in contact with professional hunters and their clients, and Joy and I made many friends among both. The majority of the *clientèle* were United States citizens, next came Latin Americans and last Europeans; there were few British among these. Most were keen and good sportsmen and it was a pleasure to meet and to help them. But there were exceptions, people who had no real interest in either the animals or the country. Their sole ambition was to kill the maximum number of animals allowed by their licences with as little delay and discomfort as possible, after which they would return to their homes with a bone-yard of indifferent trophies. One can only suppose that such people come out to Africa to hunt merely in order to establish some sort of status among their acquaintances back home. There was also the 'know all', who claimed to have hunted everything in the New World and was not prepared to take advice from anyone. Usually such a man would not allow his hired hunter to fire a shot in support, even if an animal was about to get away wounded. As a result, animals would often be wounded and lost, or the hunter would be left with the unenviable and hazardous task of following up and finishing off a dangerous animal in dense cover. More than one hunter has been killed or seriously injured under these circumstances.

I well recall my friend 'D', one of the best-known professionals in the country, coming to my camp almost in despair because his client, a haughty American, had given instructions that 'D' was not to fire a shot under any circumstances. While we were talking, a man came in with news about elephants which had raided crops during the night. As it was still early, I suggested to 'D' that it might be a good idea for him and the client to accompany me. This would give the latter the opportunity of seeing at first-hand the difficulties of shooting elephant in thick bush. This I thought perhaps might alter his ideas on the subject. The three of us set off on foot with the guide and a gun bearer. After half an hour's walk we entered the area of particularly dense thorn bush where the raiders were said to be spending the heat of the day; it was stifling hot, there was not a breath of wind. The client whispered to 'D' that he had seen enough and would like to go back to camp. 'D' turned to him in shocked surprise and insisted that, having offered to help me shoot the elephants, they were bound to see it through. Presently we heard the gentle flapping of great ears and the rasping of rough skin against a tree. From a standing position it was impossible to see the elephants. By lying prone I could just make out their feet between the stems of the bushes. Silently we crept forward until I could discern the head of an elephant—in fact there were two of them. We waited for several minutes until one moved, offering a shot at the brain. I fired and it fell to its knees but was up in an instant and started to move off. 'D' fired with better aim and the animal collapsed. Here was a perfect object lesson for 'D's' client. Had it not been for 'D', it is likely that the elephant might have got away, or led me a long and tiring chase before coming up with it. We returned to camp firmly convinced that the American would see the folly of persisting in his attitude, but a few days later he went out with 'D' to hunt an elephant, still adamant about not permitting 'D' to shoot. The elephant was wounded. Poor 'D', ill with fever, followed until he could go no farther. He had to be rushed to hospital and was found to be suffering from sleeping sickness. The elephant was never seen again.

Not all American tourists were like that one; I know one elderly gentleman who has come to East Africa year after year with the fixed ambition of shooting an elephant carrying tusks of not less than a hundred and thirty pounds a side; rather than shoot anything smaller he has allowed his licence to lapse time and again. There are also not a few who have come out with the full intention of shooting big game but who, when it came to the point, have laid aside their rifles and reached instead for their cameras.

Like the majority of hunters, I too have wanted to shoot a monster elephant and have spent hundreds of hours trailing big specimens. There was, for instance, an almost mythical elephant said to live on an island in the Tana River and to carry gigantic ivory. Many people hunted for him without success. On one occasion Joy and I spent two days on the island; it was covered in dense vegetation and in places with swamps and tall reeds. There were numerous elephant paths criss-crossing the island and several trees had plainly been used as regular resting places. At one of these we found very large foot-prints which our local guide assured us belonged to the big elephant. We followed up the spoor and came upon it with its head buried in a climber which made it impossible to see its tusks. The guide urged me to shoot as he felt convinced it was the one we were after but I was loath to take the chance without seeing the ivory. The light had gone and there was no time to make further investigations. Perhaps I should have taken the gamble. Now I am glad that I did not shoot. There is something infinitely sad in the death of one of these mighty beasts. It is like destroying a living monument of the past.

One of the main problems I had to contend with was the illegal trade in ivory, rhino horn and leopard skins, carried out in the Northern Province mostly by Arab and Somali traders; the main outlets being across the borders into Ethiopia and Somalia and to a lesser degree southwards to Nairobi. Many and devious were the methods used to smuggle out the trophies, by camel, caravan and motor lorry. Ivory and rhino horns might be concealed inside bags of maize meal, inside apparently sealed oil drums, soldered up in cans of cooking fat, and scores of other hiding places. Leopard skins might be packed inside a lorry-load of goat and cattle skins, rolled up in bedding or hidden inside a spare tyre.

Sometimes our searches took us to improbable quarters. Not infrequently, prostitutes supplied us with invaluable information regarding the illegal trade in rhino horns, ivory and leopard skins. One day I received information that there were rhino horns concealed in a hut in the 'red light' quarter of Isiolo township. Accordingly, the next morning two scouts and myself carried out a search of the place and discovered a bag containing three rhino horns hidden under a bed. The owner of the hut, a prostitute, declared that the horns had been brought to her hut the same morning by a 'friend'. The friend admitted buying the horns from an unknown Turkana. Another hut near-by was searched and a deep hole discovered under a bed. The owner, another professional, said that an Italian client had hidden rhino horns in the hole but they had quarrelled and he had removed them. We then went to the Italian's camp and searched his house. Two elephant tusks were found carefully hidden in the thatch of the roof. The Italian denied all knowledge of either the ivory or any rhino horns. Unfortunately for him, three people had seen a Turkana enter his house one evening carrying a bag containing long objects. When arrested the Turkana admitted selling the ivory to the Italian. According to his story, he was taking the tusks to the District Commissioner's Office, to hand them in and claim a reward, when he met an acquaintance who said, 'Don't take them to the office, you'll get far more from the Italian'.

12: *V I Ps and other guests*

FROM TIME TO TIME in the course of my duties, I was called upon to take out visiting VIPs, scientists and others, interested in wildlife. One of these was a Scandinavian zoologist. The second day out from Isiolo, we camped on a broad sandy river-bed called Lodosoit a few miles east of the Mathews Range. There was abundant water just under the surface of the sand, and the place was much frequented by elephant, rhino and other animals. The only site for the camp offering shade was in a small grove of acacia trees beside a large game trail. As we were about to retire I warned our guest that it was likely that numbers of elephant and rhino would use the path during the night, but that he was not to worry as the animals' only aim would be to slake their thirst and it was most unlikely that they would interfere with the camp. About three a.m. I went out and was surprised to see a light still burning in our guest's tent, and found the tall, slim young man sitting on his bed fully clothed, complete with hat and heavy knee-boots. Apparently my reassurance about the elephant had failed to act. Tactfully I remarked 'You are an early bird! We don't usually get up at this hour. I suggest you go back to bed; the boy will bring tea at six-thirty!' He was to experience more alarming episodes before we parted.

While striking camp in the morning I fell into conversation with some of the local Samburu who had come to water their stock. They told me that a few weeks before our visit an elderly Samburu and his wife, while on the march, had spent the night on a dry river-bed called Sandait about six miles away. During the hours of darkness the old man had been seized by a lion. After a struggle, he had succeeded in driving it off but not before he had been badly mauled. At daylight he sent his wife off to find water, the nearest being at Lodosoit. When, some hours later, the woman returned, there was nothing left of her husband except a few bones and a drying pool of blood. This was not far from Kitonongop where I have already described my futile hunt after the cattle-killing lions.

Some days later we made camp under a few trees by a little spring. As there were no recent traces of elephant and rhino using it, I deemed it quite safe. In the early hours of the morning, our guest, worn out by many sleepless nights, had fallen asleep but his sub-conscious must have warned him that he was still in darkest Africa for he woke with a start, and saw the enormous posterior of an elephant outside the door of his tent. He sprang out of bed still with his faithful boots on his feet (he seemed determined to die with his boots on) and leapt into the back of the truck, landing among empty water cans which set up a tremendous clatter. The elephants, of which there were upwards of thirty, panicked, and for a few frightening seconds we were the centre of a trumpeting and milling herd. On such occasions there is nothing much one can do except wait quietly for the disturbance to subside. Firing shots or blowing whistles merely increases the confusion and the danger of being flattened. Now we waited and presently all became quiet again and we returned to our interrupted slumbers. (Elephant on occasion can move soundlessly, and several times they have come into my camp and no one has been any the wiser until morning when their great footprints have been seen.)

The next adventure to befall our guest was of a different nature. He was most anxious to get some photographs of some of the graceful Samburu girls, so my Game Scouts persuaded a bevy of the local beauties to deck themselves in their barbaric splendour. He got his photographs. Then there was a pause while the girls looked at him expectantly. Not taking the hint, he turned away and suddenly found himself the centre of a circle of indignant females. With growing alarm and embarrassment, he turned to me and asked what they wanted of him. I said 'Quite obviously they have taken a great fancy to you and, if you want to get away whole, you had better throw a handful of money on the ground and while they scramble for it, jump into the truck and drive off fast.'

Another guest was a film producer whose object was to make a film about the work of a Game Warden. He questioned me closely about my duties and determined to film a romantic story about poachers. For a fortnight, I 'chased poachers' over jagged lava fields, across the Uaso Nyiro River and up the precipices of Mount Lololokwe where the cornered and desperate gang hurled rocks upon me which I was supposed to dodge. One of these boulders nearly put a premature end to the film and its producer. In vain, I pointed out that when it came to running after poachers, I relied mainly on my fleet-footed scouts and usually contented myself with directing operations. But no, he would not hear of it. He said that public sympathy would at once side with the poachers if they saw them being pursued by a gang of hefty Game Scouts armed with rifles. I must face the odds alone, also, there must be a 'love' interest and the poachers must have personable young women as accomplices. The idea of Adukan, who was to play the part of leader of the poachers, pro- ducing anything in the way of 'love' interest' seemed to me a little far-fetched. However, I took the producer to several Turkana villages to look for 'love interest' but he described the girls as quite unsuitable. Finally my driver Ibrahim had a brilliant suggestion: he would take the lorry to Isiolo and collect a bevy of Turkana prostitutes. In due course they arrived in high glee, clearly intrigued at the notion of 'Bwana Game' (myself) re- quiring a whole lorry-load of them. The final scenes were shot in a large Rendile village near Laisamis and included a beautiful Rendile girl in a setting of camels and palm trees. According to the producer this was just what the film-going public relished.

My second safari to the Boni country was carried out in November 1945 in the Game Department truck together with Joy. We determined to find a route through to Kiunga, a small Bajun village on the coast, close to the Somalia border. Wending our way through the Boni Forest with its park-like country was comparatively easy but when we reached the belt of the dense coastal bush our progress became painfully slow. It took three days to hack a way through the tough vegetation, a distance of not more than thirty miles. The Bajun villagers were greatly excited at our unexpected appearance, many of them had never before seen a motor vehicle. They are an attractive people with an admixture of Arab blood and the pleasing manners which go with it. The men are excellent sailors and possess an unrivalled knowledge of the coastal waters. The village is situated in a grove of coconut palms just below a headland on which stands a large crumbling double-storied house. This was said to have been built before the turn of the century by the old East Africa Company. The ground floor was used as the Mudir's (local African magistrate) court and office, and contained cells for prisoners. The upper floor was reserved as the residence of the District Commissioner, Lamu, who periodically visited Kiunga by steam launch. We took possession of his quarters, expecting to stay three or four days. But we had reckoned without the weather. The day after our arrival it started to rain, and continued raining almost without a break for the next month, rendering our only route out completely impassable. The country inland turned into a vast swamp with several unfordable rivers. Luckily, we were able to communicate with Lamu and obtain supplies by means of a native dhow which did a more or less regular trip every week. Cornell, the District Commissioner, very kindly sent us papers and magazines. The time passed pleasantly enough and we would have enjoyed our enforced stay had it not been for constant anxiety about getting back to my work. Already I was likely to be in trouble for risking the trip so close to the rainy season. We explored the lovely little off-shore islands with their fine beaches and the superb coral reefs. Fortunately, we had brought diving goggles and a harpoon gun and were able to keep ourselves supplied with tasty crayfish and other sea food. We walked along the beach to Ras Kiamboni, on Dick's Head, and explored the ancient Arab ruins, just across the border in Somaliland.

At the end of a month I had almost decided to take the truck to pieces, pack it aboard a dhow and sail down to Lamu and reassemble it on the mainland at Makowe. Then, at last, the weather broke and after ten days the ground dried sufficiently to allow us to essay the journey back. The going was none too easy, the truck was constantly getting bogged down in soft ground, entailing hours of back-breaking toil, jacking the wheels up and packing logs and brushwood underneath. At one point, we had to bridge a river which on our way to Kiunga had been a dry watercourse. It took us six days to cover a little over fifty miles.

Joy and I had been so enchanted by Kiunga that in succeeding years we often spent my local leaves there. The easiest way to get to the place was to motor to Lamu, hire a dhow and sail up the coast.

On one occasion I timed my leave so as to start from Garissa, rather than my headquarters at Isiolo, thereby saving a day's journey. The morning before leaving, a report came in that elephant were eating up a rice field on the banks of the Tana River, quite close to the township. Joy, a guest, Game Scout Lodogia and I set off on foot to deal with the situation. There was a motley following of shopkeepers, cooks, house-servants and loafers, who, in spite of my protests and warnings, tagged on behind to see the fun. Recently I had been issued by my department with a large bore Very light pistol with the idea of using it to drive away marauding elephant rather than having to shoot them. I was most anxious to try it out. Soon we came on a group of six bull elephants happily stuffing themselves with great sheaves of rice, their stomachs rumbling in contentment. From about seventy yards I fired the pistol. Unfortunately my judgment was at fault; the blazing missile fell on the wrong side of the elephants. Their reactions were almost instantaneous, and exceeded my expectations. They stampeded in panic, straight towards the onlookers. Some sought safety in trees, others in the crocodile-infested waters of the river. It was a tense moment. The elephants divided and were passing on both sides of us within a few feet; then, one of the bulls, seeing us, charged and I was obliged to shoot him. When the dust of battle cleared, our guest had disappeared. With my heart in my mouth, I looked around

fully expecting to see a flattened corpse. Then, much to my
relief, I heard a small voice from up above say 'I got out of your
way so that you could shoot'. With that there was a scrambling
and a thud and he appeared out of the leafy branches of an
enormous fig tree. As he was unarmed, he had acted with commendable wisdom and agility.

The next day we were joined by two more guests, Derek and
Hilda Haggie, friends of Joy's; they had recently arrived in
Kenya to settle. We started off for Lamu and the first night
camped near a little village on a river called Masabubu. It is
edged by a narrow belt of forest which affords beautiful camping
sites, where from under the shade of giant acacia trees, one can
overlook the water. But, 'every rose has a thorn'; in this case
the thorn consisted of a multitudinous insect life, including the
nastier species, such as large hairy spiders, scorpions, and centipedes, towards which Hilda seemed to have a marked phobia.
Even the harmless sausage fly sent her into near-hysterics, and I
began to feel some misgivings about the advisability of taking her
on the trip.

The following day we arrived at Makowe; from here we and
our gear were ferried across to Lamu island. Leaving the rest of
the party at the one and only hotel, Petley's, I set off to hire a
dhow. There was no lack of willing dhow owners anxious to
convey us to Kiunga at the moderate price of forty shillings a day.
The only snag was the dhows themselves. These picturesque
craft are used largely for transporting dried fish and, as a result,
in the course of years, their timbers become impregnated with an
overpowering scent of decayed fish. To anyone who is not a good
sailor, a voyage in one of the dhows can prove trying. After inspecting several, I chose the one that appeared to be the least
offensive as to smell, although the state of its rigging and tattered
sail did not inspire confidence. The quickest and safest route lies
outside the barrier reefs in deep water, but to take it would have
meant many hours' sailing without touching land. Since the only
form of convenience on board consisted of an open 'throne' pro-
jecting over the side, the women objected strongly to this plan
and insisted on taking the longer and slower route inside the

reef which winds through lagoons and mangrove swamps and can be travelled only at high tides. Since we were in no hurry, the time factor did not matter, so apart from spending several uncomfortable hours high and not so dry in the middle of mangrove swamps, there was nothing against this plan.

On the third day, we reached a point where the lagoon was blocked by a headland. In order to get round it, a narrow and dangerous channel through the reef had to be negotiated. The entire party decided that they would rather walk across the headland to the next lagoon while the boat brought the gear around. Our two up-country servants, who were to look after our belongings on the boat, viewed with mounting alarm our preparations to leave them to the tender mercies of the ocean and the dhow with its Bajun crew. When on the point of mutiny, I decided to give them moral support by accompanying them, together with Pippin, Joy's cairn terrier. Our attempt to traverse the channel nearly ended in disaster and we were obliged to turn back. As the dhow put about, it missed a half submerged coral head by a few inches. The Nahusa skipper informed me that it was too dangerous to make a second attempt, a statement with which I heartily agreed. The remaining alternative was to go back the way we had come and try another channel through the reef, which was said to be much wider and easier. It was a relief to get out into deep water away from the treacherous coral although we still needed to make the re-entry through the reef into the lagoon where we were to meet the rest of the party. But now I was told that this *mlango* (channel or gate-way) was even narrower and more tricky than the one we had failed to make. As we approached the reef I could not see anything except an unending line of breakers. The wind was on-shore but fitful and felt as if it might drop at any time. However, there was no turning back now—we had gone too far. Just as we seemed about to hit the reef, a gap appeared. At this moment, the wind died, leaving the sail limp and drooping. Even the Bajun showed signs of near-panic, and one of them cast a packet of rice into the waves as a peace offering. Others held the sail out with their hands to catch the least breath of air. Astern I saw an enormous wave bearing down upon us. I held on tight with Pippin under one arm. The prospect of having to swim for it and try to land on the jagged and knife-sharp coral among the breakers was not inviting. By the grace of God, the wave broke before hitting us and its after-flow pushed the boat through the gap into the calm waters of the lagoon. The remainder of the voyage lay along mangrove creeks and, apart from having to wait for high tide, we experienced no more difficulties.

Once again, we took up our quarters in the Kiunga house. Besides Pippin, Joy had her mongoose, Maeterlinck, a creature of boundless curiosity and indomitable independence. Whenever camp was packed up and we were ready to move off, Maeterlinck would always be missing. Once he was found wrapped up inside the tent. Luckily, one of the men heard faint squeaks coming from the bundle and we rescued him just in time before he was smothered. On other occasions, he would be found in the engine of the truck or had taken himself off for a walk, necessitating a prolonged search by all the men. At Kiunga his favourite haunt was the village where, contemptuous of the dogs and cats, he would investigate each hut in turn. The people soon got to know him and would come hurrying to tell of his latest escapades. On a subsequent safari along the Tana River he disappeared one morning and we never saw him again. As he was a mature mongoose, well able to look after himself, we like to believe that he found himself a mate, begot many little Maeterlincks, and lived out his allotted span as nature intended.

A few days after our arrival, a deputation of villagers came to me and begged me to deal with marauding elephant which were nightly raiding their crops. As I was supposed to be on holiday and none too keen to kill elephant at any time, it was only very reluctantly that I agreed to help them, especially as it meant a two hours' walk in the evening to reach the scene of the depredations. Our guests, Joy and two Bajun accompanied me on the expedition. Long after dark we arrived at the clearing in the thick bush where the Bajun were attempting to grow sorghum. There were no elephant around. However, the owners of the cultivation assured us that they would appear during the course

of the night. In order to be sure of making an efficient job of
shooting one or more elephants in the darkness, it was essential
to have a reliable person holding the spot-light, which would have
to be switched on at exactly the right moment and focused on a
vulnerable portion of the elephant's anatomy. Hilda volunteered
for the job. With some misgiving I agreed, wondering how a
person who nearly fainted at close contact with a sausage fly,
would react in the face of a possibly angry elephant. We had a
long wait and had reconciled ourselves to spending an uncomfortable night lying on the hard ground, when soon after midnight, one of the cultivators woke us to say that the marauders had
arrived. Silently, we crept forward until I was able to discern
the dim bulks of five elephants. We approached to within fifty
feet. I whispered to Hilda to focus the light on the head of the
nearest of the elephant and to switch on. Without the least
hesitation or fumbling, the beam shone true and unwavering on
the target, enabling me to shoot the animal through the brain.
When the unfortunate necessity arises, there is much satisfaction
in bringing off a clean brain shot. One moment the elephant
is alive and the next dead, without suffering or knowing what hit
him.

13: *Preparations for moving the Turkana*

IN APRIL 1949 the Government decided to move the Turkana tribesmen out of Isiolo district. Over the course of years, they had infiltrated into the area without authority and had amassed much livestock which was over-grazing the country and posing an ever-increasing problem. It was proposed to round them up together with their stock and trek them back to their own country in the Rift Valley. The distance was about two hundred miles and involved crossing plains and mountains with very meagre water supplies and grazing. Some two thousand men, women and children and eighteen thousand cattle, sheep and goats and donkeys were to be moved so it was essential to reconnoitre the easiest route well beforehand. As I was the only Government officer with extensive knowledge of the country, I was asked to help. Our safari consisted of Joy and myself, the District Officer from Isiolo, six Game Scouts, four tribal policemen, two personal servants and thirty pack donkeys and six mules for riding, my dog Kim and our pet serval cat Shockerly, Shocker for short. It had been arranged that we should all assemble on the Uaso Nyiro River about fifty miles west of Isiolo for the start of the safari. After our arrival, a day was spent in packing and organising the loads in pairs. At one point there was a heated dispute between the District Officer and his tribal police over an enormous box which turned out to be a commode. Being devoted Moslems, the tribal police did not like handling such an article and, indeed, it was absurd to think of taking it on a donkey safari; it was left behind.

One of the mules belonged to the Government. It was well known to me, having once been the property of Colonel Abbay from whom it had earned the name of Shaitani (devil). Although an excellent animal in many respects, it had the regrettable habit of heading for home at the first opportunity favourable to itself and most inconvenient for its rider. For this reason when Abbay died, I sold it to the Government on behalf of his estate, omitting to mention its peculiarity. I offered the District Officer one of my mules to ride but he declined, saying he wished to try out Shaitani and that he was an experienced horseman. On the second morning all was ready; we mounted our mules and gave the order to march. Shaitani marched all right, but in the wrong direction, pitching her rider into the river. It was only her reluctance to enter deep water that prevented her from making for Isiolo. The next morning when we were ready to move I noticed that a tribal policeman had been delegated to ride Shaitani. All went well for the next two hours, our mules leading the way with the pack train strung out behind. The country we traversed was thick thorn bush, the home of rhino and elephant and we had to keep a sharp look-out for these creatures.

At one point we passed five bull elephants, one of which carried magnificent ivory, at least a hundred and twenty pounds a side. Suddenly without warning, as was her wont, Shaitani deposited her rider in a thorn bush and headed for home. Luckily the mule paused to pass the time of day with the donkeys who were far behind, and was caught. Thereafter she behaved like a perfect lady throughout the safari.

During the next ten days we crossed the El Bata plains and descended into the Rift Valley, for the most part following well-worn and ancient trails, stopping at the infrequent water-holes and springs to assess their capacity for watering large numbers of livestock. Grazing was scarce and we came to the conclusion that the trek could be accomplished successfully only in May or late November, just before the end of the rainy season. After crossing the Sugota Valley and the river of that name we reached a little water-hole called Cigiria. It was baking hot. (As I have already said, the Sugota Valley is probably one of the hottest places in Africa.) On the march Joy complained of feeling unwell and by the time we reached the water it was obvious that she had a high temperature. We hastily pitched a tent for her under the scanty shade of a few doam palms. Her temperature registered a hundred and five degrees. I gave her a cold sponge down followed by hot tea and aspirin and in a couple of hours, much to my relief, she was back to normal. Cigiria was no place in which to be taken seriously ill. It was inaccessible by motor transport and the only means of communication was by a runner with a note.

Poor Kim had developed very sore feet through marching over the hot sand and lava rocks. In order to give him some relief I put him on one of the more lightly laden donkeys where he could sit in comfort between the twin loads. Later he often took advantage of this means of transport and seemed to enjoy the ride.

At length, fifteen days after leaving the Uaso Nyiro River, we reached our destination at Kangetet near the Kerio River. Sixteen years earlier when Nevil Baxendale and I had walked along the Kerio there had been many elephant. Now there were none, and according to the local Turkana, none had been seen in this area for years. The heat and trials of the marches had somewhat frayed tempers and a trivial incident which should have been forgotten as soon as it arose, led to such strained relations between Joy and the District Officer, that our two camps had to be pitched several hundred yards apart and communication carried on by a system of chits. Fortunately for all concerned this ridiculous state of affairs was brought to an end by a passing missionary. The same who had tried to make me see the light in my trading days; he arrived in a jeep, the District Officer begged a lift and left us to complete the return safari on our own.

Having surveyed one possible route for the great trek, I decided that on the return journey I would investigate another farther to the south. It led us through country I had not seen for twenty years. The plumed Turkana and Suk still stalked bareskinned with spear and head-rest through the land, and there were no dust clouds, raised by hurrying motor transport, to mar the landscape. Karpeddo slumbered in the heat, unaltered, except for the addition of one Asian store where we were able to buy provisions. For meat, we either purchased sheep from the tribesmen or where there were none, I shot a gazelle or some guinea-fowl. In this Kim helped me, for he never failed to secure a wounded animal or bird. He was a huge tawny-coloured animal, a cross between mastiff and ridge-back. The local Africans often asked if he were some kind of European lion, for they had never before seen a dog of his size and colour.

It took us fifteen days to reach Maralal, over the top of the eastern wall of the Rift Valley. On the way, we stopped two days in order to let Joy paint the portrait of a Suk chief. Although this route offered better grazing for stock, it traversed extremely broken and rugged country with many steep hills and had the added disadvantage of crossing Suk territory where trouble might develop between the Turkana and the Suk; I therefore recommended the northern route.

It was not until July 1951 that the preparations for the actual trek were completed. Then, once again, I was called upon to assist, and helped to collect the Turkana and their stock at the point of departure, which was on the Kipsing river-bed about thirty miles west of Isiolo.

Soon the concentration of large numbers of stock attracted the attention of lions and hyenas. One evening, after an exhausting day spent in counting stock, while I was sitting on the verandah of my tent enjoying an after-dinner drink, Kim got up with bristling hair and started to growl, looking intently into the darkness. I picked up a torch and in its beam saw a lion a few yards in front of the tent slinking away. Early next morning the Turkana came to report that during the night one of their donkeys had been taken. I set off together with Lodogia and another scout and two Turkana. We came to the place where the donkey had been killed and afterwards dragged off to the edge of a dense thicket of henna bush on the bank of the river-bed. The thicket was about a hundred yards long by about forty in width. We circled it, to see whether there were any lion tracks leading out. Finding none, we entered at several points, but in spite of throwing in stones and making a good deal of noise, could neither hear nor see any signs of the lion. At length, my men decided it must have gone and went to look for spoor.

I, however, was not satisfied that the lion had left and decided to investigate a particularly dense patch of the thicket which consisted of an impenetrable mass of henna bush which had been bent over by the last big flood and now formed the roof of a sort of cavern. I crawled on my stomach under the branches until I was daunted by a completely dark tunnel. For several minutes, I lay, peering into the blackness, then I was joined by Lodogia. I could see nothing, but Lodogia said he saw something of a lighter colour than the surrounding gloom. Eventually my attention was drawn to a tiny light patch on which the sun's rays fell; it was no larger than a match-box but it appeared to rise and fall gently. Since there was no wind, I realised that the shaft of light must be falling on the body of the lion and that its breathing was causing the movement. It was impossible to make out on what part of its body the sunlight was playing or which way the animal was facing. It was only some twenty feet away—much too close to take chances. Either I must call it a day and clear out or take a shot and hope for the best. I wished fervently that I had never entered the wretched thicket, but having done so and located the lion, it would not have looked good to withdraw before the expectant Turkana who was waiting outside. I was not keen on firing my heavy 470 rifle from the prone position, thereby risking a broken collar-bone, nor was it the best of attitudes from which to repel a charge. But, as the minutes passed, the tension became unbearable so I took aim at the circle of light and let fly. There was a cloud of dust caused by the blast of the rifle, a slight grunt from the lion and then silence. When the dust cleared, I could still see the light patch, but now it did not move. Was the lion dead or tensed ready to charge? After a few more moments of suspense, I told Lodogia to fire. Nothing happened. We cut our way in and found a very big lioness dead. The light had been shining on her chest as she sat facing and watching us. I have often wondered what would have happened if the sunlight had been on her hind end!

At last everything was ready for the great move, food depots had been established along the route, armed police and tribal police escorts mustered and medical comforts arranged for the sick. It only remained for George Low, the veterinary officer, to make a last inspection of the stock and then we would be off. A big, genial, dark-haired Scotsman, Low, a stock inspector, had been in Kenya for many years and both he and his wife were good friends of ours. When he arrived, I could tell by his face that something was wrong. He had discovered foot and mouth disease among the goats. There could be no great trek! How the Turkana rejoiced! They gathered around George, shaking him warmly by the hand and forthwith organised an impromptu dance in his honour. The proposed trek back to their barren hills and sandy plains had been very unpopular, and, moreover, their most prominent witch-doctors had prophesied that it would never take place.

While helping to collect the Turkana I had visited a huge camp on the Uaso Nyiro River, containing fifteen families of South African Dutch farmers out on their annual holiday. The scene suggested the Transvaal at the beginning of the century, only instead of covered wagons and spans of oxen, there were motor lorries of every size and make. Checking up on licences, I found that a dozen men had full game licences, and that several had special licences for elephant. Although such people are, as a rule, respectable and law-abiding folk, their main aim is always to shoot everything allowed by their licence, regardless of size of trophy, and to turn every scrap of meat into biltong (dried meat), and generally, as most of them are extremely good shots I felt alarmed at the likely slaughter which I was powerless to prevent. In this frame of mind I left the camp and within two miles came on a party of eight bull elephants close to the road. Two carried very fine ivory. I was certain they were doomed unless I could do something to save them. They were in a shallow valley in fairly open country so I thought it might be just possible to drive them gently down to the river and across it into the Game Reserve where they would be safe. Using my Landrover, I got them moving down the valley and in an hour had the satisfaction of seeing them cross the river.

During the first quarter of 1951, the Northern Province experienced one of the worst droughts within living memory. From many places reports came in of animals dying of thirst and starvation. In particular, the Lorian Swamp had completely dried up. As I felt most concerned about the plight of the elephant which normally lived on and around these swamps, I set off with Joy on a journey of about a hundred and sixty miles to investigate.

The swamp which is about eight miles long and in normal times covered with reeds six to eight feet in height was now a bare dusty plain. A little water was left at the bottom of the Sabenna wells near the centre of the swamp, twenty feet below the surface and quite out of reach of wild animals. Somali tribesmen laboured day and night drawing water for their thirsty and starving livestock. All round the wells lay the bodies of dead and dying animals, indeed, they were so thick on the ground that driving in my Landrover it was literally impossible to avoid running over decaying carcases.

Walking along the dried up bed of the Uaso Nyiro River which passes through the swamp we witnessed the most gruesome and pathetic sights. At one point there was a pool of semi-liquid mud containing a score or more of rotting carcases and in the midst a seething mass of dead and dying cat-fish. Further on we came on the bodies of two cow elephants and a little calf embedded in the drying mud. Next to them was a camel cemented into dry mud. As we watched it slowly raised its head. Somalis standing nearby laughed at our astonishment and told us that the poor brute had been there over a month, without food or water. A merciful bullet put an end to its sufferings. The tribesmen had seen so much of their stock perish that they were past caring and had made no attempt to dig the camel out. A pall of gorged vultures and carrion storks, too lethargic to move out of one's way, covered the ground and overall a stench of death and corruption hung like an invisible fog.

The Somali chief, Abdi Ogli, an old friend of mine, complained that the surviving elephant were so desperate for water that they were coming to the Sabenna wells at all hours of the day and night, scattering and trampling the stock clustered around the drinking troughs. Women carrying water back to their villages had been chased until forced to drop their containers and fly for their lives. Men working inside the wells dared not leave for their homes until their clothing was dry for fear that the elephant scenting the moisture would give chase. One elephant in particular was feared because of his truculence. Thinking this might be exaggeration we went to the wells and waited. The sun had just set, hundreds of head of stock were waiting to be watered and scores of men and women were working in the wells. At the end of half an hour we saw the dim outline of an elephant hurrying across the flats towards the wells. Without pause he swept in among the stock from one well-head to another sucking up the water in the troughs, regardless of the yelling Somalis who threw sticks and clods of earth. The stock barely moved to give him way. It seemed imperative to shoot him before he killed someone. But equally essential that I kill him with one shot, as there were far too many people around to risk wounding him with the possibility of his running amuck. After much manoeuvring I finally got a clear view of him across the mouth of a well and, while Joy shone a torch on his head I shot him through the brain, felling him instantly. Abdi Ogli informed me that eleven elephants had died of thirst in the neighbourhood of the wells. How many more had died farther away was not known. A number of the Lorian elephants had gone up the river in their search for water. At a place called Gubatu about eighteen miles up-stream they had been set on by bands of Boran young men, who, taking advantage of their weakened state, caused by hunger and thirst, had speared many without much risk to themselves. It was never known how many were massacred but a patrol of Game Scouts sent to investigate obtained positive evidence of fifteen killed, including small calves. Probably the drought and the Boran between them must have accounted for not less than fifty, almost half of the normal elephant population of the Lorian swamp. It was surprising that the instinct of the elephant had not warned them to leave the swamp before it was too late, and a still worse misfortune that the Somali tribesmen had not moved in time to the permanent water at Wajir sixty miles to the north. Final estimates suggest that some forty thousand head of stock perished from thirst and starvation.

At last, when it seemed that the surviving elephants were doomed, the rains started up-country and brought the river down in flood and the situation was saved. It was a most interesting sight to see the water literally creeping down the parched river-bed which was criss-crossed by deep cracks and dried up wells, each of which had to fill up before the water could flow on.

In normal times, the Lorian elephant live in complete harmony with the Somalis and their stock and it is a common sight to see cattle, sheep and goats feeding among a herd of elephant, often tended by small boys. Soon after the water arrived, I saw a big bull elephant enjoying his first mud bath in months on the edge of a pool. Two small boys arrived with a flock of sheep and goats. The elephant withdrew and stood thirty yards away with every sign of impatience, waiting for the animals to finish their drink. He took tentative steps back and forward, flapped his great ears and plucked reeds with his trunk and waved them in a threatening manner and then finally returned to his bath.

Nature went from one extreme to another. The terrible drought was followed by exceptionally heavy rains and floods. The swamp and adjoining Habaswein plains were flooded, cutting off all road communication with Wajir and other posts to the north. Lorries laden with supplies which had tried to get through were caught by the water and remained immovably stuck in the mud for over two months. When the water subsided sufficiently, I helped to organise donkey transport over the ten miles of flood flats until the ground dried enough to permit motor transport.

14: *To Europe via the Congo and the Sahara*

AFTER LIVING for more than twelve years in the old thatched house which by now was almost a ruin, I prevailed upon the authorities to allocate funds for a more permanent dwelling. In some ways, I was sorry to leave this house, in which I had lived ever since it had belonged to the Browns. It was comfortable and picturesque. The bougainvillaea which covered the walls made a tremendous splash of colour and the garden was full of drought-resistant succulents, but the roof leaked badly and the time to go had come.

After months of agitation a meagre £1,500 was forthcoming and that on the condition that the site should be within the Isiolo township. The idea of living cheek by jowl with other government officers did not appeal to us, and finally, through the influence of George Low who had been appointed a member of the committee detailed to choose the site, one was accepted about three miles away from the township, at the foot of a range of hills. It had a fine view looking northwards and was ideal from our point of view. The only serious drawback was that there was no water supply and all our water had to be fetched by lorry or donkeys. Fortunately, my brother Terence (he was not a trained architect but clever with his hands and good at designing houses) undertook to build the house. Although small, when completed, the house was far larger than any the Public Works Department would have provided for the price.

One of my evening amusements was to indulge in carpentry. This is thirsty work so I was in the habit of taking a bottle of whisky to the workshop. Joy frowned upon what she described as my 'excessive drinking'; therefore, in order to avoid unnecessary trouble, I used to put the bottle within easy reach on a shelf just above the work-bench among those containing turpentine, linseed oil and other substances associated with a workshop. One evening I was hard at work planing a piece of wood, when I stopped for a rest. I automatically reached up for a refresher. I put the bottle to my lips and took a mouthful; luckily I did not swallow—it was rust remover! I spat it out instantly but, even so, my mouth was sore for several days afterwards. My friend Gerry Dalton, a National Park warden remarked, 'It was just what you needed after all the water you have been forced to drink.'

It was always an up-hill struggle to obtain the bare necessities of equipment from Government. A letter I felt obliged to write to the District Commissioner in Isiolo illustrates the point:—

ANNUAL PLEA FOR OFFICE FURNITURE

Once again, it being the beginning of a bright New Year, I would submit my application for a few additional pieces of office furniture.

By dint of almost superhuman patience and the good-will of many Administrators over the years, it has been possible to accumulate:—

1. A fine office.
2. One linen cupboard of ancient but honourable vintage.
3. Two office tables.
4. One superb filing cabinet.
5. Two dining-room chairs which rock and pinch.

One visitor seated before me, suddenly screwed up his face with a look of excruciating pain. For a moment I feared he was the victim of a seizure. He was! It was the chair! A rock in the right direction soon released him.

This kind of incident means little to the calloused backsides of Game Wardens, but not so to the tender behinds of film stars and other illustrious visitors.

Is it right or fair to expect a visitor, not only to risk rupture to the person, but to dignity as well?

Would it be possible to let me have a few chairs? I do not expect them to be easy, but perhaps a little easier than the ones I have at present.

B.G.   N

Some letters I received contained strange requests:

Principal Livestock Marketing Officer to Game Warden, Isiolo

WATERING OF ELEPHANTS

I understand that a large herd of elephants have taken to watering on our borehole on the Isiolo quarantine holding ground.

With a view to making a possible charge for watering fees, could you please inform me how much water one elephant will drink in twenty-four hours?

To this I replied:

Game Warden, Isiolo, to Principal Livestock Marketing Officer, Kabete

... Elephants, like humans, vary a great deal in their capacity to take drink. The more abstemious are probably content with a mere eighteen or twenty gallons. Others, fond of lifting their trunks, may consume thirty or even forty.

While always being happy to give your department every assistance I must make it clear that my influence with the local elephants is regrettably weak, and I find myself unable to give any assurance that they will willingly comply with a request to pay watering fees. ...

In 1953, my chief William Hale decided that it was high time I went on leave to Europe. I had not been out of Africa for over twenty-nine years and had accumulated something over seven hundred days since I joined government service in 1938. A good reason for taking my leave now was that recently the regulations had been changed. In future, leave if not taken when it fell due, would be lost.

Joy and I decided that rather than go to Europe by sea or air, we would motor in my Landrover, towing a trailer, via the Sahara. This, of course, created a problem for Government as it was almost unheard of for an officer to travel to Europe in such an unorthodox manner, so there were no regulations covering such a

contingency. Finally it was agreed that I should be granted
money equivalent to the cost of a sea passage to England for
which I was supposed to account to the last halfpenny.

We were strongly advised not to take a trailer and warned that
if we did, it would certainly have to be abandoned in the sands of
the Sahara. Although I have no love for trailers, I had had plenty
of experience with them under desert conditions and felt confident
of getting through. In the event it turned out that the trailer
was an infernal nuisance, not because of any difficulties in nego-
tiating the desert, but owing to broken springs, burst tyres, a
broken coupling and the trouble of parking it when passing
through cities.

We left Nairobi on the 21st of March, and travelled through
Uganda. We met our first hurdle at the Belgian customs post,
on the Congo border, in connection with firearms. Apparently,
these were not allowed in without a special permit which could
only be obtained at Stanleyville. I had a rifle and a shot-gun.
Luckily the Belgian customs officer was a kindly person and when
he saw that Joy was on the verge of tears he relented and let us
pass. Throughout our long journey we found that Belgian and
French customs officials, both European and African, were invariably polite and helpful. A sorry contrast was the border post
at Maiduguri in Nigeria. Here we met with petty officialdom at
its worst. We arrived in the heat of the day and I was suffering
from an attack of malaria and had a high temperature. Nevertheless, the African officer made me unload the car and trailer completely in the broiling sun, and no one offered to help although
there were several of his men lounging about.

The drive through the Congo and part of French Equatorial
Africa tended to become monotonous as practically the whole of
our route ran through the vast Equatorial forest where visibility
was limited to the road ahead and a few yards on either side,
only occasionally relieved by rivers. These we had to cross by
ferries, some powered, others, which consisted of dug-out canoes
with a platform lashed across, driven by a team of paddlers.
We had brought two small tents and whenever possible camped
at night, for one thing this saved us money, which was convenient,

as the existing currency restrictions limited our finances considerably.

At a little village in French Equatoria Joy acquired a young banded mongoose. We named him Crampel. He was a tremendous character and in a very short space of time adapted himself to our nomadic existence. He had great ideas of making himself comfortable and chose to travel in the canvas bucket which we used to keep our drinking water cool. As soon as we stopped, Crampel would wake up and survey the situation. If it met with his approval and it was not too hot, he would get down and start hunting for insects while carrying on an animated conversation in varying squeaks. Poor little Crampel, at one of the stops he must have eaten some poisonous insect. He became ill, refused all food, and during the next few days grew steadily weaker. At Kano Joy took him to a vet, but he died that evening. For the brief space of fourteen days his happy nature had endeared him to us, and it was with heavy hearts that we went on.

It was with relief that we left the gloomy forests and unattractive scenery of Nigeria and got out into the open desert. By now it was late in the season and during the middle of the day the heat was like the breath of a furnace, and we had to make frequent halts and turn the car into the wind to let it cool down. The route across the sands was marked at intervals of about a mile by iron posts. Often, in order to avoid patches of particularly soft sand, it became necessary for us to make detours, then we would lose sight of the posts for a time, but so long as we took care to return within sight of them fairly rapidly, there was no danger of becoming lost. The sunsets and dawns over the desert were indescribably beautiful. Far from being an empty expanse of sand, the desert contained much of interest. We passed many hills and rocky outcrops, and on one of the latter we saw prehistoric rock engravings of animals such as giraffe and elephants, which suggested that in the remote ages in which these had been made, the country must have been covered with vegetation. Wells were few and far between, and in several the water was a hundred or more feet below the surface. Luckily we had brought a long length of rope which enabled us to draw up water in buckets and keep our containers filled. These containers held about thirty gallons, which would be sufficient to keep us going for a long time in case of break-down. Much of the desert was similar to areas of the Northern Province of Kenya, but on a much vaster scale.

At length we reached the Hogar Mountains which lie in the centre of the Sahara, and rise to a height of ten thousand feet. They are the home of the veiled Tuareg. After spending a couple of days visiting places of interest in the mountains, we continued our journey to Algiers, intending to cross from there over to France, but, instead, we decided to have a look at Morocco and finally ended up at Tangier from where we crossed over to Spain. It was here that our money troubles began. Luckily I was able to borrow £50 from a Spanish nobleman whom we had met in Kenya while he was on a hunting trip, but after travelling along the Riviera into Italy, and thence northwards into Joy's native Austria, we again ran short of cash. Once again I succeeded in borrowing another £50 from another nobleman who had once been out on safari with me. Finally, on the way to England, we stopped a few days in Paris. I had never been to the city, but Joy knew it fairly well. One evening we went to see the Follies. After the performance, when starting back for our small hotel, Joy and I had words. Suddenly, without warning, she got out of the car and disappeared. The reader may think there was nothing to worry about, perhaps just a splendid opportunity for a night out! But Joy had all our money and I could not remember the name of the hotel nor the name of the street. Moreover I dared not seek the aid of a policeman as the first thing he would naturally ask me would be where I was staying and if I said that I did not know, he would most probably take me in charge. At this late hour the streets were almost deserted apart from a few belated revellers and odd women wandering about. After driving for some time, not knowing where I was going, in desperation I accosted one of the women hoping she might speak English. Although she seemed extremely friendly and willing to help, I had the feeling she misunderstood my need. Just as dawn was breaking, I recognised a street where we had stopped to enquire about accommodation. I knew our hotel was close by and found it without further difficulty. Joy, of course, had arrived several hours earlier and was wrapped in untroubled slumber. There were further words.

On the 7th of September, four and a half months after leaving Nairobi, we arrived at Dover. During the next two months we toured the Highlands and visited friends and relations, most of whom I had not seen for nearly thirty years.

Then I returned by sea to Kenya and Joy stayed on in England.

15: *The Mau-Mau*

KENYA WAS NOW in the throes of the Mau-Mau rebellion and soon after my return from leave I was attached to the military forces. My task was to visit British units in the field and report on the capabilities of their native trackers and weed out the duds. I spent five strenuous weeks on patrols through the Aberdares forests above Nyeri, looking for the elusive Mau-Mau. It was an interesting experience, not unlike hunting dangerous game, although it was made more difficult by handicaps inseparable from military operations. The greatest to my mind was *noise* in infinite variety. The clicking and clanking of odd bits of equipment, mess tins, etc., the coughings and cussings (it was said that the Aberdares parrots now prefixed everything with a soldierly adjective) the hacking of bamboos when making camp, and at last when all was quiet, along would come an aircraft and circle overhead, noisily demanding to be spoken to over the wireless set. Everyone within a mile was alarmed and knew the exact whereabouts of our position. It was a wonder that we ever made contact with the enemy, and in fact, most of our contacts were with the larger fauna such as elephant, rhino and buffalo. This was no bad thing in itself as it kept the men alert and on their toes. More than once my knowledge and experience enabled me to identify the sounds and signs of these creatures, thus avoiding unnecessary encounters.

I worked with units of the Buffs and Devons. Most of the men were National Service youngsters in their late teens or early twenties and were a cheerful lot. During the first few days I felt like Grandpa, and I wondered whether I would be able to stand up to these fit young men and whether I could hump the unaccustomed pack, and sleep, inadequately clad, on the bleak moorlands. However, in a few days I was fit and I found that I could keep going with the best. The standard of tracking was poor and some of the trackers had no right to describe themselves as such. Others were plain lazy, or frightened, and the few who might have been some use were often handicapped by being burdened with wireless sets or other spare gear. The only piece of good tracking I saw done was by one of my own men and resulted in the capture of a wounded gang leader.

One day an American journalist arrived at company headquarters. He was most anxious to have first-hand experience of a real forest patrol. So, after he had assured us that he was well equipped for the trip, it was agreed that he should accompany us on a two-day patrol. At dawn the next morning we were all loaded up like mules and ready to march off when R appeared with a rifle in one hand and a leather suit-case in the other. However, after he had been more suitably equipped he came with us and proved himself a delightful companion and thoroughly game. Later on he produced a suitably bloodthirsty story called 'Murder Patrol'.

Just when I began to feel that I was doing a worthwhile job, I received orders to join the trackers' training school at Nanyuki as an instructor. This task did not appeal to me and I was therefore much relieved when I was given permission to return to the Northern Frontier Province.

Soon after I got back to Isiolo, it became clear that I could not carry on my normal duties for there was plenty of evidence to suggest that gangs were becoming increasingly active in the Northern Grazing Area of the Meru District, adjoining Isiolo, and that it would no longer be safe to leave my men on their own in outposts, for their arms and ammunition would be too much of a temptation for a resolute gang to disregard. It would therefore be necessary to organise them into an anti-Mau-Mau force. In view of my knowledge of the country and of the people, the Administrations of Meru and Isiolo asked me to help in this task.

According to information, the Meru Northern Grazing Area was being used by gangs as a centre in which to recuperate after being harassed by forces in the Mount Kenya forests and on farmlands. My task was to give them no rest and chase them back again.

On our first patrol into the area, three British soldiers were attached to me; they included a Bren-gunner. I mounted them on my spare mules while the Game Scouts went on foot. We were following down a little stream, the scouts on one side and myself on the other, when suddenly there was an outburst of firing from the scouts who had flushed a gang. We spurred on our mules to join in the fray. The river at this point flowed through a narrow channel only four feet across under high banks. From the corner of my eye I saw the mule ridden by the gunner come to a dead stop on the edge of the bank. The rider sailed gracefully over its head and landed with a loud splash in the water. He took no further proceedings in the action. In spite of the many shots fired, due to the woeful shooting of my scouts, no one was hit and the Mau-Mau vanished into the bush.

One day we received a report of a gang, said to number over two hundred, close by in the vicinity of some springs called Maji-ya-Chumbi (Salt Springs). We set off to investigate, and when nearing the water heard shots and saw figures running. We prepared for action but luckily I looked through my glasses and saw two Europeans. They turned out to be a well-known professional hunter and his elderly American client out shooting birds. I suggested that it was a little unwise to go bird-shooting in country reputed to be swarming with Mau-Mau. The elderly gentleman seemed a little taken aback and remarked; 'You don't say! Genuine Mau-Mau?!'

On another night, in pouring rain, ex-Game Scout Lakalesoi arrived breathless at my headquarters with the news that his *manyatta* had been plundered by a gang of seventeen Mau-Mau, two men had been shot and all his cattle carried off. Following at a safe distance he had seen the gang disappear up a valley into the European farming area. At dawn I set off with a friend in my Landrover, which was filled to capacity with Game Scouts. After a drive of sixteen miles across country we came on the fresh track of the gang. Leaving the Landrover, we followed up on foot. Near the head of the valley and across it, we saw the gang driving the cattle before them. Luckily before opening fire on them I took a look through my glasses; it seemed to me that some were wearing uniform; if so they might not be Mau-Mau. I positioned the men with orders to fire the instant I gave the word, then I showed myself and shouted to the gang to halt and lay down their weapons which consisted of six rifles and an assortment of spears and bows and arrows. Reluctantly, they complied with the order. I then discovered that they were a party of Meru Home Guards, who had taken it upon themselves to do a bit of rustling on the side as a reprisal for a cattle raid carried out on Meru stock by Samburu *moran*. They admitted to raiding Lakalesoi's *boma* and shooting two men. They were taken to Isiolo under arrest, together with the looted stock.

There were constant rumours of a gang hide-out in an isolated range of hills called Shab, north of the Meru country. It was alleged that this gang was being fed by Somalis who had a village at the foot of the hills. With great secrecy a large-scale operation to comb the hills from end to end was mounted. Those taking part were a company of Northumberland Fusiliers, a police unit, hundreds of Meru Home Guards and my Game Scouts and, in addition, a police spotter aircraft. Starting at dawn, at the southern end of the range, two-thirds of the hills had been covered by dark, leaving only the northernmost peak uncovered. All exits were blocked and at first light a mortar section of the Fusiliers plastered every yard of the hill with bombs. Then the force went in. Not a trace of a terrorist was discovered and the only casualty was a Fusilier who got in the way of a rhino and was slightly injured. About a year later a film company looking for a site to stage some blood-curdling episode, tumbled by accident on the hide-out we had expended so much energy trying to locate. It was well hidden behind an enormous rock and contained even a pen for goats.

While following up the tracks of a gang, my men one day captured a straggler, a youth, foot-sore and starving. After being given a good meal and time to recover from his fright, I asked him why he had joined the gang. He told me that his sole reason was that he had been persecuted by the headman of his location for non-payment of tax and so, as he had no money to pay the tax and did not want to go to jail, he had 'gone into the bush', as joining Mau-Mau was often called. There were many like him, and also not a few who had no political convictions but joined for the sake of adventure.

Out on patrol in two Landrovers with a section of The Royal Inniskilling Fusiliers, I thought it would be fun to give them a surprise, so, driving the leading car, I veered across country up the slope of a low hill and suddenly jammed on the brakes within two feet of the edge of Magardo crater. The crater is about half a mile across and some six-hundred-feet deep, with sheer walls on three sides. On the east there is a narrow cleft in the lip with a precipitous path winding down to the floor to a little brackish lake with, near its edges, a few sweet-water springs. As this is the only water supply for a long way around, it is used by the Boran and Meru tribesmen to water their stock. Meru women also come from afar in large parties to collect the saline deposits and carry them back to their homes. Near the entrance to the cleft there are many small caves where, in normal times, small Meru traders set up stalls to sell tea and sugar and the drug miraar to the Boran. It is also a centre for the illegal trade in leopard skins and rhino horn, and often I had carried out surprise raids on the caves. On this occasion the crater floor was packed with cattle, an odd camel towered over them and there were more coming down the path. As animals both descending and ascending could move only in single file, it would take nearly the whole day to water a fair-sized herd. Water for household purposes was drawn by Boran women from the springs and loaded on to the camels in woven fibre containers to be carried to their villages six to eight miles distant. Judged by any standards it was a unique and remarkable scene. It was, therefore, with astonishment almost amounting to awe that I observed a soldier with his head buried in a 'penny dreadful'.

For a time it was thought that the Mau-Mau might be procuring firearms smuggled in from Somalia. The most likely route lay along the Tana River. I was therefore asked to carry out a patrol along the river and endeavour to find out whether there was any evidence to support the story. I arranged for my donkeys and mules to meet me at Kora on the river about a hundred miles up-stream of Garissa. While awaiting their arrival, I went by Landrover along an old disused track to Balambala, a small trading centre some forty miles down-river. I asked the police constable in charge of the post whether there had been any Mau-Mau activity recently in his beat. He looked at me blankly for a few moments and then asked whether it was a *mau* (canoe) I required or did I want a *mamba* (crocodile)? I disclaimed any interest in canoes or crocodiles and left it at that, having come to the conclusion that Balambala was not a hot-bed of Mau-Mau!

The march up the river which I had wanted to do for a long time was most attractive and interesting. At one point we passed impressive falls which were not marked on any of the current ordinance maps, and I wondered whether I was the first European to see them, though, almost certainly, some of the early travellers must have passed close by and perhaps seen them.

At a Boran village I came on a Somali who seemed a suspicious character. After questioning him closely, I told him that I was convinced that he was a gun-runner, the penalty for which was hanging. This so frightened him that he readily admitted that he was an illegal trader in ivory. To prove his innocence he produced a rather decayed elephant tusk for which he said he had paid fifty shillings and added that he had been offered another tusk which he had declined as it was too heavy to carry. By his own admissions he had rendered himself liable to at least a year's imprisonment, but, having taken a rather mean advantage of him, I had not the heart to charge him and, instead, appointed him an honorary prisoner for the duration of the safari, and my gun-bearer. He proved himself to be staunch and loyal and at the end of the expedition I enrolled him as a Game Scout, and never had reason to regret it.

Almost constant patrolling continued for many weary months. At one time a company of the Royal Inniskilling Fusiliers was camped near my house. This made life easier for me and relieved me of the anxiety of leaving Joy alone with only a couple of Game Scouts to guard her. My scouts were now attached to the company to act as guides. They got on well with the 'Johnnies' as the Africans call the British soldiers and much appreciated the good rations. The soldiers were a remarkably well-behaved lot, and many took a keen interest in the country and in its wild life. Through the kindness of the commanding officer, the scouts received much-needed range practice under the eyes of keen instructors and, as a result, their standard of shooting improved immensely. The average British soldier looks upon arms drill as a necessary but boring duty. Not so the scouts who were constantly importuning NCOs to put them through their paces. We made several lasting friendships and when the time came for the company to leave, we were all extremely sorry to see them go. Soon after they left, my small force was augmented by a section of mounted *dubas* (tribal police) from Moyale on the Ethiopian border. Many times they proved their worth in action.

There was, of course, the dark side of the picture. The grim and the tragic. For many both European and African there were the long nights of ceaseless tension, the waiting, the watching, the listening behind locked doors and shuttered windows for the sounds of stealthy foot-steps. The anxiety of what the dawn might reveal. The sadness of betrayal by the nearest and most trusted. Only those who lived through it know the grimness and the tragedy. But, as the President of Kenya has said, all the hate and bitterness are past and done with and must be forgotten. It is the future which matters. A future which we all fervently hope will be one of peace and happiness for this wonderful country.

IN JULY 1955, I was asked to help with arrangements for a trip to Loingalane on Lake Rudolf for His Excellency the Governor of Kenya, Sir Evelyn Baring and his family. Knowing that some of the party wished to try fishing on the lake, I borrowed a boat from a friend and took it up a few days before the main party arrived. Before leaving Isiolo I made secret plans for Joy to come to Loingalane after the Governor's visit, on the excuse of painting some of the local tribesmen. If all went well, we hoped to cross over the lake to Von Hohnel or South Island. It was necessary to keep the project secret as if it had become known to the authorities, we would not have been permitted to carry it out. Indeed I had good reason to know what would happen if the secret were let out. A few years previously, I had arranged with P, a District Commissioner, to do the trip in two folboats (canvas kayaks) and we had actually got the canoes out from England for the purpose. Then the Provincial Commissioner heard of it and considered it too dangerous and forbade us to go. Probably he had visions of having to organise search and rescue operations, and perhaps of being obliged to write letters of condolence to our nearest and dearest.

Ever since I had crossed the lake with Nevil Baxendale in 1934 it had been my ambition to visit the grim-looking and mysterious island known locally as The Island of No Return. Also, as no one had set foot on the island since the disappearance of Dyson and Martin in 1934, I hoped to find some clue to their fate. Circumstances having at last placed a boat at my disposal, the temptation was too great to resist.

Joy arrived on the 24th, having met the Governor's party on their way back when there had been some demur about letting her go on without an escort. We decided to attempt the crossing the following day. I arranged with my men about signals: on the evening of our arrival on the island, I would fire off a Very light, which was to be answered by my driver Ibrahim who would have the Landrover on a ridge overlooking the lake and would switch the headlights on and off three times. On the following evening the same signals would be repeated; they would indicate that all was well. I impressed on the men that so long as they saw the single Very light, on no account did I want any fuss made or alarm created, even if we were away for a week or more— which was possible as the weather might well prevent our return. The distress signal would be three Very lights; if they saw them my driver was to go at once to the Police post at North Horr and signal the District Headquarters at Marsabit. The men were very upset and uneasy about the venture, as the El Molo had told them tales of a demon who lived on the island and had assured them that anyone who went there would never come back. Yet, in spite of their fears, Godana Dima and another scout volunteered to accompany us, but there was no room for them in the boat.

The 25th was not favourable as there was a high wind all day and white horses on the water. The 26th started even worse but by noon the wind suddenly changed and began to blow from the west—a sure sign that a calm would follow. We hurried to our starting-off point, a small bay some six miles south of Loingalane and got the boat ready. It was a flat-bottomed dinghy about fourteen feet in length. We lashed down two motor-car inner-tubes and empty petrol-cans for buoyancy; installed the larger of two outboard engines and stowed the smaller in case of emergency. The large engine was a 5 hp Britannia, rather too heavy for the dinghy, but it was fast and I estimated it would get us across in about an hour, although it left a freeboard at the stern of only two inches. The small Anzani engine of about 1 hp was much more suited to the boat but gave only half the speed. I thought that if we got caught in a storm, I would heave the Britannia overboard and use the Anzani. Forward, I lashed two iron mortar bomb boxes containing our food, cameras, Very lights, and ammunition. In addition we had a 303 rifle, a 22, fishing tackle, and a spare can of petrol.

By four-thirty, the white horses having gone to sleep, we set off. The motor behaved beautifully and in an hour and a quarter we landed in a little cove on a gently sloping sandy beach. The water was crystal clear and we could see huge perch and tilapia cruising about. We unpacked the gear and drew the dinghy up the beach and then set off to look over our surroundings. We found that we had landed on a small island, cut off from our objective by a thirty-yard channel. The shore of the main island looked extremely uninviting, jagged lava running straight into the lake, with only one little beach where a landing would be possible. Hurriedly we returned to the cove, packed up and started off again, rounded the north end of the little island and made for the beach across a half mile of calm water. On the beach we saw an enormous crocodile, quite the biggest I have ever seen; at a guess I would say not less than twenty feet in length. The beach consisted of a twenty-yard stretch of pebbles and sand between two lava flows, it was well sheltered by the little island and a headland. There was not much time left before sunset, so we busied ourselves making camp. I was anxious above all to find a resting place secure from crocodiles and other animals, as I imagined that if any wild life existed on the island the creatures would have no knowledge or fear of human beings. We made our beds in a cleft in a rock about twenty yards above the shore. I say beds! Joy had a single blanket and I a cotton *kikoi* (loin-cloth) and for mattress, loose pebbles. By dark we were more or less settled in. Soon we saw the headlights of my Landrover across the water. I sent up a Very light which was promptly answered as arranged, followed up with a fireworks display of 303 tracer bullets. Evidently my men were pleased that we had arrived safely.

About nine p.m. the south-east wind started and through the night it increased in violence until it was a howling gale, sweeping down in cold tearing gusts. Sleep was almost impossible and long before dawn we were shivering with cold. It was a relief to get up, hunt for fuel and boil tea to warm our bones. Just as dawn was breaking, I noticed the Landrover lights. Evidently faithful Ibrahim wanted to make sure the demons had not eaten us during the night.

The first day on the island we spent in climbing to the top of the central range of volcanoes, the highest of which is about 1,500 feet above the lake level. The going was exceedingly bad, and even dangerous, up a vast lava flow. A false step and a fall could mean a nasty cut from the knife-sharp lava which had cooled into fantastically broken and twisted shapes. Near the summit we came on a flock of seven goats; they let us approach to within forty yards and then made off into the hills. In appearance and colour they were no different from any flock of Samburu or Turkana goats. They were in excellent condition and altogether more healthy looking than the average native goat.

Most of the hills on the island were extinct volcanoes with well-defined craters; these and the intervening sheltered valleys supported a certain amount of vegetation which consisted of frankincense bushes, sterculias, a few caraluma and odd tufts of well-cropped grass of the kind found all along the lake shore, which after inviting you to sit upon its smooth green surface, repels you with sharp prickles. From the top of the central volcano, we had a fine view of the greater part of the island. The whole of the eastern side was a mass of lava flows, exposed to the full force of the gales, and with few possible landing places. The western side, on the other hand, consisted of gently sloping soft volcanic rock or tuff, offering excellent beaches for landing, there was more vegetation and even a few straggly acacia trees, but for the most part the island was bare rock. Through our glasses we saw four more flocks of goats numbering about sixty animals. Several of the hills in the centre and to the south were surmounted by stone cairns, presumably put there by Dyson and Martin in the course of their survey work. Before returning we too built a cairn and Joy collected specimens of vegetation.

By four-thirty p.m. we were back at camp. The lake was exceedingly rough with waves dashing against the rocks and sending spray flying thirty feet in the air. We spent the remainder of the afternoon trying to render our camp a little less uncomfortable.

We built a wall across one end of the cleft as a wind-break, collected a supply of drift-wood and removed the larger and sharper pebbles from our beds. Soon after sundown we again exchanged signals with the men.

On the 28th, after another gale-ridden and comfortless night, we set off southwards along the shore with the idea of trying to find some traces of Dyson and Martin's camp. The going was even worse than on the previous day as we had to cross numerous lava flows instead of keeping along them. There was a well-marked water level some forty to fifty feet above the present lake level. Evidently no volcanic eruptions had taken place since the water dropped. At one point between two lava flows, I noticed what might have been an ancient level at least a hundred feet higher, no doubt prior to the eruptions. On our way south we passed two small lagoons, swarming with crocodile of every size; they appeared to be almost as shy as on the mainland. Among them were shoals of tilapia, apparently quite unconcerned at the presence of the crocs. Close by was a small herd of goats; they allowed us to approach within thirty yards and take photographs. We continued along the shore and found two small beaches where a landing might have been possible, but no signs of any old camp. From the top of a flow we could see the coast-line stretching to the south end of the island in unbroken lava flows running down to the water. Jagged half-submerged rocks, extremely dangerous for navigation, could be seen well out from the shore. Everywhere were cast skins of snakes; they were of two species, the striped sand snake and the spitting cobra. We saw two more small herds of goats feeding on caperis bushes and the spiky grass. The following morning, after another stormy night, we were foot-sore and our shoes were in tatters, so we decided to stay around camp, mend our shoes and collect fire-wood. On one of the trips to collect wood up a valley to the north, we came on fragments of pottery; these lay along what might have been a rough path, just above the highest water mark, some forty or fifty feet above the present lake level. Later we found more fragments in a similar position. We also came on a rough stone wall about eighteen inches high and three feet long beside a path. There seemed no purpose for the wall. It might have been put there to mark the path or perhaps was the work of children at play. We found no indications of habitations, such as fire-places; but anyone living on the island would most certainly not choose the eastern side for his abode, and I thought it was likely that a search of the western side of the island would be more likely to reveal traces of its former inhabitants. I shot two tilapia of about five and six pounds off the rocks with my 303 rifle; provided the lake was not too rough, there was no difficulty in obtaining fish in this manner whenever required.

Suddenly, while wandering about the camp, I saw the neck of a bottle sticking out from a heap of stones and a further search revealed rusty old bully beef and sardine tins. We had found Dyson and Martin's camp—within ten yards of our own! Evidently they were tidy-minded men and had buried their camp litter before leaving. This would appear to give further support to the idea that they had packed up and left the island and had met disaster on the way across to the mainland.

On the 30th, having mended our shoes (I always carried an awl and waxed thread for the purpose), we set off for the north end of the island. We toiled along for over three hours over very rough lava until we reached a wide bay with a good pebbly beach. On a high-water level about twelve feet above the present level, we found, among other debris, a four-gallon petrol drum, corroded with rust, and near it a length of red motor-car inner tube. Both the drum and inner tube were obviously very old, the former being of a type common before the war. I had read in old records at the Provincial Commissioner's office at Isiolo that Dyson and Martin had carried a four-gallon drum of petrol and another of water in their boat, so this no doubt had been left by them.

At this point the island became a peninsula. The bay already described had a corresponding bay on the west coast divided by a ridge half a mile across. There was an isolated lava flow which dropped down the eastern side of the ridge. Beyond were two hills with craters composed of fairly smooth tuff, dropping at a steep incline into the lake, forming the north end of the island.

At the foot of the incline, we saw an astonishing sight; thousands of tilapia were packed along the water's edge, many with their backs above water, hungrily gnawing at a thick pink deposit which covered the rock. Further out were more big shoals that looked like dark clouds. As we watched, the shoals would break up and the fish come to the rock to feed. Never in my life had I seen so many fish. Perch and other species, of which there were plenty, did not appear to take any interest in the pink food. Later, while shooting a tilapia, the bullet stunned some small fish; among these was a little fellow about an inch and a half in length, which was a deep carmine red with blue spots on its head.

By the time we reached the north end, the lake had calmed down considerably and had we been at camp I might have been tempted to make the crossing. We hurried back, but by the time we reached camp white horses had again appeared on the water.

The next two days we spent in and around camp; our shoes were beyond repair, food was running low and we were becoming anxious about getting back and did not wish to miss any opportunity the weather might give us. Our signalling arrangements with the opposite shore worked perfectly. Punctually every evening the car lights had appeared and we replied with a single Very light. Actually we could have carried on thus for at least another week without undue hardship, by living on fish and possibly shooting a goat for the sake of its fat. Perhaps we might even have eaten crocodile eggs for breakfast, for I noticed that there were holes all along the coast wherever there was sand, dug by the crocodiles to lay their eggs. (I think it possible that the crocodiles from the mainland came to the island to breed; this would account for their shyness.)

The morning of the 2nd of August did not look at all promising, a strong wind was blowing and a heavy sea was running. However, by midday, the wind changed and started to blow from the west, and I felt certain there would be a calm in the late afternoon. About four p.m. I judged the lake to be sufficiently safe to have a try. We packed up and set off, but on rounding the little island found the sea still too heavy for safety, so we returned to our beach. An hour later conditions had improved considerably and we made the crossing in a little over the hour, to find Godana Dima and the other volunteer waiting for us on the shore. I asked how they knew that we could cross over this day. They said that a Rendile girl, famous for her second sight, had foretold that we would come today; so they had walked from Loingalane in the morning to wait for us. Ibrahim and my sergeant, being more sceptical, only turned up at sundown to make the routine signals. We had a great welcome, both from my men and the local Rendile and El Molo. The headman of the El Molo in particular, was much interested in our stories about the goats and the vast number of fish and said he would go over with his people and make the island their home.

Apart from the goats which must have numbered well over two hundred, and two species of bats, the island contained a great number of snakes which had no natural enemies there apart from birds of prey. It was certainly the most snaky place I had ever been in. On the morning of our return while packing up, I found a young spitting cobra in Joy's bed. She must have slept with it. I omitted to mention the matter to her until we had arrived safely back at Loingalane.

Samburu legend relates that a long long time ago what is now the lake was a big dry valley with villages in it. One morning a pregnant young woman took her flock of goats out to pasture and came upon a spring bubbling out of the ground. Having nothing better to do, she idly picked up a stone and started hammering away at the orifice of the spring. Suddenly it burst open and a great gush of water spilled out, flooding the land. The woman fled with her goats to the hills which soon became an island. In due course she gave birth and peopled the island. Unfortunately, her descendants inherited her idle and vandalistic nature and spent their spare time hammering away at the tops of the hills. A subterranean demon (the same who had taken exception to the activities of the woman) was so disturbed by the continual knocking that he caused craters to appear on the hills and swallow up all the people. So now we know why there are goats and craters and no people on the island!

PART THREE

Elsa comes into our lives

17: *Life and death of a Kenya lioness*

AT DAWN, one January morning, it was in 1956, Ken Smith and I set off from our camp at Melka Lone to look for a man-eating lion. Ken was a Scotsman, ten or twelve years younger than myself; he had come to Kenya after the First World War and joined the Game Department. He was very interested in game conservation and extremely keen on his job; we had first met when he was a Game Warden; later he had taken over the Garissa District from me. This lion we were after had carried off a young Boran tribesman a few weeks previously, near the Tana River. It was a gruesome story. One dark night five men were asleep in their *boma* together with their flock of goats and sheep. One of the sleepers was wakened by a slight noise and discovered that the man next to him was missing. He roused the others and they soon realised that a lion had taken their comrade. At first light, the four remaining men and others from a neighbouring *boma* followed up the well-defined trail which led into the dense riverine jungle bounding the river's banks. A short way on, they came to the pitiful remains and heard the deep warning growl of the lion. The Boran are courageous hunters but the almost impenetrable vegetation where visibility was reduced to a few feet, daunted them and they gave up.

Accompanied by three Boran and Game Scouts Godana Dima, and Kikango, we went by Landrover to a range of low rocky hills reputed to be the favourite haunt of the man-eater. Lions in this hot arid region often lie up on hill tops for the sake of the coolness during the heat of the day. We walked along the foot of the hills hoping to come on fresh spoor leading up. After about an hour we came on fresh tracks of a lioness. We followed thinking she might lead us to the lion. The going was difficult, over and between great granite boulders. We had just crawled through a passage between two giant rocks when there was a furious growl and the lioness appeared on a rock above us, looking extremely truculent. We had no wish to shoot a lioness but she was much too close and looked as if she might charge at any moment. I signalled Ken to fire. At the shot, the lioness disappeared. We advanced cautiously and found a heavy blood trail, leading further up the hill. There is nothing more dangerous than a wounded lioness—a bundle of concentrated courage, strength and ferocity, armed with nature's most formidable array of weapons. We crept on step by step over the crest of the hill and came to a huge flat rock where the tracks were lost. I climbed on top to obtain a view. Ken skirted the rock below. Suddenly I saw him pause and peer under the rock, then he raised his rifle and fired both barrels. There was a savage growl and out came the lioness straight at him. I could not shoot as Ken was in the line of fire. Fortunately Kikango was standing alongside him and fired, causing the lioness to swerve and I was able to kill her. She was a big lioness in the prime of life with her teats swollen with milk. Now, I knew why she had been angry and faced us so courageously. There must be cubs nearby. We retraced our steps and found the place where she had been lying at the foot of a rock face. But there was no sign of the cubs. I told the scouts and the Boran to search over the hill carefully while Ken and I sat down and discussed the hunt over a Thermos of tea. Presently I heard faint sounds issuing from a crack in the rock. It was the cubs! Both of us put our arms in as far as we could reach. There were loud infantile growls and snarls just out of reach. We cut a long hooked stick and after a deal of probing dragged out three little lionesses, not more than ten days old. Both of us were filled with remorse and I particularly blamed myself for telling Ken to fire as I should have known by the behaviour of the lioness that she was defending her litter and unlikely to charge home had we retreated. No more was ever heard of the man-eater.

We carried the three little cubs back to the car. Two of them spat and growled the whole way. The third and smallest of the litter seemed quite unconcerned and made no protest. Back at camp Joy was waiting for us and the first question she asked was —'Did you get him?' I pointed into the back of the car and said: 'Look what we have brought you!'

At once Joy took absolute possession of the cubs. Ibrahim was sent fifty miles in the Landrover to Garbatula, the nearest trading centre to purchase a case of evaporated milk and a feeding bottle. In the meantime, I devised a teat out of a piece of sparking plug lead with the wire core removed.

How little did Joy or I imagine that the story of the smallest of the three cubs, and the cubs she herself would have one day, would be translated into thirty-three languages, sell several million copies, be made into a film and, as we hope and believe, make a lasting impact on the way in which human beings regard and treat wild animals.

Since Joy's books have made Elsa famous the world over, it would be pointless for me to repeat the story which has been told in *Born Free*, *Living Free* and *Forever Free*.

I shall therefore confine myself to a brief outline of this period of my life for the sake of the continuity of my story.

The three little cubs, Big One, Lustica and Elsa lived at our house at Isiolo until they were six months old, by which time they had become quite a handful and it became obvious that we could not continue to keep three fast-growing lionesses indefinitely as pets. After much heart-searching we finally decided to send Big One and Lustica to the Rotterdam Zoo and retain the smallest of the three, Elsa. A friend of ours kindly offered to fly to Holland with the two lionesses under his care. A few days later we received a cable to say that they had arrived safely.

Elsa, left alone, became extremely affectionate and dependent upon us. She accompanied us everywhere, even on a holiday to the shores of the Indian Ocean and on a foot safari with pack donkeys and mules to Lake Rudolf.

When Elsa was nine months old, we took a holiday at the coast; soon after our return, it became necessary for me to go and deal with two man-eating lions at a place called Merti on the Uaso Nyiro River some hundred and twenty miles from Isiolo.

These lions had, over a period of three years, killed and eaten about twenty people of the Boran tribe. Many and gruesome were the tales told of their marauding. On a dark night one of the lions forced his way into a *boma* and seized a youth, who called loudly for help as he was dragged off but none dared go to his aid except for two dogs who ran up barking. The lion dropped the man, turned on the dogs, and chased them away. He then returned to his victim who continued to call for help until his cries faded into the distance.

Late one evening a woman with her baby strapped to her back was hurrying home along a path when she met the two lions. In panic she tried to climb a tree, but was clawed down and devoured together with her child.

Normally, the Boran would have gone after the lions, but the Merti man-eaters overawed them, partly because of their extreme cunning and boldness and the fact that when hunted, they would always retreat into the dense riverine jungle where it was impossible for a man to poise and throw his spear, partly because superstition added to the general fear. It was said that before embarking on a raid, the lions would repair to an open sandy place and make rows of depressions in the ground with their toes and there, using pieces of twigs as counters, they would play the ancient game of *bau* (a game of unknown antiquity and origin, resembling chess and played almost all over Africa; it is also connected with predicting the future). If the omens worked out to their advantage, the lions would raid a *boma* and claim a victim. Another story had it that they were the spirits of two holy men, murdered by the Boran long ago, now come to seek their revenge. Superstitious awe and the fact that on two previous occasions I had tried and failed to get the lions, and others had been equally unsuccessful, convinced the Boran that these lions were supernatural and that any attempt made to hunt them was a waste of effort. Given this attitude, little help could be expected from the tribesmen. All this background added to my determination to kill the lions this time, however long and difficult the task.

We set off from Isiolo prepared to camp for a month if

necessary. Joy had Elsa in the back of her truck. John, a young officer of the King's African Rifles on leave, two game scouts, Ibrahim and myself were in the Landrover with trailer. We were fortunate to find a good camping place a couple of miles short of the Merti trading centre, under some fine acacia trees about half a mile from the river. The camp was near the riverine jungle but set well in the open, a necessary precaution when dealing with man-eaters, which are less likely to raid a camp placed in the open. After pitching camp, we went to the trading centre which consisted of three mud, wattle and corrugated iron shops owned by the Somalis, to get the latest news of the man-eaters. We were told that they had been heard roaring up and down the river almost every night for the past month. They had not taken a human victim for the last three months, but had raided a quantity of livestock, and a few nights previously they had forced their way into the back-yard of the principal shop and taken a donkey.

I sent for the local chief and elders and told them to inform their people up and down the river that as soon as the lions killed again, news must be brought to my camp without delay. They seemed full of enthusiasm and promised to give every help. I then broached the subject of providing an old and infirm cow, camel or donkey as bait for the lions. Immediately their enthusiasm evaporated and their faces fell.

'There are no infirm camels, cows or donkeys within a day's march,' they said. 'How about this moribund donkey I see behind the shops?' I asked. 'Ah! That one! Truly it is old and not likely to live long, but the owner is away on a long safari so we will send men to find another animal.'

Much experience has taught me that it would probably take me days to wring a 'kill' out of the Boran. I therefore went off in my Landrover to look for a zebra, which at this dry time of year were very scarce in the parched desert country surrounding Merti. Finally, after covering over forty miles, I managed to get one and towed the carcase with the Landrover into the riverine jungle close to the river-bank and about a mile from camp. I secured it to a stake under a large acacia tree. In the lower branches of the tree, about twelve feet off the ground, we built a *machan* or platform. For the next three nights John and I kept watch. Nothing happened, although we heard the lions roaring away up river.

The fourth night, being weary from lack of sleep, for we had spent the days trying to follow up the lions' spoor, we slept in camp. That night the lions came to the kill. As it was imperative to get a fresh beast in position without delay, I went to the trading centre to enquire whether there was any news of the 'kill' promised by the chief and elders. I was told: 'Yes, men have gone to distant *bomas* to look for one, but have not returned yet.' The moribund donkey was still tottering about behind the scenes. I told my men to go and fetch it. It was led into the main street, a deathly silence fell on the assembled onlookers as I stepped out of the Landrover, gun in hand and, feeling like a junior officer in charge of a firing squad at an execution, I felled the poor old moke with a bullet in the brain. Instantly there was a roar of laughter. 'What will Abdi say when he gets back and finds that his old donkey has gone to feed the lions?'

Again we sat up over the donkey for three nights without avail. The fourth night we rested in camp; the lions came! I was beginning to think the Boran might be right and that the lions were indeed the spirits of holy men or, more likely, devils. After this I changed my tactics and hunted the lions by day, following up their spoor in the dense bush. Twice we got up close, only to hear them break away ahead without the chance of a shot. The nightly vigils were a great strain for Joy who, from the camp, heard the man-eaters roaring almost every night, often very close and wondered whether the presence of Elsa might encourage them to come into camp.

Never in my experience had I come across lions which covered such long distances in the course of a night. One morning together with Joy we followed the spoor down river until dusk without coming up to them. On two occasions we found that they had covered at least thirty miles during a night. Hunting on foot was most exhausting owing to the heat and because we had to walk in a crouching position through tunnels in the thick vegetation and the presence of rhino and elephant did not make it any easier.

We had already been out three weeks and I could not afford to be away from my headquarters for much longer, so I decided to move camp across the river to the southern edge of the bush, and again try sitting over kills. The rains had started up-country and the river showed signs of rising, so the move had to be made without delay if we were to get across the ford below Merti. We packed up camp and arrived at the ford early in the morning to find that the river had indeed risen considerably during the night and was still rising but I deemed it just fordable for the cars. I unhitched the trailer from the Landrover and removed the fan belt to prevent water from splashing over the ignition system, and crept in using the lowest gear and four wheel drive. All went well and I crossed without difficulty although the water was above floor level. Next, Joy's car entered the water with Elsa in the back. It went bravely on until mid-stream when the engine spluttered and died; nothing would make it start again. Hurriedly we hitched on a tow rope and hauled with the Landrover. The rope parted! By now the back of the truck was awash and it was heeling over at an alarming angle. It had to be unloaded quickly. First we let Elsa out; she plunged joyously into the water and thought it great fun to try to duck the men as they struggled with the heavy loads. Finally we had to chain her up. When, at last the truck was empty, and we again fastened the tow rope then, with all hands pushing and the Landrover pulling, we managed to get it across. Another half hour and it would have been too late for the river was rising fast.

Camp had to be made on the spot in thick bush as it took all the rest of the day to dry out the loads and the engine of Joy's car. By next morning the river was overflowing its banks and we had to move to high ground. For two nights it rained solidly and the country turned into a quagmire. This I thought meant the end of the hunt, however I managed to find a zebra and put it out for the lions. It was not an ideal situation, as there was no suitable big tree for a *machan*, however, we built a rather inadequate platform in the top of a large bush, scarcely eight feet off the ground. John and I took up watch soon after dark. An hour later, we heard the two lions, one roaring by the ford half a mile away and the other across the river. The roars from the direction of the ford gradually drew nearer—that lion was in fine voice. The last roar, barely fifty yards away, fairly shook the *machan*. Silence followed, and I could picture the lion stealthily creeping up—towards the kill I hoped, not towards us. Presently, I heard the unmistakable sound of the animal tearing at the carcase. I waited for him to settle down to his meal. It was a dark and cloudy night and we could not see anything. Gently I nudged John who switched on the torch. The lion had his tail towards us and his head buried inside the carcase, offering a poor shot but, as he turned up his head to look at us, I aimed for his neck and fired. There was a deep grunt and he leapt in the air and then made off uttering loud gurgling sounds; obviously he was hard hit and I was confident of finding him dead near by at dawn.

As soon as it was light enough to see, my two scouts arrived and together we started to follow up the spoor. There were great gouts of blood along the tracks which led straight into the riverine jungle. A very nasty proposition for us if the lion was still alive. We advanced cautiously step by step, pausing every few moments with ears strained to catch the least sound. Suddenly there was a growl and I caught a fleeting glimpse of two lions making off. Evidently the second man-eater from across the river had joined his friend. We went on; again there was a growl and we heard the lions break away ahead. I thought: the next time, the wounded lion will certainly charge.

By now the blood trail had almost disappeared and it was difficult to follow the pug marks in the uncertain light. We were carefully examining the ground when a game scout behind me tapped me on the shoulder and pointed back. There, fifteen yards away, I could see the head of a lion watching us over a low bush. I shot him between the eyes with my heavy rifle. He was a big lion, nine feet five inches from nose to end of tail and in the prime of life. As there appeared to be two bullet holes at the back of the head, apart from the one between the eyes, I was convinced he was the lion I had wounded. To make sure we went back along his tracks which led in a half circle to where we had been standing when I fired. I concluded that the other lion had escaped across the river as, after firing, I had heard a splash.

That night we again sat up over the zebra hoping the remaining man-eater would turn up, but merely got drenched to the skin for our pains. We heard a lion across the river but, as the water was too deep to ford and too dangerous to swim, because of the crocodiles, the only possibility was to construct some sort of a boat. Using the steel frame of a camp bed and a small tent, I fashioned a canoe. It was a great success but unfortunately could carry one person only in safety. I crossed the river and walked to Merti to enquire whether anyone had seen or heard the second man-eater. There was much amazement and excitement at the news of the death of one of the man-eaters; now, at last, the Boran were convinced that the lions were not immortal, and became keen to help me find the second.

On the way to Merti I had crossed the tracks of a lioness. (It was probably her roars we had heard during the night.) Now I began to have doubts about whether the lion that I had killed was in fact the one I had wounded. The expanding bullet from my heavy rifle had smashed its skull and possibly the two holes at the back of the head could have been caused by fragments of the same bullet. I recrossed the river and found a party of six young Boran at the ford. All were armed with spears and readily agreed to help look for the, possibly, wounded lion. Together with Joy, we went to the scene of operations and after a careful search came on the fresh spoor of a lion which I felt certain must belong to the wounded lion, although there was no blood to be seen.

As it was getting late, I suggested to the Boran that they return early the next day with their best hunting dogs and then we would continue the search. In the morning, we met the Boran as arranged; they had brought a dozen unlikely looking hunting dogs which they assured us were not afraid of lions. Once more we entered the jungle. After a short time I noticed that the dogs were not displaying much eagerness for the hunt in spite of encouragement from their masters. A few moments later, the leader of the pack suddenly turned and with his tail between his legs headed for home, followed by the rest. We all expected to hear a roar followed by a charging lion. But nothing happened, and after pausing with ears and eyes strained, we moved on. Presently we heard the excited barking of baboons ahead, a sure sign that they had seen something alarming, either a lion or a leopard. As I was stooping to pass under a branch something light caught my eye, lying under a bush. It was the lion apparently crouched ready to charge! I was about to fire when I heard the loud buzzing of flies and realised he was dead. We found that the bullet fired from the *machan* had torn his throat, missing the spine but probably damaging the jugular vein. It was incredible that he could have survived two nights with such a terrible wound. He was a really magnificent lion, not as large as his friend, being nine feet from tip to tip, but a much handsomer animal. Unfortunately, the skin was ruined and not worth taking.

Why these two lions should have taken to man-eating is a mystery; both were in perfect condition without any infirmities and about middle-aged, as lions go. In spite of the suffering the two had caused the Boran, I could not help feeling a shade of remorse at destroying two such magnificent animals, and sorrow for the agony the wounded lion must have endured before death released him. The hunt had taken twenty-four days of unceasing effort. Maybe the spirits of the two holy men are now at rest and will trouble the Boran of Merti no more.

At length, in April 1958, when Elsa was over two years old and almost full-grown she started to take an unwelcome and increasing interest in the local livestock and made it plain that her days at Isiolo were numbered. After the almost free life she had led with us, it would have been sheer cruelty to banish her to life-long captivity in some zoo. Finally we decided to try to rehabilitate her back to the wild. The area chosen for the experiment was near the southern border of Kenya, known as the Mara Triangle in Masai country, containing vast herds of game and many lions.

This region was nominally under the jurisdiction of the Royal
National Parks of Kenya but owing to lack of staff it was con-
trolled by my friend and colleague Lynn Temple Boreham, the
Senior Game Warden in charge of Masai. He knew the country
and its lions intimately and went to an immense amount of
trouble to pick a good camp site for us and to help us generally.

After obtaining three months' leave we moved Elsa to her new
home. Although she revelled in the complete freedom and
wonderful surroundings, she was extremely nervous of the local
lions. All our efforts to introduce her to likely looking suitors
were a failure until we decided to let her do the choosing in her
own good time, which would certainly happen when she came
in season. The climate did not suit her, being much colder and
wetter than the semi-desert conditions of Isiolo and of her birthplace and we had arrived in the height of the rainy season which
made matters worse. At the end of two months she was taken
seriously ill with some infection which could not be diagnosed
and at one time we feared that she would not survive. However,
after a course of antibiotics, she got over the fever and started
to pick up condition. Just when life had returned to normal and
it seemed Elsa was acclimatised and beginning to go out on her
own, the dead hand of officialdom clamped down. We were
ordered to remove her out of the area, the reason given being that
the rehabilitation was taking longer than anticipated and that
the tourist season would be opening shortly. I expect someone in
high places had visions of Elsa entering the tents of VIP visitors
and causing nervous breakdowns. It was a sad and unexpected
blow and in my despair I went to see William Hale who showed
sympathy for our problem and agreed that we might take Elsa
to the River Ura, a small tributary of the Tana River in a remote
and uninhabited part of the Meru district, less than thirty miles
away from her birthplace. Although the thick bush country of
Ura was a poor exchange for the game paradise of the Mara
Triangle, it lay within my territory so I could keep an eye on
Elsa during the course of my normal duties. In the end the forced
move turned out to be a blessing in disguise.

The change of climate worked wonders for Elsa; within a few

weeks she was the picture of health with a shining coat and rippling muscles. Also, being in the environment in which she was born, she took naturally to the conditions.

Soon my leave was up and I had to return to my duties at Isiolo where I was besieged by complaints from the residents of the township about damage by elephant. I quote extracts from my reports of the time.

'There were many complaints from Isiolo residents of damage to gardens by elephants. Opinion seemed divided, with the majority in favour of chasing the elephants away without causing them serious bodily harm. This was easier said than done. I carried out many patrols at dead of night and at break of day. Three times the offenders were located and plastered with bird shot in their behinds. This was only partially successful. On the third occasion, being weary of sleepless nights, I determined to kill one. But when it came to the point I could not do it; they looked so peaceful and happy in the early dawn with their bellies bulging with the good things from the gardens, so I again gave each a charge of bird shot followed by thunder-flashes. I fear that sooner or later I will have to bow to growing indignation and really shoot one. But I would beg the residents of Isiolo to reflect. All over the world there are beautiful gardens but where else in the world is it possible to sit on your doorstep and watch an elephant quietly enjoying your cannas? But my sympathies are with the inmates of Isiolo hospital. One night the elephants came and discovered that an outside ward had walls of just the right height and roughness for enjoying a really good old scratch. Backwards and forwards they rasped their skins for hours. As a patient described it—"We dared not go outside to relieve ourselves".'

'A bull elephant on the Veterinary Quarantine Area took to chasing cars and tractors. As there were large numbers of perfectly respectable and law-abiding elephants in the area at the time, it was felt that in fairness to them, the identity of the culprit must be established beyond doubt before taking lethal action.

On three occasions likely looking elephants were approached to within provocative range; in every case they gave way with politeness. At the fourth attempt, the chaser of motor vehicles was located in a little valley and shot in the act of chasing the Senior Veterinary Officer who had come with me to see the fun and take ciné pictures. The camera did not come into action.'

'Other elephants brought themselves into disrepute by indulging in mud baths in the Isiolo water supply and interfering with horticulture. Game Scouts shot five close to the scenes of their crimes, including a fine old bull which was well known to Isiolo residents and over the past ten years was often to be seen at all hours of the day peacefully feeding in the prison gardens oblivious of passing traffic and village urchins who came to throw stones at him.'

'I often wonder what future generations will think of us for destroying noble and rare living animals in order to preserve a few square yards of indifferent vegetables and flowers. But such is *progress*. Mankind, the least attractive and most expendable of nature's creatures, is ever the most destructive of life.'

The current District Commissioner of Isiolo, reading my report, sent the following comment to the last paragraph: ' . . . in order to restore the dignity of the species *homo sapiens* I should like to draw your attention to the last seven verses of the first chapter of the first book of Moses called Genesis.'

As I am not a scholar of the Bible, I cannot think of an apt quotation in response but I believe the Koran says: 'There is no kind of beast on earth, nor fowl which flieth with its wings, but the same is a people like unto you . . . unto their Lord shall they return. All God's creatures are His family and he is the most beloved of God who trieth to do the most good to God's creatures.'

In February 1959, Joy left for England, taking with her the manuscript of *Born Free*, the story of Elsa. Later I heard from her that she had offered it to several leading publishers in London, all of whom turned it down. Almost as a last hope she took it to a small but discerning publishing house, the Harvill Press who, becoming enthusiastic about the book, gained the interest and support of their larger associate, Collins. After that, *Born Free* never looked back.

At this time the Ura country was not a Game Reserve. I could therefore go out hunting with Elsa and shoot animals she was actually stalking. This gave her the opportunity to come to grips with her prey and develop her inherited knowledge of how to kill efficiently. On one occasion, while walking through the bush, she stopped and put up her head, sniffing the wind. Then, very cautiously, she moved forward with myself following. Suddenly there was a loud snort and a big male waterbuck started to break away. A lucky shot brought it down. In a second Elsa was on it and had it by the throat and did not relax her grip until in a minute or two the animal was dead. Instinctively she knew the correct grip so as to avoid the sharp flailing hooves. This is the normal method of killing, by strangulation and not by breaking the neck as many people imagine. As soon as the animal was dead, Elsa gnawed a hole in the tender skin between the hind legs, drew out the entrails, a small portion of which she ate, burying the rest. She then seized the carcase by the neck, straddling it between her forelegs and dragged it into a shady thicket thirty yards away.

All her actions were carried out with quiet deliberation, as if she had been doing it all her life. Wild creatures *know* everything about life and how to cope with it from birth, requiring only practice to become proficient. We poor humans *know* nothing and from early infancy have to be taught everything.

We left Elsa to guard her 'kill' against vultures for the rest of the day and against hyenas and jackals at night. One frequently hears stories of lions carrying their victims away by swinging them over their backs. All I can say is that I have never seen it and will believe it when I do. It is true that lions will carry light animals such as dogs or small gazelles in their mouths but anything larger is dragged in the manner described.

The months sped by with Elsa living the life for which she had been created, just as capable as any wild lioness of looking after herself. She had many a fierce battle to maintain her territorial rights against a rival of her own kind until in due course she reached fulfilment and mated with a wild lion and produced three fine and healthy cubs. In spite of her complete freedom and independence, she never lost her affection and friendship for us. Periodically we visited her in her domain. Always she gave us a joyous welcome.

Christmas 1960, Elsa's cubs had passed their first birthday. The two males, Jespah and Gopa must have scaled one hundred and fifty pounds apiece, their manes were just sprouting. Little Elsa, the female, perhaps twenty-five pounds lighter, was the shyest of the three.

Joy went to considerable pains to organise a Christmas tree with all the trimmings such as candles, presents, etc. suspended from the branches. The preparations were watched with much interest by the lions. At a moment when Joy had her back turned Jespah took the opportunity and seized my present and ran off with it into the bush, chased by Gopa, Little Elsa and myself. Perhaps he was unable to contain his impatience to see what was wrapped so carefully in glittering cellophane. Very soon it revealed itself as a shirt. By means of diversions with the lions' own presents of plates of bone marrow garnished with cod liver oil, I was able to rescue it undamaged although mud-stained and crumpled.

It was a happy and fairy-like scene, the pin-points of candle light flickering against the background of rustling palm trees, the quiet river below and the lions now replete, sitting around us at their ease. Was there a hint of sadness as we wondered whether we would see the like again?

A not-so-welcome Christmas present was an official request from the Meru District Council to remove Elsa and her cubs out of their district, the reason given being that in the future she might become a danger to the inhabitants. Elsa had been on the Ura River for over two years without harming any person or property. Therefore the request for her removal seemed unjust and unreasonable, to say the least. But no doubt there was more behind it than the reasons given. Although it is doubtful whether the Council had any legal powers to expel Elsa before she had committed any offence, it was thought wisest to move the family out of reach of local politics. If the Council did not want Elsa in their country, there were others who did. There were offers of sanctuary from Tanganyika, the Rhodesias and South Africa.

The dilemma placed me in a very difficult position. Hitherto I had been able to combine my work with the care of Elsa as she was within the area of my operations. If she had to be moved, this would no longer be possible. According to government regulations, I was already due for retirement, having reached the age limit. But, for the sake of convenience, it had been agreed that I should carry on until the end of 1961. I did not wish to resign but at the same time, under no circumstances, was I prepared to abandon the rehabilitation of Elsa and her cubs or to leave them to their own devices in strange country. I put my dilemma up to Ian Grimwood, who had recently taken over as Chief Game Warden from William Hale. Grimwood, the last Chief Game Warden under whom I served, had come from the Game Department of Northern Rhodesia. He was a very fine man and we all had a great respect for him. I told him that I was quite prepared to resign if there was no other way out of the difficulty. Largely through his help and understanding, this did not become necessary.

As a result of Joy's book *Born Free*, a growing number of people in many parts of the world were becoming interested and sympathised with the plight of our lions. However, before deciding to take them out of Kenya, Joy and I agreed that I should carry out a reconnaissance along the eastern shores of Lake Rudolf where I was fairly confident of finding a suitable locality.

It was my good fortune that Ken Smith was given permission to go with me on the trip. Early in January we set off while Joy stayed at Elsa's camp. It was my intention to explore some of the valleys in the Longendoti range of hills which we had passed on the foot safari with Elsa. No one had attempted the

Elsa and Jespah
The cubs at Elsa's grave

Little Elsa and One Ear
Little Elsa finds me

Leopard drinking out of bath by night

Hyena cubs at entrance of burrow

trip in a motor vehicle and it would be necessary to find a route accessible to a heavy lorry which would be required to move Elsa and the cubs. Each driving a Landrover, Ken and I reached the lake at Alia bay, immediately north of the hills. Much to our surprise, we found large herds of cattle grazing along the shore and even eating the lake weed, standing up to their bellies in the water, an easy prey for the crocodile which abound in the bay. A very severe drought had forced the Rendile tribesmen to venture farther north in search of grazing, away from their normal haunts, which lie well to the south of the hills. We camped on the lake shore and early the next morning started across country along the eastern foot of the hills looking for a way over them but the slopes were much too precipitous and broken by deep gorges. It would have required a major engineering feat to get a road through. Reluctantly, we had to abandon the idea of reaching the valleys on the other side of the hills. After very rough travelling for about twenty miles, we arrived at a large sandy river-bed which I knew debouched into the lake at the southern end of the range. The sand was reasonably firm for the cars and by keeping the throttles wide open in third gear we made good progress down the river-bed, occasionally coming to a stop in drifts of soft sand. It was hot work for the cars and their occupants with the temperature over a hundred and a fierce following wind. Halts were frequent to let the cars cool down. The river-bed was bounded by a thin belt of trees offering the only shade in the surrounding desert. Herds of oryx, Grevy's zebra, giraffe, Grant's gazelle and gerenuk had taken advantage of the shelter from the burning sun and we passed many of these animals which stared in astonishment before galloping away. The lake was reached in the late afternoon at Moite, where the river-bed we had travelled along forms a small delta jutting out into the water. There were large herds of Grant's gazelle feeding on the coarse spiky grass along the shore and also, much to my dismay, a small herd of cattle and goats belonging to a Turkana family who had no business to be in the area. We flung off our clothing and rushed into the water and lay soaking for an hour getting the heat and grit out of our bodies. The next day we spent at Moite exploring the possibilities of the country as a home for Elsa and her cubs.

On the north side of the delta was an expanse of thick bush, much favoured by hippo, which would have offered good cover for the lions. There was enough shade under acacia trees to establish a fairly comfortable camp. At the foot of Moite hill we found a little spring of fresh water which, cleaned out, would have been sufficient to supply the camp. Compared to Elsa's camp on the Ura River, the environs of Moite were grim, to say the least. Bare sand and lava rock, blazing heat swept by fierce winds, made tolerable only by the waters of the lake. It was subject to periodic visitations by Rendile tribesmen and their stock which might prove an overwhelming temptation to the lions. But at least it was remote enough to be out of reach of political complications and it might be possible to come to some arrangement whereby the tribesmen kept clear of the immediate vicinity of Moite. There was sufficient game for the lions' needs and a few of their own kind for company. The route we had come by was certainly not practicable to a heavy lorry and, if Moite was to be the place chosen, a better route would have to be found. We set off eastwards along a broad ridge which would have afforded an ideal landing ground for the largest aircraft; if only it had been possible to persuade the Royal Air Force to lend one of their huge Beverly transports, the whole undertaking of moving Elsa and her family would have been simple. But, of course, this was out of the question. 'What!—fly wild animals in a military aircraft? Who has ever heard of such a thing?'

Unfortunately, the ridge narrowed after a few miles and led up to broken lava country and we had to abandon it and take to sand luggas (dry water courses) again. As none of them led in the right direction we could follow them only for short distances and then crossed over rough ridges to the next lugga and had to repeat the process for thirty miles until we reached the Alia bay track again.

It was decided to carry out a further reconnaissance north of Alia bay. We came on large herds of topi, numbering several hundreds, besides herds of oryx, Grant's gazelle and zebra. In many ways it would have been an ideal situation for Elsa and her cubs. But the remoteness of the area and the fact that it was subject to the passage of rifle-armed raiders from across the Ethiopian border, rendered it unsafe for the lions, also the strict security regulations in force would have precluded Joy taking part in the release operation and camping. Moite was the only hope and we had yet to find a passable route. We decided to return and try from Loingalane about sixty miles to the south of Moite. On the way my Landrover broke a half shaft in the back axle while struggling out of deep sand. Fortunately, as it had a four-wheel drive, I was able to reach North Horr police post using front wheel drive only and being helped out of bad places by Ken's Landrover. We reduced our baggage to the bare minimum and continued in the one car.

On leaving Loingalane, we turned north along the route I had travelled several times before on foot. We camped on a dry river-bed called Serr el Tommia (the River of Elephants—although elephants had long forsaken this part of the lake). I had good reason to remember the place as it was here that Nevil Baxendale and I had built our boat in 1934. We reached Moite without much trouble; it was certainly an easier route than the other two we had tried but that was all that could be said for it. There were long stretches of soft sand, heavy going for a laden truck and several big sand luggas to cross. We came on a few lean and hungry looking Turkana tribesmen who were subsisting by catching fish and trapping game. Of the latter occupation they took good care to hide all traces and, as a screen of respectability, kept a few miserable goats. At one of the encampments we saw a remarkably handsome Turkana girl with a figure of perfect proportions. One of our men remarked that she, at any rate, had not been living solely on a diet of fish and that several giraffe must have gone towards building up her physique.

Soon we turned back and headed for Isiolo.

After two days there clearing up urgent office work, I returned to our camp. Joy told me that Elsa had been unwell for the last few days and was off her feed but when later I saw her, she appeared to be in excellent condition with a shining coat. I told

Joy that I did not think there was anything seriously wrong and persuaded her to go to Nairobi to deal with urgent business affairs and to consult Ian Grimwood about where Elsa and her cubs could be placed, since Joy was not at all keen on the idea of taking the lions to Lake Rudolf. Next morning, very reluctantly, she left for Nairobi.

During the next three days Elsa's condition rapidly deteriorated until it was plain that she was desperately ill with a high fever. She would eat nothing and in the later stages seemed unable even to drink water. As soon as I had realised the seriousness of her condition, I had sent my lorry driver off to Isiolo with a message to Ken Smith, who was standing in for me, asking him to get a vet to me as quickly as possible and to warn Joy by telephone. By the third evening it became obvious that Elsa could not last out the night. It was heart-rending to witness her acute distress and be helpless to relieve it. I thought of ending her suffering with a merciful bullet but there was still the faint chance that the vet might arrive.

As the palm trees took shape against the dawn, Elsa rose to her feet and moved quickly to the front of the tent, paused a moment and then collapsed. I held her head in my arms. Her great tawny eyes opened wide, looking before her with a gaze concentrated on some mystery unseen. She uttered a great and terrible cry. Our Elsa was dead.

18: *We try to keep in touch with Elsa's cubs*

I SHALL NOT describe in detail how Elsa's three cubs were chased away by wild lions and lost to us for over six weeks until they were discovered raiding Tharaka tribesmen's villages sixteen miles away on the Tana River; how Jespah was wounded in the rump by an arrow shot by an incensed stock-owner, or the difficulties of capturing the cubs and transporting them nearly seven hundred miles to the Serengeti National Park in Tanganyika. All this, and an account of their release and of our subsequent months of search for them, the reader who is interested will find set out in Joy's books: *Living Free* and *Forever Free*, so I will confine myself to saying that, on the 4th of May 1961, Elsa's three cubs were released in the Serengeti National Park. The authorities permitted us to camp at the place of release until the 8th of June in order to help them with food and to establish them in their new home.

At seventeen months, the cubs were still too young to be left to their own devices. Normally, in the wild state, cubs remain within their pride together with their mother until they are at least two years old and are experienced enough to branch off on their own. But all our pleas to be allowed to stay with the cubs for a longer period fell on deaf ears and we were obliged to leave. We felt particularly anxious about Jespah who still had the arrow head embedded in his rump with about an inch and a half of its shank protruding outside the skin. Although it did not appear to interfere with his activities or his health, we believed it would remain a potential source of infection unless it sloughed out of its own accord or was removed surgically.

We were no longer allowed to camp near the cubs and keep them under observation but, in the capacity of tourists, we could at least stay at Seronera, the park headquarters, in one of the recognised camp sites and drive out daily, a distance of about thirty miles, to look for the cubs. However, the regulations permitted travelling only during the hours of daylight which in effect meant that the early mornings and late evenings, which were the most likely times to find the cubs abroad, were spent by us in travelling backwards and forwards. For a week in July we were granted the concesssion of sleeping out in our cars at the place where we had last seen the cubs. During these few days we saw the cubs together for the last time.

In the course of the next two years, Joy and I spent nineteen months searching for Elsa's cubs. Sometimes both of us were together, at others, I was alone.

During pauses in the search I had other assignments. In the first three weeks of August 1961 I joined Julian McKeand at Lugari near the border with Uganda in a rescue operation the object of which was to endeavour to move Thomas' kob off European farms, where they were interfering with farming activities, and transport them to the Mara country not far from where we had first released Elsa; there they would be safe and not come in conflict with human interests. Julian was a young man who had first been on the fisheries side of the Game Department but later came to me for a short term. He was keen and very able and it was a loss to the department when he left to become a professional hunter. One of his last activities in the Game Department was a bongo hunt. This kob-rescue operation was his own idea and he carried it through at his own expense. To capture the animals we used a self-activated hypodermic syringe containing an immobilising drug. This was shot at the kob from a gas operated gun. The drug used was succinyl choline chloride with addition of atropine (2 gms. and 1 gm. respectively, diluted with 200 ccs of water). We found that a female kob weighing about 150 pounds required 2 ccs of the solution to become immobilised sufficiently to effect its capture. Julian and I used an open Landrover, while one of us drove the car the other did the shooting. By driving carefully it was possible to approach the kob to within forty yards which was the extreme effective range of the gun. After being hit, the animal might run three or four hundred yards before the drug took effect. It was necessary to follow it closely; after five to eight minutes it would usually go down. We then had to jump out quickly and tie the animal's legs together, give it injections of tranquilliser (largactil), and penicillin and as soon as possible get it into the cage truck which would be waiting in the distance. The kob recovered quickly from the drug and would struggle violently before the tranquilliser took effect. They were extremely powerful creatures and it required three hefty Game Scouts to hold one down. On a good day we were able to capture up to eight animals. As soon as they were safely inside the cage-truck it was sent off to Mara, a distance of about three hundred miles. The animals travelled surprisingly well and out of thirty-four taken to Mara, only two died on the journey. The idea was that as soon as they reached their destination they were to be put into an enclosure where they would stay for a week or ten days until they had fully recovered from the journey and had settled down, when, it was hoped, they could be released and move away quietly without panicking. In the event, soon after arrival, the first load of kob broke out of the enclosure and scattered to the four winds. No one had realised what incredible jumpers they were. They could clear twelve feet without difficulty and dive through the thickest thorn *boma*.

Up to a point, the experiment was successful. We proved that it was possible successfully to capture the animals by means of the drug and to transport them a long distance. Where it failed was at the receiving end where the arrangements were inadequate. The cost of the undertaking was high. It was estimated that a kob captured and transported to the Mara cost about £30. After three weeks Julian and I found that the kob on the Lugari farms were becoming exceedingly wary and difficult to approach within effective range; consequently costs started to mount and the experiment had to be abandoned. Later, other methods of capture were tried but without success.

Out of seventy-four kob shot at and hit with the drug-filled syringes, twenty-three escaped for various reasons, such as failure of the syringes to work properly, failure to locate stricken animals before they had recovered from the drug and badly placed shots. Nine died under the drug, probably due to the drug entering a large vein or artery and acting too violently. The ideal point of impact was the rump but under field conditions and due to the shortcomings of the gun, this was not always possible.

In September I finally left my job in the Game Department, after twenty-three years' service, and handed over to Ken Smith. I was sorry to leave as I felt that I still had many years of useful service left in me but at least I was glad that it was Ken who was taking over the country I had come to know and love so well. Officially, I was now on leave, of which I was due 928 days, pending retirement.

Luckily, I was able to rent a house belonging to the Kenya National Parks which was only seven miles from Isiolo and close to where my first headquarters used to stand.

Early in November, after settling into the new house, Joy and I set off for the Serengeti to renew the search for Elsa's cubs. Relegated, as before, to 'tourist' status, we were obliged to camp close to Seronera in one of the official camp sites and drive out daily to look for the cubs.

To start with, we concentrated our attention on the country in the immediate vicinity of 'Cub Valley'. As the weeks passed we went farther and farther afield. Most of the country we covered had no roads or even car tracks. We made our own way across the plains and through the hills to places where no car had ever been before. We continued the search for nearly six months, which included the rainy season, one of the wettest on record. Often the rivers were in flood and barred our way. Twice we were cut off and had to spend the night out. On the first occasion, the Landrover became hopelessly bogged in a steep-sided gully. We toiled until dark, digging down the banks, jacking up the wheels of the car and stuffing brushwood under them. Then I harnessed myself to a block and tackle and pulled with all my might while Joy put the car into four wheel drive. All to no avail. It started to rain heavily and we were forced to take shelter inside the car, Joy on the front seat and myself in the back. In the course of the night the water rose in the gully to the level of the floor. It was bitterly cold and we had no warm clothing. At daylight we made a further attempt to extricate the car but after three hours of effort decided it was hopeless and prepared to abandon it and walk the twenty miles to Seronera. Since we were miles off any beaten track, there was little chance of being rescued. Just as we were about to set off we heard the noise of car engines and shortly afterwards two Landrovers appeared. A kindly American who had his camp near ours, hearing from our servants that we had not returned, reported the fact to the Warden and, together with some Park Rangers and a second vehicle, came out to look for us. Fortunately, they had noticed the fresh tracks of our car turning off the road and had followed them. With a Landrover towing and the men pushing, we managed to get the car out of the gully.

Our next night out was on Christmas Eve. We had crossed the Balangeti River in the morning without difficulty but on the way back in the late afternoon found it in high flood. As there was no point in spending the night on the river-bank, we returned to near 'Cub Valley' and slept in the car on the top of a small hill, hoping that the car lights, which were switched on at intervals, would be seen from afar and attract the cubs. But the only visitors during the night were a couple of hyenas. By morning, the river had gone down sufficiently to make the crossing and we hurried to Seronera to forestall any rescue party which might be sent out to look for us.

A method we often employed in the hope of attracting the cubs was to leave a lighted lamp hanging in a tree overnight in some conspicuous place. On the third occasion, when we went to the lamp in the morning we found marks in the long grass at the foot of the tree which showed that three lions had lain under the lamp during the night. We felt sure it must be the cubs, for why should wild lions be attracted to the light and apparently spend some

B.G.   Q

considerable time lying under it? For a week we carried out an intensive search of the hills and valleys in the neighbourhood but although we saw several lions none resembled Elsa's cubs.

Every few days we would stop at 'Cub Valley' to see whether the cubs had come to Joy's car which we had left in the valley as an attraction. Only once did we find a lioness near it, this momentarily raised our hopes, but closer investigation showed that it was an old animal.

Later, we met a party of visitors who told us they had come across a young lion with a crippled left hind leg who seemed uncommonly interested in their car and showed no nervousness when approached closely. He had been seen far out on the central plains about thirty miles east of 'Cub Valley'. As we were anxious to follow up any clue, we spent a week searching for him until at length we found him in the company of three other young lions. Although he was of the same age as Jespah, there was no resemblance.

In spite of many disappointments, our daily trips were always full of interest. Constantly we kept a look out for concentrations of vultures which would lead us to lion kills. On dull mornings, we would stop frequently and listen for lions roaring. Often the behaviour of game would indicate the presence of a lion. For instance, if we noticed that animals were looking intently in one direction, it would nearly always mean that they had seen lions.

Several times we came on lions which resembled the cubs and spent hours observing them for familiar characteristics and mannerisms, only to be disappointed. One test was to approach in the car to within forty yards and then get out and show oneself and call. Usually they would take alarm and move away or in some cases show resentment such as crouching and growling. If still in doubt, we would put down a bowl of water and a dish of cod liver oil. Only once did a young lion come boldly up to the bowl and drink. Unfortunately, he was too young to be one of our cubs.

A pride of seven young lions frequently visited our camp at Seronera. One night I was woken by a yell from Joy. A lion had tried to enter her tent. A few nights later I heard them in front of my tent and looked out to see a young male reaching up the trunk of a tree and tearing a new canvas water bag which I had hung there to shreds. Next, there was a disturbance in the kitchen and by the light of a torch I saw a lioness going off with a large empty cardboard carton. Then there was the hyena who became the bane of my life. Every few nights he would come into my tent and steal various items of food. Cheese and bacon were his favourites. When I locked these in an iron box he tried to go off with the box. He seemed to have an uncanny instinct for knowing when I was asleep. Among unopened cans of food he invariably chose Ideal Milk which he would carry off a short distance, then pierce the can with his teeth and suck the contents. Once he entered my men's tent and stole a pair of shorts, whether for personal adornment, in order to impress his fellow hyenas, or for consumption, it is difficult to say. At length, in desperation, I set a rat trap baited with a piece of bacon. This gave him the surprise of his life and a sore nose and it was a long time before I was molested again.

In the dry weather I had my canvas bath put in front of the tent and watched a lioness, a leopard and a hyena drinking out of it and managed to take flashlight pictures of the last two but I had to discontinue the practice for fear of losing the bath.

A remarkable sight out on the plains was a pair of ostriches with a flock of over a hundred half-grown chicks. Obviously, they could not all have been the offspring of the single pair. It would therefore seem that these birds organise a kindergarten with a pair of adults delegated to look after it.

Attracted by the sight of vultures sitting in trees and circling overhead, we found two fine big lions, obviously twin brothers, who had just killed a huge bull buffalo. Less than a week later they killed another near the same place. One of the lions had a bad limp; evidently he had not come unscathed out of the battle with the buffalo.

At the end of March Joy left for Nairobi and as the roads were bad I accompanied her over the worst part to Ngorongoro Crater. At night, on my way back, where the road skirts the lip of the crater, I saw a magnificent lion sitting beside the grave of Michael

Grzimek who, a few years earlier, had been killed in the crash of his light aircraft while carrying out a survey of game. Somehow, it seemed a fitting tribute to a man who, together with his father, had given so much towards the cause of wild life.

As the Serengeti Park was closed from the 1st of April, I camped at Lake Lagarja just outside the south eastern boundary. It was a long way from 'Cub Valley' but it was possible that the cubs might have moved in this direction. I found that the camp had been pitched near a pair of mating lions. I stayed for five days and during this time the lions performed the sexual act about once every twenty minutes throughout the day and night, and they were still at it when I left.

In the middle of June we returned to the Serengeti and carried on the search throughout the southern half of the park and even extended it outside the boundaries. Almost every day we would come across lions, on occasion over thirty. Many we came to know well as we passed them again and again. Although it was disheartening to go out week after week without finding a trace of the cubs, the daily trips were never monotonous as there was always something interesting to see and new valleys and hills to explore. One day travelling along the southern bank of the Balengeti River, we saw a big lion on the opposite side. Looking at it through binoculars, Joy said it appeared to have an injured jaw. But as I saw it apparently snapping at flies I thought she was mistaken and drove on. A week later we were driving along the north bank of the river and at the same place came on the lion at close quarters. He was a most pitiful sight; his lower jaw was shattered and resting limply on his breast. He was terribly emaciated and could not have eaten for a month. I felt it my duty to put him out of his agony.

Before taking any action we drove to a ranger's post three miles away with the intention of getting the African rangers as witnesses but the post was deserted and as there was only an hour of daylight left we returned to where we had left the lion. He was not there, but a few minutes later we heard baboons barking by the river and found him coming slowly up the bank. He had been to the water to drink. He sat down in a little plain. I drove up to within twenty feet. In spite of his terrible state he was full of dignity and looked straight into my eyes calmly and unafraid. I believe he knew what was about to happen and welcomed it. A merciful bullet put an end to his weeks of suffering. The injury to the jaw looked as if it had been caused by a bullet which could have been fired by a poacher or even a visiting sportsman, as at this point the north-western boundary of the park was no more than fifteen miles away. I wished some of the many people who come out to Africa to shoot lions could have been with me this day.

In shooting the lion I had, of course, committed a serious breach of the regulations. The proper course for me to take would have been to go the sixty miles to Seronera and report to the warden who, if he had not been too busy, would have come out the next morning to shoot it, by which time the lion might have disappeared. As a precaution against possible repercussions, we took a number of photographs of the lion before and after death. My act of mercy did not meet with the approval of the authorities, and as a mark of their displeasure my rifle was taken from me. Henceforth, I was obliged to continue the search unarmed.

Joy left for England on the 11th of September. A week later I found my way into a little valley in the Nyaroboro hills which we had not visited before. About noon, I stopped under a tree and was having a late breakfast when I heard a zebra snort in alarm and saw it trotting past, pausing and looking back. A few minutes later I saw a lioness approaching. When about sixty yards away she stopped and, turning at right angles, walked past without looking at me, although I was in the open and plainly visible. She went into a small gully where I could see the black tip of her tail swishing about, a sign of indecision. A few moments later she came out of the gully and again walked past, looking straight ahead, but a little closer this time, and climbed into a small bushy tree where she was completely hidden by the foliage. Through my binoculars I could see her eyes watching me intently. This was very strange behaviour for a wild lioness. She was about the age of Little Elsa and a fine big animal. I got up and walked about, calling to her, and then continued my breakfast, while she sat in the tree watching me. As I was still uncertain, I got into the car and drove slowly past the foot of the tree. The lioness came down and started to follow. I stopped; the lioness came up to within fifty feet and sat down gazing at me calmly while I got out of the car and lit the lamp and hung it in a tree and put out a bowl of water and a dish of cod liver oil. By now I was almost certain it was Little Elsa. But as it was getting late I could not wait and left her. During the next fortnight I saw her on seven occasions. Always, as soon as she heard the car, she would appear and come up and drink the water I put out for her and take a little of the oil. On the last occasion I was driving up into 'Little Elsa's Valley' when an eland got up and ran ahead of the car. Suddenly a lioness sprang up and rushed it, almost catching it. I thought it was Little Elsa but on getting closer found that it was an old lioness with only one ear. Just then Little Elsa herself appeared coming down the hillside to meet me. The two met and it looked as if there was going to be a fight. Little Elsa had her ears laid flat and 'One Ear' the hair on her back up. After a time they calmed down and Little Elsa came close to the car and drank the water and the oil. I left them sitting near each other.

For the next six weeks I went frequently to 'Little Elsa's Valley' and searched the surrounding country but did not see her again. I had hoped that by maintaining contact with her she might eventually lead me to Jespah and Gopa. Finding her in such fine condition at least encouraged me to continue the search for her two brothers, particularly as the place where I had found her was not more than eight miles from 'Cub Valley'.

On one of my visits there I saw two male impala engaged in a desperate battle; both were bleeding from wounds inflicted by the other's sharp horns. As I watched three other males came racing up snorting loudly and broke up the fight by getting between the contestants and driving them away from each other with lowered horns.

Another time I came across a female wildebeest being attacked by two hyenas. Already her tail had been bitten off and her udder torn open. With much difficulty I managed to drive the hyenas away. I then stopped the car beside the wildebeest who was extremely exhausted and waited until she had recovered sufficiently to rejoin the herd which was grazing a few hundred yards away. It was astonishing that none of the herd bulls had come to her rescue as they would have had no difficulty in dealing with the hyenas.

On another occasion, I saw a zebra foal being attacked by seven wild dogs in the distance. I raced across the plain in my car but by the time I arrived on the scene, a matter of three or four minutes, it was too late. The unfortunate foal had been literally ripped asunder. While this was taking place the parent herd of zebra was standing by watching a hundred yards away without making any attempt to interfere.

In the middle of November I returned to Isiolo. It had been arranged that I should take over from Ken Smith for four months while he was away on leave. I was very pleased to be back on the old job. Soon after Ken had left I received an urgent request from the District Commissioner at Wajir to deal with a man-eating lion which had killed and eaten five Somalis between Wajir and the Lorian Swamp. Among its victims were a couple of clandestine lovers who had gone out into the bush to spend the night together. Apart from human prey, stock was being taken nightly.

I made my camp on a desert rain pool called Akalar which was rapidly drying up and had only about a fortnight's water supply left. The night of my arrival lions killed sixteen goats and sheep two miles away. As soon as the report came in I set off and found that the flock had been carelessly left out at night; therefore it was hardly surprising that it had been attacked. Only two out of the sixteen animals killed had been eaten. Normally, lions do not kill more than sufficient for their requirements but in this case it was plain to see by the marks on the sandy soil that most of the goats and sheep had been killed by half-grown cubs who, like mischievous children, knew no restraint. I sat over the carcases that night fully expecting the lions to return but, much to my relief, they did not turn up as I had no wish to shoot lionesses and cubs. During the next ten days camels and cattle were killed almost nightly by the lion reputed to be the man-eater. Every night I sat up over the remains but the lion was too cunning to return to a kill and instead raided afresh.

Owing to the drying up of a pool, the tribesmen were moving out of the area to the permanent wells at Wajir, over forty miles to the north, so there remained only two villages which narrowed the field for the lion. I decided to anticipate his next move and prepared to spend the night at the larger of the two villages. At midnight there was an uproar from an enclosure containing calves. I rushed to the scene only to find the lion making off. He had killed a large calf but had had no opportunity to drag it away to eat. I felt certain he would return to claim it and in order to make things easy for him had the carcase dragged outside and waited for him. But he was more intelligent than I imagined. About two hours before dawn he again attacked at the opposite end of the village and carried off a sheep. As soon as it was light, Godana Dima, a Somali and I set off following the pugmarks. The sheep had been carried some four hundred yards away and completely eaten. We followed expecting that the lion would not go far after his meal. But it was noon and fiercely hot when we came to a dried-up swamp which was dotted with shady bushes. Under one of these we saw a dark shape. As we were all exhausted and did not relish the thought of chasing him farther, I fired, hoping the bullet would strike a vital place. There was a roar and out came the lion straight at us. My second barrel brought him down a few feet away. He was an old animal with broken and blunted teeth and below average in size. According to the Somali, certainly the man-eater. As we returned to the village, Godana Dima and the Somali broke into a song of triumph, hearing which the women and girls came running out uttering their traditional ululations of welcome. It was a satisfactory end to what I hoped would be my last lion hunt.

Normally lions drink plenty of water but under desert conditions they become completely independent of water and will live months, in fact, from one rainy season to the next, without a drink. Obviously, they must have moisture in some form in order to survive; this they obtain from the blood and body fluids of their prey. In the same way, elephant, rhino, giraffe, greater and lesser kudu, oryx, warthog and other animals have adapted themselves to do without water for long periods. In their case the necessary moisture is obtained from various desert plants.

Early in June, Ken Smith having returned from leave, Joy and I once again set off to carry on the long search in the Serengeti and resumed the daily trips through the country which had become so familiar, meeting many old friends among the lions and other animals. On the 30th July we went to the valley where, ten months ago, I had last seen Little Elsa in the company of 'One Ear'. Close to the same place we saw three lionesses, including 'One Ear', with six cubs. Shortly afterwards we came on two lionesses and a lion eating a buffalo which they had killed during the night. The lion was a big animal and had a scar high up on his left hind leg, approximately where the arrow head had lodged in Jespah. He was about the same age and showed other characteristics which recalled Jespah. He was much preoccupied chasing vultures away from his kill and gave us little attention. Could it be that at last we had found Jespah? Unfortunately it was getting late and we could not watch him for more than a few minutes. The older of the two lionesses showed some interest in us but did not resemble Little Elsa. As only a small portion of the buffalo had been eaten I felt confident of finding them next day still at the kill.

The following morning we left Seronera before light and hurried to the valley but the lions had gone during the night and we never saw them again in spite of an intensive search of all the surrounding hills and valleys, which lasted for many days. We again came on 'One Ear' among a pride of nineteen lions and a large male known as 'Half Tail' whom we had seen many times.

Now Joy had to leave for an extended lecture tour and I was

once again alone and carried on the search for another two weeks without finding any trace of the lion with the scar or of Little Elsa.

I had then to return to Isiolo after which I went back to Serengeti, determined to find the lion with the scar and resolve our doubts. I changed my tactics and rather than drive the whole day across country I would select a likely place with a good vantage point and scan the country through binoculars for the tell-tale vultures, and call.

During my daily excursions I often passed a burrow containing three generations of hyena cubs, six in number. At first, as soon as they saw the car approaching, they would dive and remain underground until I had passed. One morning, I stopped the car twenty yards from the hole and placed a freshly-opened can of corned beef at the entrance. A few minutes later a head appeared, then another and another until there were six eagerly sniffing the delectable aroma of the beef. The youngest, a few weeks old, were the boldest and the first to partake of the unexpected manna. Often I had seen half-grown hyena cubs but never the very young. The two smallest were completely black without any markings. Their burrow was shared by a bee-eater who had its own little hole a few inches inside the entrance. After the expenditure of a few more cans of bully beef the heads appeared as soon as they heard my car. They would disappear when they saw me walk forward to deposit the beef but as soon as I moved away, came out and ate quite unafraid.

I also became familiar with five little half-grown jackals who used always to wait at the same place for free handouts of bully. They were much bolder than the hyenas and almost took the meat out of my hand. The two strongest would arrive first but invariably start to fight fiercely while their weaker brethren took the opportunity to finish the meat.

One morning I came on two buffalo bulls, both emaciated. One was lying dead: his comrade, although much agitated at my proximity, would not leave his friend whom he kept on nudging, urging him to get up. Both were the victims of rinderpest and I did not think the survivor had long to go.

At a small spring which I visited frequently, I saw a pride of seven lionesses with five cubs of not more than six weeks old. Stopping the car thirty yards away I called to the cubs in the manner in which Elsa used to call hers when they were very small. Promptly they stopped playing and came up to within twenty feet of the car.

On another occasion I came on a very fine blond-maned lion sitting on a termite mound. Driving up to within twenty yards, I started to imitate a lion roaring softly. No human lungs are capable of producing a full-throated roar but my efforts immediately aroused his interest. He became alert and looked this way and that, walked around the car, clearly puzzled and unable to locate the sound. He was a lion I identified on many occasions as the black tassel on the end of his tail was missing.

Late one afternoon I was hurrying back to Seronera through a heavy rain storm with visibility reduced to a few yards when suddenly a lioness got up almost in my path. Immediately I recognised her as Little Elsa. She was in the company of an older lioness and a young lion about eighteen months old. Recognition was mutual and Little Elsa came up to within a few feet of the car. Unfortunately, it was late and I had to get on. Early next morning I was back at the place where I had left them but they were nowhere in sight. As it was a dull and wet morning I waited hoping to hear them roaring. (Lions frequently roar late into the morning in dull weather.) Sure enough, after half an hour, I heard roars in the distance and going to investigate, found Little Elsa and her two friends. They were sitting watching a small herd of wildebeest. Soon Little Elsa got up and, followed by the others, started to stalk the wildebeest. It was a careful and well-planned stalk which would have been successful but, at the crucial moment, a strange lioness appeared from the opposite direction alarming the wildebeest. The stranger was treated with reserve and there was no greeting ceremony. However, they all sat down together, the stranger a few feet away from the others. Suddenly, without warning, Little Elsa and her friends set upon the lioness who had to fly for her life and was chased some distance. Soon afterwards the three were joined by a young lion in very poor condition apparently suffering from some disease. There was no resemblance to either Jespah or Gopa. During the next three days I had no difficulty in locating Little Elsa and her friends and spent several hours in their company. Then the weather broke and heavy rain and floods made it impossible to reach their place for ten days. After the weather cleared up I returned day after day but never saw Little Elsa again.

On Boxing Day I was out in the central plains near Lake Lagarja together with two American school teachers who had travelled across Africa in their caravan. We came on two lions and a lioness. The two males were big animals with very short manes. In many ways they bore a strong resemblance to Elsa's cubs. One of the lions got up and, followed by the others, came towards the car. I put down a bowl of water and a dish of cod liver oil. The lioness drank the water and one of the males upset the dish of oil and carried it away in his mouth while the second male licked up the spilt oil. It was late and we could not stay more than a few minutes. I returned the next morning, determined to spend the whole day with the three and study them carefully. They had gone and it was not until thirteen days later that I saw them again near the same place. I stayed over five hours in their company watching carefully for old familiar habits and mannerisms but in the end was forced to the conclusion that they were not Elsa's cubs.

A few days later I visited 'Cub Valley' for the last time. I called each of the cubs by name: Jespah, Gopa, Little Elsa. Three times my calls went ringing across the valley but there were only the echoes of the cliffs for answer.

The search for Elsa's cubs had occupied more than nineteen months during which time I had looked at more than five hundred different lions, lionesses and cubs. The fact of finding Little Elsa in such fine health meant that her two brothers had at least the same chance of survival. It is possible that somewhere in some hidden valley of the five thousand square miles of the park they may have their place.

In spite of the differences of opinion with the National Park authorities I will always remain grateful to John Owen, the director, for granting sanctuary to Elsa's cubs in the first place and the many acts of kindness and help from him and Myles Turner and other members of the park staff.

19: *Making the film* Born Free

IN APRIL 1964, the Open Road Film Company engaged me as their technical adviser for making the film *Born Free*. This included the story of Elsa from the time of her capture to the birth of her cubs. (The whole of the book *Born Free* and part of the sequel *Living Free*.) It had been decided by the director and production manager of the company to rent a small ranch of about seven hundred acres at Naro Moru near the foot of Mount Kenya and make it the base of operations. Being situated at an altitude of over six thousand feet, the country bore little resemblance to the area in which the Elsa story took place, the altitude of which was under three thousand. Also, being in the lee of the mountain, Naro Moru is notorious for its bad weather, a circumstance for which the company had to pay dearly in the following months. Neither was the site ideal from the point of view of working the many lions which had to be used in the production. It was surrounded by farms and ranches and consequently heavily populated. My suggestion for shooting the picture in Elsa's own country, near Isiolo, or in the Meru Game Reserve, was turned down for various reasons such as remoteness, lack of good roads and accommodation, the danger (very slight) of attack by Somali 'shifta' gangs and for reasons of health and comfort.

Not unreasonably, the director who had had experience of filming animals thought it would be necessary to use circus trained lionesses for the principal parts, requiring intimate scenes with the two stars representing Joy and myself. After, it is said, looking at hundreds of lionesses in Europe, he finally chose two rather elderly circus-trained animals, Juba and Astra, owned by a dealer in Germany. These were due to arrive by air together with two cubs and two female handlers on the 22nd of May. Meanwhile we were busy erecting the enclosures to contain them. These consisted of strong link-mesh wire netting nailed to twelve-foot posts with an overhang of three feet at the top. The enclosures, of which there were two, had an area of over six thousand square feet each and were attached to a small wooden house in which it was proposed to shoot many of the scenes depicting Joy's and my life with Elsa at Isiolo. Portions of the two main rooms were wired off with access to the enclosures.

On the appointed day Juba and Astra arrived, two fine big lionesses of something over fourteen years and ten years respectively and two male cubs of the latter, aged four months, accompanied by Monika, a twenty-three year old Austrian circus girl who had had over three years' experience of working with lions, and Ruth, a Valkyrie-like German girl aged eighteen, also with some experience of handling wild animals. The girls took up their quarters in the wooden house where they slept in the rooms with the lions, divided from them by wire. Naturally lions are clean creatures, if given the opportunity, but this proved to be a somewhat unhygienic arrangement as the girls insisted on locking the lions inside the house at night.

From being a foreman of works I was now appointed body-guard to Monika and it was my duty to stand by with a loaded rifle while she put the lions through their paces inside the enclosures. This gave me a legitimate excuse to move my quarters from the main house which by now was rapidly filling up with film personnel, and pitch a tent close to the lion compound. Most of the people of the unit were extremely nice and friendly but their way of life was not mine. There were too many dramas and 'goings-on' for my peace of mind. I felt safer with the lions.

It was necessary to train the lions to ride in and on top of cars. For this purpose I had first to teach Monika to drive the Landrover which was to be used. I had never before tried to teach a woman to drive. It was an interesting and, not infrequently, a hair-raising experience. It fixed me in my determination never to become a professional instructor. It was impossible to get Monika to take the lessons seriously. A near-miss or horrible grinding of gears was always the signal for helpless laughter. The language difficulty did not make it any easier. But, in spite of jolts to the nervous system, we had much fun together. By the end of the picture Monika had become quite a proficient, though light-hearted, driver.

Early in June, the two actors, Virginia McKenna and her husband, Bill Travers, arrived, and shortly afterwards started to train with the lionesses under the care of Monika. Both had insisted in their contracts with the company that no doubles would be employed for their scenes with lions.

After a few weeks, it became apparent that Juba and Astra were too old and temperamentally unfitted to take the part of Elsa. Their circus training and life seemed to have dried up their natural, friendly natures. There was always an uneasy feeling that they were measuring one up, waiting for a false move to take advantage. It was quite impossible for Virginia and Bill to behave in a normal carefree manner in their proximity. Even Monika would not enter the enclosure without a couple of sharp sticks in her hands and would never turn her back on them. The relationship was completely different from that which Joy and I had enjoyed with Elsa. It was obvious that *Born Free* could not be made with these animals. Apart from anything else, they looked what they were, a couple of elderly and rather embittered lionesses.

Fortunately, at this time, the company acquired a nine months' old lion and lioness from the Second Battalion of the Scots Guards which was returning shortly to England. Fortior and Unita, commonly known as Boy and Girl, had been the battalion mascots and were thoroughly used to being handled. Also, we were lucky in obtaining the temporary services of Sergeant Ron Ryves who had been in charge of the lions and had a great love for them. Therefore they entered the new life at Naro Moru joyously and were happy from the outset. They slept in Ryves' tent which, of course, helped greatly to overcome the strangeness of their new surroundings. In a few days the Travers had established friendly relations with them and these

Boy

were maintained throughout the picture in spite of a most unfortunate accident to Virginia.

One morning she and Bill had taken Boy and Girl out on to the plains to exercise them. Lions at that age are extremely playful. Boy jumped on Virginia, and, catching her off balance, threw her to the ground. In falling, one of her ankles was broken in two places. Bill, who was some distance away, ran to her rescue. The lions, seeing her down, naturally thought it was all part of the fun and were bent on continuing the game. Bill had to carry Virginia to the car which was several hundred yards away while, at the same time, fending the lions off. Then having got her into the front seat of the Landrover, he had to entice the reluctant lions into the caged-in back portion. No one could have blamed Virginia if she had decided to abandon the film, but, after leaving hospital and when a few weeks later she felt herself strong enough, she continued her relationship with the lions.

In July, the Kenya National Parks organisation loaned a very fine sixteen months old lioness called Mara from their animal orphanage at Nairobi. Mara had been found abandoned when a baby near the Mara river in southern Kenya. She had been brought up as a family pet by a farming couple and when about nine months old, handed over to the orphanage. Evidently, the life of confinement had affected her nature. Now, finding herself in completely new surroundings, she showed signs of being distinctly dangerous. It was thought she could not be used and would have to be returned to the orphanage. However, I liked the look of Mara and had faith in her and therefore took it upon myself to try to win her trust and affection. I had a tent pitched up against her enclosure and placed my bed within a few inches of the wire, from where I could talk to her, scratch her head and feed her delicacies through the wire at night. After about a week, by which time she had become thoroughly accustomed to my voice and scent, I ventured into her enclosure. She showed great affection but was extremely possessive, clasping me around the body, frantically sucking my clothing and refusing to let me go. It was necessary for another person to distract her attention with a piece of meat before she would leave me and give me the opportunity to slip away. For two weeks I spent an hour daily in her enclosure until she had grown calmer and less possessive. Then, as a supreme test of my confidence in her, my tent was moved inside her enclosure. For the next three months she slept regularly in it, usually stretched out on the floor along-side my bed and sometimes on it. Although many of the nights were far from reposeful, particularly when Mara decided to share the bed, she never gave me cause for anxiety regarding my personal safety.

It was now possible to take Mara out on to the plains together with Bill Travers and an assistant and allow her to run free for two or three hours almost daily. When Virginia had recovered from her accident, we frequently had morning coffee, seated around a table in the lioness' enclosure or a picnic lunch out in the plains with Mara lying peacefully asleep beside us. Being young, playful and exceedingly strong, she could be a real handful and many a time sent us sprawling on the ground. It was always necessary to exercise her thoroughly before allowing Virginia to come in contact with her. One of our favourite games was for me to lie flat on the ground hidden behind a tuft of grass. Mara would stalk me with great stealth, belly low to the ground in proper lion fashion and then there would be the final lightning rush and she would land on top of me. Always she kept control of her formidable claws and never hurt me. (Incidentally, when playing with lions, one should never pull away from their grip, as in doing so, the animal will instinctively dig in its claws.)

There was quite a lot of game on the plains, such as Thomson's gazelle, impala, water buck and warthog. Mara soon developed a lively interest in hunting and at times we had difficulty in recovering her and suffered from the ever-present fear that she might get among cattle or sheep.

One night, on a location some thirty-five miles from Naro Moru, she climbed out of her temporary enclosure and raided a cattle *boma*, a mile away, and mauled two steers. Fortunately, the cattle guards had the sense to run to the camp and inform us. Another trainer and I jumped into a Landrover and were at the scene in a few minutes. Luckily Mara had not followed up the stampeding cattle although she was just about to when we arrived. Much excited, she came up to me, hugely pleased with herself. She would not get into the back of the car until finally she followed me in and the two of us were locked in together and were driven back to camp. On another occasion, while exercising on the plains, she caught a baby water buck but, in spite of her excitement, she permitted Bill and me to rescue it out of her paws.

Our next addition was Henrietta. Of the same age as Boy and Girl, she was a pathetic creature, all skin and bone and highly nervous. The story goes that she was the sole survivor of a litter of cubs which had been run over by a tractor in one of the Uganda National Parks. She was placed in the Entebbe animal orphanage who now loaned her to the company. Our director was not impressed and described her as useless for taking any part in the film.

A few weeks of good feeding and personal attention worked wonders and she blossomed out into a beautiful young lioness. She was a born clown and full of fun. The Africans named her 'Memsahib Makofe' (Lady Clout) as she had the habit of smacking with her fore paws, sometimes none too gently, although she never put out her claws. From being the Cinderella, she became the star performer, whenever Girl and Mara failed to carry out a difficult scene, Henrietta saved the day.

There was one scene, somewhat fanciful and unnatural, in which Elsa was supposed to appear in camp herding a young elephant. Girl was chosen for the part, together with Eleanor, a three year old cow elephant. In order to get the two accustomed to each other, Eleanor was let into an enclosure where there were two guava trees laden with fruit of which she was inordinately fond. While Eleanor was busy stuffing herself, Girl was introduced. It was plain that she did not much care for the elephant and was nervous of her, although Eleanor herself paid not the slightest attention, being far too preoccupied with the guavas. When replete, Eleanor was led out for a walk, and we managed to induce Girl to follow, albeit reluctantly.

For the shooting of the scene a long wired enclosure was constructed, well camouflaged behind bushes. At one end the cameras were set up and at the other a small holding cage for the lion. In theory, Eleanor would start from the lion end and, attracted by a bunch of bananas, hurry towards the cameras, when Girl would be released and, it was hoped, follow the elephant. In the event, nothing would persuade Girl to follow. The director and producers were all but tearing their hair. The film was costing in the region of £2,500 a day. It was out of the question to use Mara as she might injure Eleanor. There remained only Henrietta who had not had any contact with Eleanor. She was brought along and secured in the holding cage from which she watched the elephant with evident interest. As soon as Eleanor was well on the way to the bananas, Henrietta was let loose and without hesitation sped after her and, coming up from behind hooked a hind leg, almost bringing poor Eleanor to the ground. The take was repeated no less than six times.

Another scene required Elsa to ride sedately on the roof of a Landrover through an African village and past a bus load of tourists. Henrietta was the obvious choice as she loved sitting on the roof of a vehicle in motion. Everything was set up ready; there was Henrietta lolling at her ease on the Landrover as it slowly entered the village. The cameras had started to turn. Suddenly Henrietta spotted a cockerel pecking busily in front of a hut. She was off the roof in a flash, scattering villagers and tourists; after a short chase she grabbed the cockerel and calmly sat down to eat it while the unit waited with some impatience on the part of the director and producers. At length, with difficulty, we managed to induce Henrietta to resume her position on the Landrover and started her off. It was not to be! She espied another chicken which had been overlooked and was peering nervously around the corner of a hut. After a considerable chase through and around huts, she got it and bore it in triumph back to the Landrover. By now the director and producers were practically speechless but this in no way deterred Henrietta from doing justice to the second bird. In the end they got the scene.

Another tricky item was a bedroom scene in which the lioness was required to lie on a bed and then play around in a room under glaring lights and in front of close-packed cameras and crew. Again I recommended Henrietta as she was in the habit of spending most of her leisure hours sleeping on a camp bed in her enclosure although she had never been in a brightly lighted room. It was therefore necessary to get her used to the conditions. I volunteered to rehearse her for a week by spending the nights with her in the room. An enclosure was attached to the end of a corridor leading to the bedroom, allowing her easy access in and out. The first night Henrietta was a little nervous and hesitant but when she saw me through the corridor lying at my ease on a comfortable bed, she could not bear to be out in the cold, came through the passage like a whirlwind and landed on my chest, then she set out to explore the room. The first object to draw her attention was a blue enamel chamber pot under the bed. This she seized and smacked from one end of the room to the other: finally she placed one huge paw in it and slid across the polished floor. This became a nightly performance, until she was exhausted, when she would lie quietly on the bed and sleep. Before dawn I would be woken up by feeling a rough tongue rasping my face and her heavy body pinning me to the bed. On the day Henrietta carried out her act with Bill perfectly although, much to my regret, a waste-paper basket was substituted for the chamber pot.

Among my special charges apart from Boy and Girl, Mara and Henrietta, there was Ugas, a very fine young lion aged three years, who had been picked up as a small cub near Wajir and after being kept as a pet for a few months by a policeman, was sent to the Nairobi orphanage from where the company had borrowed him for the duration of the film. He was a most friendly and good-natured creature and inclined to be playful when his size and strength rendered him a somewhat rough playmate. On one occasion Mireille, a Swiss girl handler who had joined us, and I were training Ugas to charge down an enclosure. He was put into a small holding cage at one end while the girl stood by the door of a second cage at the far end with a large piece of meat.

I released the eager Ugas who rushed towards the meat. As soon as he reached Mireille she tossed the meat into the cage, Ugas followed, and was shut in. This arrangement worked perfectly for several days until one morning the director and one of the producers came to watch progress through the wire. Mireille as usual took up her stance by the door of the cage while I released Ugas, but instead of rushing into the cage after the meat he missed the door, ran around and jumped on poor Mireille. I ran to her assistance whereupon Ugas left her and jumped on me. There was nothing vicious about it; it was all in good fun. But for the spectators it seemed as if he was attacking us in earnest and the producer looked quite shaken. After this incident we found it best to take Ugas out on to the plains and let him have a good run until he was tired and then work him; handled in this way he was perfectly easy.

Joy arrived at Naro Moru in mid-July after her extensive lecture tour in the States. As the author of the Elsa story she was bound to be hypersensitive to the possibility of sentimental fiction replacing fact in some of the scenes. The producers, in the final scene, at first intended to show Joy gathering the cubs up in her arms and cuddling them, whereas in the actual story nothing of the kind occurred, mainly because it would have been exceedingly rash and foolish for Joy to have touched the cubs in Elsa's presence, not knowing what her reactions would be, and, also, because the whole point of the Elsa story was that we were trying to give her back to the wild and the last thing we wanted to do was to make pets of her cubs. Fortunately, in the end, Joy's views prevailed.

Altogether twenty-four lions, lionesses and cubs were used in the picture. Apart from cubs, my five lions and to a limited degree Astra and Juba, none of the other grown lions could be handled, largely because they were kept permanently confined and given no opportunity to run free on the plains. I am firmly convinced that it is the boredom and frustration of captivity which makes lions dangerous. One of their strongest senses is that of smell. To deprive them of the chance to exercise it is tantamount to depriving a human being of all reading matter.

It was a revelation to me to see how absorbed my charges would become in the many interesting scents encountered on the plains.

Many times the Travers and we trainers urged that a camera should accompany us while out exercising the lions, for it was then that the lions behaved in a completely natural and un-inhibited manner and offered many opportunities of superb shots. But for various reasons, one of which appeared to be a trade union rule which required a camera to be manned by a crew of several persons, it was deemed impractical. The script of the film was undeniably a fine piece of work, especially considering that the man who wrote it, as he himself admitted, knew nothing about lions. But it surprised me that it was adhered to almost like holy writ. This resulted in many interesting and often charming shots being missed, simply because they were not in the script.

During these months the inadequacy of the circus lions became apparent. Try as they might, poor old Juba could only be used in one scene where she was cast to represent a dead lioness. Astra was made to play a scene where she was supposed to chase and catch a wild pig. She chased the pig all right but when it came to catching it, the half-grown warthog had other ideas. It turned and charged Astra and chased her out of the picture. The shot was retained I believe for its comic effect. Mara had to finish the scene which she did creditably. Another scene in which Mara had to take over from Astra was of 'Elsa' sitting in a tree. Evidently Astra's circus training had not prepared her for tree climbing. With the aid of step-ladders and concealed plat-forms, Astra was finally persuaded to mount the tree and promptly fell off, after which nothing would induce her to go up again. The first time Mara was introduced to the tree she bounded up the trunk and liked the situation so much that she spent most of the day lying out on a branch and did not come down until the evening meal time. However, Astra did play a difficult fight scene with flying colours, largely due to the patient and skilful training of the girls. It gradually became obvious to everyone that the African lions were temperamentally and, because of age, much more suitable material than the circus lions.

Of course, no one could have foreseen this when the circus animals were purchased.

Late in October the unit was scheduled to move to the coast to film the scenes of Elsa in the sea. After much discussion it was decided that Girl and Mara should play the scenes. I would have liked to include Henrietta but considerations of expense ruled her out, although I am certain she would have given her money's worth and more. It was a long and tiring journey of nearly five hundred miles over bad roads and by the time we reached the camp on the sea, the lions were completely exhausted and somewhat battered. Mara and Girl, who normally were not on friendly terms, spent the first night pressed up against each other through the wire for company. Mara had stood the journey better than Girl who was very much distressed at being parted from Boy. In fact, after two days, it became obvious that Girl would be useless without her brother and he had to be sent for.

The site chosen for the filming was most attractive with a stretch of fine sandy beach close to the camp and small coral islands half a mile off shore easily accessible at low tide. The camp itself was in a grove of coconut palms. But to my dismay, within four hundred yards was the village of Watamu, containing innumerable children, goats and chickens. Once out of their rather flimsy enclosures, there was nothing to stop the lions from entering the village. I was appalled at the risk. The Travers were equally alive to the dangers and between us we insisted that the beach and the camp be wired off on the landward side. This was done at considerable extra cost. The sole occupants of the camp were a professional hunter, myself and Nuru (the original Nuru who figured in the Elsa story, although his part in the film was played by an African actor) and some African staff. The rest of the company stayed at hotels in Malindi, fourteen miles away. This was a perfectly happy arrangement as far as I was concerned. My tent was close to the lions which helped to reassure them in the strange surroundings.

Like the original Elsa, the lions took to the sea in a surprisingly short time. Mara, in particular, showed herself to be a fine swimmer and fearless of the waves. In the case of Boy and Girl,

Bill Travers, myself and Mara on Landrover
Virginia McKenna making friends with Mara

Monika with Astra and Juba

Re-enacting the scene in which Elsa returns to camp after her
unsuccessful release

Boy taken out for exercise
Boy enjoying the walk

Girl being trained to climb

Virginia, Bill and Girl at Malindi Beach

it was the former who led the way into the water and followed us in and out of his depth the very first time we took him to the beach. The arrival of Boy had transformed Girl from a listless and sorrowful creature into her former carefree and happy self. Soon the lions were thoroughly enjoying their morning walks along the beach and, at low tide, over to the coral islets, to reach which it was often necessary for them to swim. We could not take all three lions out together in case of fights between Mara and Girl. Normally this would not have been much of a danger but being stars in the film we could not risk scarred faces.

As Virginia had more confidence in Girl than in any of the other lionesses, all the scenes requiring close physical contact, such as playing along the beach with coconuts and in the water with a football and resting together in the shade were performed by Girl. Mara was used for the more spectacular shots such as swimming in deep water and a memorable scene of Virginia, Bill and Mara together coming through the breakers on the reef. In another, Mara was supposed to swim to a fisherman's canoe containing Bill and Virginia; instead she tried to board the camera raft, causing much consternation. On this occasion Joy was a spectator, standing by a coral rock some two hundred yards away. Suddenly Mara streaked off towards her, and all in fun, jumped on her. In trying to save herself from falling on the jagged coral Joy must have pulled away. She was clawed down one arm and received a nasty cut requiring several stitches.

On one occasion, Bill, myself and Mara were resting under the shade of a rock when our two producers were seen strolling along the beach some distance away. Mara set off to stalk them. We shouted a warning and went after her. It having been impressed on everyone that it was fatal to run in the presence of lions, the producers, with commendable restraint, 'hurried slowly' and gained safety while we distracted Mara's attention.

On our return to Naro Moru, there was a change of directors, after which things seemed to go easier. I was sorry to see our first director go: he had many sound ideas about the training and care of animals. Our new director was thoroughly experienced in his craft and had the natural ability of getting along well with the personnel. He frankly admitted that he knew nothing about animals, never having worked with them but he relied on us trainers and always sought our advice when it came to using the lions.

Probably *Born Free* is one of the few animal films made without resource to the use of questionable methods to obtain results from the animals.

Working and living with the lions for the better part of a year, I naturally became exceedingly attached to my charges. The thought of their returning to lifelong captivity in zoos was utterly abhorrent to me and also to Joy and the Travers. I determined therefore to try by every means in my power to secure the freedom of as many of the lions as possible, in particular Ugas, Mara, Henrietta and Boy and Girl. And to rehabilitate them back to the life for which they were created and which was theirs by right. As the whole story of Elsa and the film are based around the theme of giving a lioness back to the wild, we not unreasonably expected the whole-hearted support of the film company to help the lions who had served it so well. In this we were sadly disappointed. With two exceptions, all the lions directly owned by the company were disposed of to zoos and in one case to a private person who had no connection with the film. These amounted to sixteen lions, lionesses and cubs. The remaining eight had been taken on loan and on hire; they included Ugas, Mara and Henrietta. Naturally, these had to go back to the owners. Fortunately, Boy and Girl, although owned by the company, were subject to a condition imposed by the original owners, Sgt. Ron Ryves and R.S.M. Campbell Graham of the 2nd Bn. Scots Guards, whereby the company undertook to fly the lions at their own expense to England, to a zoo approved by Messrs. Ryves and Graham, at the end of the film. I wrote to the two soldiers, asking their permission to rehabilitate Boy and Girl. To quote Graham's reply: '. . . After considerable consideration and discussion with Ryves we have decided to give you our permission to release Boy and Girl. We have been around looking at some of the first-class zoos and we are not impressed. We both wish you luck in this enterprise you are about to take

on and hope you will keep us in the picture every now and again
up to the time you leave them to themselves. Please pass on to
the staff of "Open Road" our appreciation and say we are both
in agreement about the lions' release; also it will save the film
unit a considerable amount of money . . .' Thus, in the end, it
remained for two simple soldiers to show the kindness of heart
and understanding to prefer freedom for their pets rather than a
life of confinement. Some months later, I was given Ugas,
largely through the personal intervention of the Minister for
Natural Resources and Wildlife.

My lovely Mara and Henrietta, who had given me all their
trust and love without reserve and who had so much enjoyed
their life of comparative freedom at Naro Moru, were consigned
back to an existence of endless captivity, the former to Whipsnade
Zoo and the latter to the Entebbe Zoo in Uganda. When they
were taken away I felt as if I had betrayed them and could not
bear to see them off.

I might have got Mara but the lady who owned her as a small
cub wrote a letter to the Press which started an avalanche of
criticism. She is a kindly person and her sole concern was for
the safety of her former pet, her main argument being that Mara
would be far safer in a zoo. Which, of course, is perfectly true.
In the same way as it might be argued that a person undergoing
a life sentence in prison is safer than the same person out in the
world taking his or her chance in the battle of life. But is this
justification for withholding freedom? Countless thousands of
men and women through the ages have fought and died for the
cause of freedom simply because they believed that life without it
was not worth living. Might not the same apply to Mara and
her kind?

The morning the Travers left Naro Moru for England they
called at Simba Camp where Joy and I were living in tents, to
say goodbye, bringing with them Dudu, their DKW four-wheel
drive car as a contribution towards the rehabilitation of Boy and
Girl. It was a most generous gesture, in keeping with their
characters. The world-wide success of *Born Free* as a film must go
firstly to the Travers who by their unfailing patience and affection

for the lions coupled with hard work and fine acting, made it possible. As I always accompanied them when out with the larger lions, I know how much of their private time they devoted to training with them. While the unit would sit in comfort having lunch in the dining-room, they would be out on the plains having a picnic lunch in company with Boy and Girl or Mara or Henrietta. The last named, we found had a craving for Skipper sardines, no other brand would do, a weakness we were able to exploit during filming when it came to persuading Henrietta to do some tricky shot.

At the end I felt that all the trials and tribulations encountered in the making of the film were worth enduring to gain the friendship of two such people as Virginia and Bill. I may add that Dudu proved its worth in the ensuing months and became the work-horse of my camp.

PART FOUR

Returning Lions to the Wild

20: *Rehabilitating Boy, Girl and Ugas*

Ideally, I would have liked to rehabilitate the lions in a remote corner of the Tsavo National Park, well away from the haunts of tourists. The park covers a huge area of over eight thousand square miles of semi-desert country where it would not have been difficult to find a suitable locality for the lions. However, the park authorities would not agree. The next area, in Kenya, most suitable would have been the desert country along the north-eastern shores of Lake Rudolf in the vicinity of Alia bay which I had looked over for Elsa and her cubs. But it had to be ruled out on account of the expense of maintaining a camp in such a remote area and the difficulty of communications. These problems could have been solved by air transport but this was entirely beyond my means.

The remaining alternative was the Meru Game Reserve, Elsa's old home. Communications were easy, the country was ideal and most important of all, the Meru County Council who owned the land and the Warden in charge, Ted Goss, were sympathetic towards the project and prepared to help in every way possible. My only reservation against the choice of this area was its size of only about four hundred square miles.

On the 25th of April 1965, Boy and Girl, aged nineteen months, joyfully jumped into the back of my Landrover, (the same although somewhat the worse for wear, which Elsa and her cubs had known so well five years ago), no doubt believing that they were being taken out for a routine run around the familiar Naro Moru plains. Little did they know that they were embarking on a new life and freedom. Being together, they endured the journey of 140 miles to the Meru Game Reserve exceedingly well, most of the time lying quietly in the back of the car. But by the time we reached the camp which had been prepared beforehand, they were very exhausted owing to the constant bumping over the rough roads.

The camp had been set up by Giles Remnant who had been my assistant with the film company at Naro Moru and knew Boy and Girl almost as well as I did. He had readily agreed to come and help me as his feelings about the lions were the same as mine. The site chosen was near the foot of a small rocky hill called Mugwongo in the centre of the game reserve, surrounded by plains on three sides and on the fourth, swamps, thorn bushes and palm trees, at an altitude of about two thousand feet above sea level. As the crow flies, it was not more than ten miles away from Elsa's Camp. The site had been enclosed with strong link-mesh wire netting, nailed to poles six feet in height, divided into a lion enclosure and the camp compound containing the tents. It had been my intention to keep the lions confined at night for the first week or two until they had become accustomed to the new conditions, but Boy and Girl had other ideas. Being tired out, they slept the night through in their enclosure. In the early hours of the morning Girl, followed by Boy, climbed over the netting of their enclosure and came to my tent. They roused me with warm greetings and Boy sat on my chest, so I had to get up and take them for a walk. We then placed thorn branches along the outside of the netting and this proved an efficient barrier, but as the lions showed no inclination to leave the camp after dark, apart from brief excursions to chase away hyenas and jackals, I did not confine them after the second night. Henceforth they were completely free to come and go as they pleased; in fact, they usually slept on the top of my car.

The education of the lions began with early morning walks for three or four hours in order to get them acquainted with the locality and to encourage them to hunt any game encountered on the way; at first, they felt the heat and were driven nearly frantic by the tse tse but there was no lack of keenness. Boy and Girl hunted everything from elephant downwards, including rhino, buffalo, giraffe, eland, zebra, oryx, etc. One morning we came upon a flock of ostriches. Boy planned a stalk, followed by Girl;

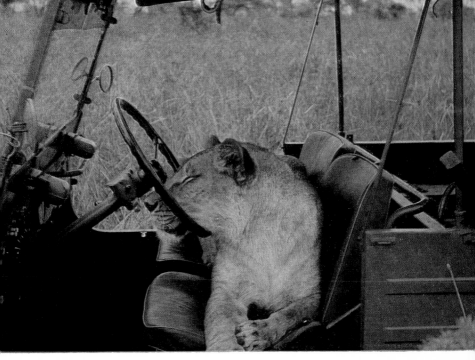

Ugas

Girl

he made a wide detour and crept up behind the birds while they were watching me, but ostriches are wary creatures, they soon saw him and were off. At first the lions ran wild chasing animals until exhausted, however they soon learned that it was futile trying to run down the swift zebra and antelope in the open, and that there was nothing to be gained by tackling such creatures as elephant and rhino—apart from the fun of it. Then they began to ignore animals which were aware of their presence and reserved their energy for stalking those which had not been alarmed.

A few days after their arrival they met their first elephant, a large bull. It was stalked with elaborate care until they were a few yards off, then a mild demonstration from the elephant sent them scurrying, but a few moments later they were back and continued the game of harrying the elephant until they were tired. (Today these great creatures are looked upon as part of the landscape and not interfered with.) A rhino which ventured too close to camp received much the same treatment. But in this case it was the rhino who finally decided to seek more peaceful pastures. On another occasion, it was a herd of buffalo which, realising that they were being threatened by lions, gathered in tight formation and charged. Wisely, Boy and Girl did not wait to contest the issue. But shortly afterwards they returned to the fray and singled out a big bull who had lagged behind the herd. They teased him unmercifully for half an hour, easily avoiding his angry rushes.

Eleven days after our arrival in the game reserve Boy developed a high fever, his temperature rising to over one hundred and seven degrees, and I feared we might lose him. Blood slides revealed that he had trypanosomiasis, caused by the bites of infected tse tse flies. I was rather doubtful whether it would be possible to push a needle into Boy without a squeeze-cage, but he did not flinch when I gave him an injection of 8 ccs. of berenil which worked wonders. In a little over twenty-four hours the fever had left him and he has never been sick since. Girl has never had a day's illness.

Daily it could be observed how Boy and Girl developed their inherited knowledge of the wild and gained experience and skill

B.G.   S in hunting. Their bodies became hard and muscular and their powers of scent, hearing and sight sharpened. Teaching them to become independent, which entailed killing for food, was made more difficult by the fact that the animals in the area were very well versed in the ways of lion and not easily caught napping, also there was a lack of smaller game such as warthogs which would have been relatively easy prey.

In order to encourage Boy and Girl to hunt I cut down their rations to one animal every eight or ten days. After a 'kill' I would drag the carcase well away from the camp. Boy and Girl soon learned to spend their day guarding it from vultures and that it was fatal to leave it even for a short time. So when they were thirsty they came one at a time to water in the camp while the other stayed with the 'kill'. From this I went on to make them guard it against jackal and hyena by night, by leaving it at the foot of the hill. It was not until three months had elapsed that Girl made her first kill. A mere baboon but, at least, a beginning. A few nights later she killed a half-grown eland. Next I actually witnessed the killing of a zebra. While out for a walk one evening we came on a small herd of these animals. Girl carried out a very careful stalk, moving only when all heads were down. The moment a head was raised she would freeze until she gained the cover of a fallen tree about forty yards short of the zebra. Here she crouched motionless while the unsuspecting herd grazed slowly towards her. At twenty paces she made a lightning rush, catching a young male. She brought it down from behind and quickly gripped it by the throat. In two or three minutes the animal was dead. I was most impressed by the efficient manner in which the stalk and kill had been accomplished. So often young and inexperienced lions made a terrible mess of killing.

On another occasion, about 10 p.m., Girl disappeared into the darkness, leaving Boy asleep on the top of my Landrover. In the course of the night I could hear him calling for his sister. In the morning there was no sign of her. This was most unusual as she never stayed away from her brother for long. I felt quite worried and so did Boy, judging by his plaintive moans and disconsolate expression. We set off together to search, visiting all the usual lying-up places within half a mile of camp. Our calls brought no response and there were no pug marks to be seen. Defeated, we returned to camp. An hour later, Korokoro, a Turkana tribesman who had helped to look after the lions at Naro Moru and who had followed me to the game reserve, reported that he had just seen Girl lying beside the carcase of an eland not far off. Hastening to the scene we found that Girl had killed a full-grown cow eland, an animal more than four times her own weight. There were signs of a violent struggle around a fallen tree. Girl herself, although very tired, was scarcely marked and had already had her fill of fresh meat. Altogether it was a remarkable achievement. It was odd that none of us, not even Boy, had heard the noise of the struggle during the night. Poor Boy, once again he had missed the boat, but he lost no time in making up for it on the vast quantity of fresh meat.

A pride of twelve lions, lionesses and cubs became persistent visitors; in particular a big black-maned lion gave me many a sleepless night. It seemed that Mugwongo Hill and my camp were within the territory of the pride which at first resented the presence of strange lions. Another night, I heard fighting and rushed out to find Boy lying on his back with Black Mane standing over him. I chased the intruder away and called up Boy who seemed unhurt and little perturbed. As is said to be the case with wolves, once a young lion makes a gesture of submission to an older and stronger one by lying on his back in a defenceless attitude, he is usually not molested further.

Lions were roaring around the camp every night and a meeting between Boy, Girl and their wild kin was bound to occur and to be a test they would have to face and overcome.

One night the pride of twelve lions came to the camp, luckily I was alert and managed to get Boy and Girl into the tent compound. A few nights later I was again woken up by growls outside and, on going out, found Boy sitting about twenty yards from a wild lioness. He did not seem in the least concerned. The lioness backed away, most reluctantly, as I approached. Girl was nowhere to be seen. Frightened, she had gone up the hill.

Boy followed her, calling, and eventually brought her back to camp. Boy, it seemed, was afraid of lions but not of lionesses. Girl didn't trust any of them.

In August the National Park authorities agreed to let me rehabilitate Ugas. When I went to fetch him at the wild animal orphanage at Nairobi I was warned that he had become danger-ous since leaving Naro Moru more than four months ago. However, he seemed extremely pleased to see me and I felt quite confident of being able to handle him. He was in the same enclosure as Mara who was booked to fly to England in a few days. She also gave me a great welcome which made it all the more sad to think of her going to lifelong captivity.

The journey back by Landrover took over eleven hours and was very trying for Ugas who would not lie still; consequently, by the time we arrived, he was badly grazed about the face and completely exhausted. I put him into the lion enclosure where he rested a whole day and night without stirring. In the morning I set him free. His first reaction was to have a brief squabble with Boy, to let him know that henceforth he was boss. Promptly Girl went to her brother's assistance, after which the three of them settled down under the shade of a tree for the day. In the cool of the evening I took them out for a walk. Ugas, now a huge lion, was just the same friendly and affectionate creature I had known at Naro Moru. He constantly rubbed his great head up against me, moaning softly to let me know how pleased he was to be back in my company.

That night, about 11 p.m., I was sitting in my tent writing while Ugas lay in front of the gate asleep when I heard a noise in the empty enclosure. Thinking it was a hyena after the remains of Ugas's meat, I ran out with a torch only. Ugas disappeared into the darkness. A few moments later there was the noise of lions fighting. I grabbed my rifle and ran to the scene in time to see Ugas and Black Mane disengage. The latter made off at my approach. Ugas came up to me with blood dripping from his mouth. He had a nasty bite above one eye and under the lower jaw. It was most unfortunate that the wild lions should have decided to visit my camp just when Ugas had been set free.

They had not worried me for over two months. During the course of the next two days, Ugas's face became much swollen and he seemed in pain. Daily I gave him injections of penicillin which he took without a murmur. Within a week the wounds had almost healed.

A week later Black Mane again started to fight with Ugas. I was out in time to prevent any damage and chased him away. But now Ugas was determined to get his revenge and set off after him. I was equally determined that Ugas should not get involved in a serious fight and followed, carrying a pressure lamp, a torch and a rifle. Boy and Girl who were not going to miss the fun came with me. Black Mane kept his distance. At intervals he would roar a challenge, to which Ugas replied in kind and doggedly followed. Finally, after stumbling over lava strewn plains for hours, I managed to convince Ugas that he had seen Black Mane off and we started back for camp, Ugas leaving many a message, doubtless insulting, on bushes as he passed. Dawn was breaking as we entered camp.

One evening, sitting over a late sundowner, I heard an odd gasping sound outside the wire. It was like the noise of someone trying to start a reluctant motor cycle engine. I found the three lions surrounding an enormous porcupine and keeping at a safe distance, although Boy already had a quill stuck deep into a paw; (later, he managed to extract it). After a few minutes the lions lost interest and lay down a few feet away from the porcupine who continued to stand his ground for fully twenty minutes, uttering the same odd sound and rattling its quills, before stalking away.

A little over a month after Ugas's arrival he was taken ill and developed a high temperature. I felt certain he had trypanoso-miasis as the symptoms were very similar to Boy's. But blood slides showed no parasites and bowing to superior knowledge I took the advice of a vet who prescribed injections of penicillin. After several days' treatment his condition remained unchanged and in desperation I injected him with berenil. Once again its effects were near miraculous and within twenty-four hours the fever left him. Berenil is a drug which in all probability would have saved Elsa's life, had we known about it at the time.

Although Ugas got on very well with Boy and Girl he would not join up with them and always seemed to prefer my company. When the three lions and I went out for walks and it was time to turn back, Boy and Girl usually found a shady place and stayed out, often for three or four days at a time. I would wait until all three had settled down and were asleep and then try to sneak away unobserved. But invariably, after a short while, I would look back and see Ugas trotting along to catch me up. There was something wonderful in possessing the love and trust of such a magnificent creature but there were times when I wished he would show a little more independence. Boy and Girl were so devoted to each other that there was no room for a third in their partnership. It was essential to find another lioness as companion for Ugas and to kill for him. How I regretted the loss of Mara and Henrietta. The former in particular had shown so much aptitude for hunting that she would have made an ideal mate for Ugas.

Boy and Girl being away, I set out, one morning, for a walk with Ugas alone. We came on two huge bull buffaloes grazing on the plains. Ugas made a careful stalk until the buffaloes, seeing me, began to gallop away with Ugas giving chase. He ranged up alongside one of them and attempted to jump on its back, he was sent sprawling in the mud and then in turn chased by the second. Poor Ugas, I could not help laughing at the expression of hurt dignity on his face.

On another occasion, Boy and Girl had been missing for three days and I set off early in the morning together with Ugas to look for them. We were crossing a little stream when I heard a buffalo snorting and grunting on the opposite side. From the top of the bank I saw it being chased by Boy and Girl and coming in my direction fast. Ugas rushed forward to intercept it and got charged for his pains. The buffalo then continued towards me. Thinking it had not seen me I waved my arms and shouted. It merely accelerated its pace and bore down on me. Fortunately, there was a small tree close by, around which I dodged as it swept past a few inches away. It spun around in its own length and came at me again. Feeling I was getting a little old to risk any more toreador acts I shot it in the head at less than ten feet, killing it instantly. A few seconds later, the three lions piled on to it. I was full of remorse at being obliged to kill the buffalo but it was thoroughly angry at being chivvied by the lions and no doubt mistook me for another of them.

A few days later I was out with the three lions when they again tackled a buffalo bull. They baited it unmercifully, through and around bushes. Every time it angrily charged one lion, the other two would be on its tail until all concerned were exhausted. Keeping well out of the way I finally drove it off by shouting.

Of the three lions, Ugas had far and away the best nose. One day, instead of following me, he led the way and soon it was obvious that he was following a scent. Unhurried, with scarcely a pause, he went nearly two miles until we came on the remains of a freshly killed Grant's gazelle. He sat down and finished off what was left and then again took up the scent until we met Boy and Girl, their stomachs bulging. Evidently, they had killed the gazelle early the same morning.

Ugas soon found out that it was only necessary for him to rear up and lean on the wire with his great weight for it to sag and permit easy access into the compound. He availed himself of the knowledge on several occasions and spent nights in my tent, stretched out on the floor alongside my bed. Once Boy and Girl followed him and I had all three lions sleeping beside me. As there was nothing much I could do about it I let them be and followed their example. They were very well behaved, at least by lion standards; that is to say I was permitted to sleep undisturbed but lions are not particular about where they urinate. They will do it lying, sitting or standing at any time and in any place, although they are most particular about where they defecate and will always move well away from their sleeping places. It is quite possible that their free and easy habits of urination have a definite purpose. Lion urine appears to be an insect repellent. I noticed this in the case of Elsa and her sisters;

their small night enclosure became heavily infested by fleas, but after a time, when the ground had become impregnated with urine, the fleas disappeared.

Girl was nearly twenty-seven months old when she showed signs of coming into season for the first time. There was little to indicate her condition apart from her behaviour. She became moody and short-tempered and would wander about calling in a love-lorn manner. Ugas's interest was aroused but his importunities were not well received. Once she went for him with such fury that, startled, he fell over backwards into the drinking trough which cooled his ardour for the time being. Even her beloved Boy felt the edge of her temper. Mating did not take place and after three weeks she returned to normal and Ugas lost interest.

By the end of the year 1965, Boy and Girl were two and a quarter years old and Ugas three years and seven months and, as an afterthought, myself a month short of sixty. As lionesses go, Girl was small but she made up for lack of weight by extreme agility. Boy was as tall as Ugas although not so heavy. Ugas, by any standard, was a big lion. Boy and Girl as a pair, were perfectly capable of looking after themselves and could have been left to their own devices. Ugas was thoroughly at home in the wild but, without a lioness as partner, he was still, to a large extent, dependent on me. Yet, in spite of their size and strength, they were amazingly gentle with me, particularly Girl, who always behaved like a perfect lady. Occasionally, high spirits would get the better of Ugas and Boy and I would find myself on the ground. But they never took advantage of my defenceless recumbent position; in the case of Ugas I could haul myself to my feet by gripping his mane. Nevertheless, I had to be on my guard, especially on cold and wet mornings as there was the danger of being caught off balance and accidentally breaking a limb. I usually carry a rifle, not as protection against my own lions but in case of an encounter with the larger fauna, aggravated by the attentions of the lions, as happened in the case of the buffalo. Also, I found the butt end of the rifle useful in fending off Ugas and Boy when they were inclined to be over-playful.

Always I walked alone with the lions, mainly because I had full confidence in them and it was not fair to expect anyone else without the same confidence to accompany me. Also, lions seem to appreciate age and are more likely to play rough with a younger man, and this was noticeable with young Giles Remnant during the four months he was assisting me with Boy and Girl.

After the arrival of Ugas, Mike Adam, a man in his thirties and of much experience, came to help me. He took all the burdensome chores off my shoulders; such as procuring meat for the lions and for the cheetah Joy was looking after, fetching water which had to be transported in a tank trailer from a river six miles away and generally maintaining the camp. This left me free to concentrate on the lions and write this book. In addition, I was most fortunate in having the services of the staunch Korokoro who had no fear of the lions and could always be relied upon to help. It was he who cut up the carcase of a buffalo while the lions were actually feeding on it.

21 : *Four cubs join the pride*

EARLY IN January 1966 I was offered four little five months old lion cubs, a male and three females, by the Bisletis, friends who lived on a large estate near Lake Naivasha. As all my efforts to obtain an adult lioness as companion for Ugas had failed, I decided to accept the offer. The owners would not hear of taking payment, insisting that they were delighted to give their cubs the chance to live out their lives in freedom, the only other alternative being a zoo.

Susua, Suki, Sally and Shaitani arrived at my camp in excellent condition, the first being the male and the name of the last meaning 'The Devil'—so called because she was the wildest of the quartet. For the first four days I kept them confined in an enclosure in order to allow Ugas, Boy and Girl to get used to them and make their acquaintance through the wire. The three big lions were much intrigued. The cubs showed not the least nervousness and crowded up against the wire to rub noses, while Ugas made soft moaning sounds, the equivalent of leonine baby-talk. Girl sat for hours apparently fascinated but at the same time would snarl at too close contact. Boy, temperamentally the most serene, seemed to accept them at once as part of the family. On the fifth morning I let them out, feeling a little apprehensive about the way Girl might react. But I need not have worried. The cubs went straight up to Ugas to greet him. He looked quite embarrassed, not knowing how to treat the situation. Then, suddenly, he leapt over them and raced off. The cubs went in hot pursuit. The other two joined in the game with surprising gentleness.

From now on the cubs were let out every morning for two or three hours to play until thoroughly tired and then put back in their enclosure to rest through the heat of the day. In the evening, they were given a whisky bottle full of milk each, sucking it through strong rubber teats. As it was impossible for me to hold four bottles simultaneously, I had to call on my assistant or Korokoro to help. If each was not presented with the bottle at the same moment as the others, there would be fights and in the *mêlée* one was apt to get clawed. Fresh milk being unobtainable, I fed them on tinned 'Ideal' milk suitably diluted, upon which they seemed to thrive. Apart from milk, they were given an entire goat carcase twice a week. These would be leapt upon and 'killed' in approved lion fashion, one, usually Shaitani, getting a firm hold on the throat and hanging on.

The cubs soon began to show their individual personalities. Susua was the friendliest and most playful but inclined to be a little rough. Suki, the largest of the females, was the most even tempered and easy to handle. Sally, a temperamental female, full of affection at times and at others almost unapproachable. Shaitani always remained aloof. Her distinctive brown eyes and lithe build reminded me very much of Elsa's sister Lustica, while her character and behaviour resembled in a marked degree that of Little Elsa.

After a week of model conduct which I felt was too good to last, Shaitani one morning when the cubs were let out, raced for Mugwongo Hill, followed by the other three where they all disappeared among the rocks and vegetation. Soon they emerged on the top of the hill and sat on a large rock where we could see them silhouetted against the sky. Calling Korokoro, I set off to try to recover them, but by the time we reached the rock they had vanished. We searched until noon and then again in the afternoon until dark without result. I felt extremely worried at the thought of their spending the night out alone; they were far too young to be able to defend themselves against leopards which I frequently heard on the hill or even hyenas. I was up before dawn the next morning and rousing Korokoro, we were about to start off to continue the search when suddenly the cubs appeared. They were very thirsty but otherwise it was plain that they had thoroughly enjoyed their adventure. A few days later they disappeared for two nights and after a prolonged search we found them hiding in a deep cleft in a rock which it was impossible for a man to enter. All our efforts to entice them out failed. At length, as the sun was setting, I saw Ugas on the plain below and called to him. He came up and as soon as the cubs saw him at the mouth of the cleft, they rushed out to greet him and after that followed us obediently back to camp.

Instead of feeding them morning and evening, I now fed them in the evenings only. This had the desired effect for by then they were usually thirsty and hungry and soon all I needed to do was to go to the foot of the hill and call. At once four pairs of large round ears would appear above the rock and the owners come scrambling down and follow me back to camp.

In spite of the many weary and anxious hours spent in searching for the cubs when they went astray, I was pleased that they were showing their independence at such an early age as this would be a vital factor in the successful rehabilitation of not only themselves but of the big lions as well. In the wild state, it is the lionesses which do most of the killing so the addition of three to my pride was a great asset. Should a member of the pride be injured and unable to hunt, there would be the others to provide food until he or she recovered. Also, four lionesses hunting as a team would find it much easier to make kills than a single animal.

Since September of last year, Ugas had been suffering from an infection in his right eye which gradually became worse, in spite of prolonged treatment by means of injections of antibiotics including penicillin, acromycin and frequent applications of eye ointments. I believe the trouble was due to a spitting cobra. At one time there was an improvement and the eye returned almost to normal, I thought the battle to save it was won. Then it again deteriorated until it became a dreadful sight, almost twice its normal size, nearly popping out of the head and much discoloured. I felt sure Ugas had lost the sight in it. It often caused him much pain which I would try to relieve with cocaine eye drops. Altogether he must have received more than fifty injections. There were times when he was too sore to tolerate another needle and would voice his objection by a low growl. On such occasions I gave him pills concealed in pieces of meat. On one occasion only when he was in pain, did he almost lose his temper with me. As I thrust the needle into his rump, he leapt up with a loud growl and seized my arm in his jaws. Suddenly, he seemed to recollect himself and just as he might have crushed my arm, he gently released it. Not even the skin was broken, only a few small bruises to show for it.

One morning when poor Ugas's eye was at its worst, he was sitting together with the four cubs outside the camp wire when there was a noise over towards the foot of the hill. They all went off to investigate. Thinking the sound might have been made by a wild lion, I collected my rifle and followed. I found the cubs sitting on a large flat rock but there was no sign of Ugas. After sitting with them for a few minutes, I returned to camp, twenty minutes later there was loud growling and Ugas appeared with blood dripping from his bad eye. He was almost mad with pain and pawing at the air. When he had calmed down a little, I managed to give him an injection of sernyl which seemed to ease the pain and put him to sleep. I at once sent a radio message to Dr and Mrs Harthoorn at Nairobi, both experienced vets who had taken a great personal interest in Ugas's case and had already made several trips from Nairobi to examine him and prescribe treatment. The following day, they flew from Nairobi and carried out a careful examination of the injured eye. It seemed that Ugas had accidentally run a sharp stick into it. As there did not appear to be any hope of saving the eye, we all agreed that it was best to remove it. (They were also sure that he had lost the sight of the eye some time previously.) The Harthoorns performed the operation next morning under a rough shelter I had rigged up over the already unconscious Ugas. It was a heart-rending sight to witness what had once been a beautiful tawny shining orb, reduced to a few shreds of bleeding tissue.

In less than three weeks, the wound had completely healed up and the stitches could be taken out. No doubt, the loss of the eye was a serious handicap to Ugas but it was astonishing how little it seemed to interfere with his normal activities. I had seen several lions and lionesses in the wild state with only one eye and, judging by their appearance they had been able to cope with life adequately.

The arrival of the cubs made it necessary to obtain a regular supply of meat to keep them well-fed during their growing stage as they would not be old enough to kill for themselves until they were about eighteen months old and then only small animals, unless in company with the big lions. As it was not practical to give them meat and deny it to their elders, either my assistant, when I had one, or myself had to go out and shoot zebra. This had to be done outside the boundaries of the game reserve and often entailed a trip of a hundred miles or more over rough tracks and across country. Most of the animals shot were obtained in places where from time to time it was necessary for the game department to thin out the zebra which were causing damage to cultivation.

By now, my old Landrover, KGR 608, which Elsa and her cubs had known, and many a time sat on and which had been used on the long search for the cubs in the Serengeti and again during the filming of *Born Free*, was at last beginning to feel its age and it became necessary to get a new one, though, for the hard work I kept 608. I did this partly for sentimental reasons, but also because it had a caged-in body which might be useful in an emergency for recovering the lions should they stray.

About a month after the arrival of the cubs I decided it was time for them to learn to share a 'kill' with their elders if they were to be integrated into one pride. I therefore let them out to share a zebra carcase but with a certain amount of anxiety as I was not at all sure how the big lions would react and whether the cubs possessed the requisite table manners customary for the young when dining with their elders. Once again, I need not have worried. Ugas, as was right, took the first helping while Boy and Girl and the four cubs waited impatiently albeit respectfully. After fifteen minutes, the edge taken off his hunger Ugas had no further objection to the others joining in and allowed the cubs to eat beside him. A lion family on a kill looks and sounds far from peaceful. There is much growling, laying-back of ears and snarling but little real violence. A common and curious habit among lions is what might be called a 'deadlock'. Two will seize on to the same piece of meat with heads touching, side by side, growling fiercely, neither giving way, often for half an hour. Any moment a fight seems imminent. But nearly always, in the end, one will quietly release his grip and move away. On one occasion Ugas and Boy started a 'deadlock' in the back of the caged-in Landrover. I was really worried as if they had started a fight in such a confined space one or both might have been seriously injured and there would have been little I could have done to intervene. Finally, Boy gave way. On 'kill' nights I left the cubs out as they were perfectly safe in the company of the big lions who would not move away from camp while the meat lasted. In fact, the arrangement suited them well as the cubs took it upon themselves to chase away the vultures with great enthusiasm while the elders could take their ease and slumber.

Early in March, Joy left for London to attend the Première of *Born Free* which was to be a Royal Command performance. She was most reluctant to leave her cheetah, Pipa, who was due to give birth to cubs within the next ten days. Fortunately, I had an assistant who took charge of her camp in order to keep Pipa under observation and help her if necessary. I myself was invited to be present at the Première of the film in Nairobi and was expected to say a few words from the stage, a prospect which filled me with dread. As the time for my public appearance approached, I decided that Ugas was too ill with his eye trouble for me to leave him alone for two nights. Accordingly I sent my regrets saying it was impossible to attend. However, the sponsors were determined that I should undergo the ordeal and I was informed that an aircraft would be sent to fetch me and fly me back the following morning. Under the circumstances I could hardly refuse. I unearthed my dinner jacket which had not been worn since our trip to Europe thirteen years ago and found that I had quite forgotten how to tie a bow tie. A frantic two hours were spent in practising tying it around a fruit can. In the event the result was hidden behind my beard and I said my piece without faltering, possibly helped by the excellent supper given before the show. This was the first time I had seen the complete film and was agreeably surprised at the result of all the trials and hard work that had gone into the making of it.

A few days later Pipa gave birth and an urgent cable was sent to Joy in London. Within a few hours of receiving it she was on her way and two hours after landing at Nairobi she was flying over *my* camp in a light chartered aircraft and dropping a message asking me to meet her at *her* camp. The next morning Pipa, after a huge meal, led Joy to her cubs which were hidden under a tree about half a mile away. Three days later Joy was on her way back to London.

At the age of seven and a half months I decided the four lion cubs were big enough to look after themselves at night and keep out of trouble. Henceforth they were never again locked up.

One dark and stormy night there was a tremendous uproar in front of the camp. I rushed out with a torch and a rifle but could see nothing in the rain and darkness. Suddenly the four cubs dashed past looking very frightened and disappeared behind the camp. The noise of fighting lions accompanied by much roaring receded towards the hill. Quickly I got my Landrover and drove around to the opposite side of the hill. With the aid of a spot light I could see five and a half pairs of eyes (the half being Uga's) glinting in the beam on top of the ridge. Presently I made out Boy and Girl and, judging by the intermittent growling, there was some high leonine drama being enacted. After calling for some time, Ugas came down the hillside unscathed and unperturbed and, with a little persuasion, entered the back of the car and was locked in and taken back to camp. But as soon as he was released he returned to the hill. Next morning, I found that the cause of all the bother was a lioness with two big cubs. Evidently my lions had seen her off.

I now started to encourage the cubs to come out on walks with me but this they would only do if the big lions came as well. It was quite a sight to see my pride of seven lions out together. As the weeks went by, the cubs gained in confidence and took

I take Girl and Boy for a walk

Resting after exercise

Girl greets me

Taking blood sample from Boy

Out walking

Rudkin and the lions
Boy and Girl harrying buffalo
Ugas, Boy and Girl at the kill
Feeding Ugas

Bottle-feeding the Bisleti cubs
Myself and the four Bisleti cubs
Two of the cubs at play
Cubs meet porcupine at night

Boy and the Bisleti cubs

Boy, Girl and three of the cubs on Landrover

to staying out whole nights, usually together with Boy and Girl. In fact, all the lions steadily became more nocturnal in their habits and seldom spent much time at camp except when hungry. On one occasion they all arrived back in camp with the exception of Girl. As it was unusual for her to be parted from Boy for any length of time, I felt a little anxious about her. Evidently Boy shared my anxiety as he kept on calling for her in a forlorn manner. Picking up my rifle I set off across a sandy plain to search for her. After walking for half a mile I came on fresh spoor which looked like hers. I called and was answered by a loud growl from behind a bush fifty yards away. A gaunt and scruffy-looking lion appeared who did not seem at all pleased to see me. In fact, his manner might be described as distinctly offhand. He stood rumbling to himself and flicking his tail about but as I did not give ground he finally moved slowly away. I then noticed a face peering at me from around a bush. It was Girl. She came up to me looking, I am pleased to say, a little ashamed of herself. And no wonder, keeping such disreputable company! She had a nasty bite in one shoulder, doubtless a love-token from Scruffy. She followed me back to the camp where her reception from Boy was noticeably frigid.

A few weeks later, after being missing for three days, Boy and Girl appeared one morning with their stomachs bulging. Boy had a wound in his rump which looked as if it had been caused by the horn of some animal. Obviously, they had made a kill. In the afternoon I saw large numbers of vultures about a mile from camp and on investigation found the remains of an oryx. Thirty yards farther on were the remains of a hartebeest. I examined the surrounding ground carefully, expecting to find the spoor of a number of wild lions. But there were the pug marks of only two, unmistakably Boy and Girl. The signs showed that the oryx had been killed some hours before the hartebeest. Probably the hartebeest had blundered accidentally on to the lions while they were feeding on the oryx and had paid for his carelessness with his life. Unfortunately, the vultures had been too long at the carcases for me to be able to save any meat.

My assistant having left for reasons of ill health I was alone for over a month until I received the unexpected help of a young American who had recently arrived in Kenya with the intention of taking a course in zoology and allied subjects at the University College at Nairobi. Since his term did not commence until September, he was anxious to gain some experience of lion and their ways. Hans was extremely keen and interested in all aspects of wildlife and had already some experience in the game departments of Zululand and Zambia. The morning after his arrival he expressed the wish to go out walking with the lions. First, I introduced him to Ugas and Boy and Girl who seemed to accept him in a friendly manner. We started off from camp, Ugas in the lead followed by us and then Boy and Girl and the four cubs. Our way led through long grass, an ideal situation for a lion ambush. Suddenly Ugas bounded out and had poor Hans on the ground in an instant. It was all in good fun but even so alarming, though Hans took it in very good part. As Ugas appeared to be in a particularly playful mood, I decided to abandon the walk. The same thing happened on the two following mornings. I feel sure Ugas knew that Hans was a young man and therefore quite capable of standing up to a little rough-housing. He had tried the same game with me in the early days but soon realised that I strongly disapproved, at my age, of being bowled over and thereafter was always gentle with me.

Although visitors to my camp were not encouraged, there was no legitimate means of stopping them, for once having paid their entrance fee at the gate, visitors were at liberty to go where they wished. One morning an enormous bus appeared at camp containing fifty Indians. All the lions happened to be at camp but the sudden arrival of the gleaming monster was too much for the cubs who promptly made for the hill. It was a strict rule that no one was allowed to get out of their vehicle unless invited to do so by myself. Usually, when a car arrived, I had it driven inside the compound from where visitors could view the lions through the wire—like a zoo in reverse, the animals being free and the humans caged!

One morning I had to go out to fetch water with the Land-rover and trailer from the river about four miles away. On my return about an hour later, I was astonished to find a party of eight British soldiers wandering about among the lions apparently on the friendliest terms with Boy and Girl who I am convinced remembered their association with the Scots Guards and seemed delighted to welcome the soldiers. They were a party from the Welsh Guards, men on leave from Aden.

Early in June I one day heard the unmistakable sounds of lions mating a few hundred yards from camp. At first I thought it must be Ugas and Girl as the latter had been showing signs of coming in season again. It would have been unwise to investigate on foot so Hans and I drove to where we had last heard the sounds but saw nothing owing to the long grass and bush. We waited for perhaps ten minutes and then again heard the lions quite close. I caught a glimpse of a lioness moving away with Ugas close behind. We followed slowly and could see the backs of the pair over the grass. By standing on the roof of the Landrover I obtained a better view. The lioness looked like Girl but I was puzzled by her shyness as when I called her by name, she again moved away. I decided not to disturb the happy couple further and we returned to camp where, much to my surprise, I found Boy and Girl. Obviously Ugas had found himself a wild girl friend. For the next three nights the mating continued within earshot of camp. The lion, when performing the mating act, utters a curious whining growl which once heard cannot be forgotten. The lioness also makes a characteristic purring noise. Purring before mating is a sure indication of a lioness coming in season.

The evening of the day on which we discovered Ugas with the lioness we saw a light aircraft fly past heading in the direction of Nairobi. At the time I wondered what emergency was causing the pilot to risk flying so late in the evening. Next morning we heard over the radio that Ted Goss had been badly injured by an elephant. About three miles from the main Leopard Rock Camp, Ted had tried to immobilise the bull elephant by shooting it with a drug-filled dart with a view to marking it with an ear tag. For some reason the drug did not take full effect. Leaving a Game Scout to watch the animal, Ted went back to Leopard

Rock to fetch another dart. On his return he found that the elephant had not moved and appeared to be in a dazed condition. So,
he walked up to within a few paces to give it the second dart.
Suddenly the elephant charged. Ted tried to get away but was
quickly caught and hurled to the ground. The elephant then
tried unsuccessfully to skewer him with its tusks but succeeded
in trampling on him, crushing a thigh and breaking an ankle.
The Game Scout, who was an experienced hunter, dared not
shoot for fear the elephant might fall on Ted and crush him as he
was lying on his back directly underneath the animal. With
amazing presence of mind, Ted managed to drag himself clear
by clutching tufts of grass, enabling the scout to shoot the elephant
through the brain. It was truly a miraculous escape from almost
certain death.

A fortnight after Ugas had found his friend, I went to look
for Boy and Girl who had been missing for three days. About
two miles from camp I found them mating for the first time. It
was interesting that Girl should have chosen her own brother
rather than Ugas or a wild lion. The following morning, when
I visited them, Boy and Girl jumped on to the roof of the car
and tried to perform the sexual act in this somewhat precarious
position. I intended to drive them back to camp but, after going
a few yards, Girl jumped down, followed by Boy. The latter
placed himself in front of the car and made it plain that he did
not wish me to drive away. In fact, when I tried to pass him, he
again moved in front and growled. He had never acted in this
manner before and I was puzzled at his behaviour. At length
they settled down in the shade of a bush and I was able to drive
away. The romance lasted four days and during this time Boy,
who usually allowed himself to be bullied by Ugas, became
exceedingly fierce and Ugas dared not approach the couple. But
there was reason to think that, owing to the inexperience of Boy,
the mating had not been successful.

Late one afternoon Joy arrived with the news that a big gang
of Shifta had raided a Meru village on the Nyambeni Hills,
north-west of the game reserve. I was advised to leave the camp
and spend the night at Leopard Rock headquarters. As all the

Camp at Mugwongo

Sam

lions were in camp busy eating a zebra carcase and would certainly not leave until it was finished on the following day, I was not prepared to abandon them as they would have provided sitting targets for the rifle-armed Shifta. Also, there had been several scares during the past months and I judged it extremely unlikely that they would bother me as there was little of any value in my camp.

All their raids up to then had been directed at trading centres where there were shops and plenty of loot. I might here explain that the Shifta, the word means bandit, had been causing a great deal of trouble in the north-eastern parts of Kenya since the country achieved independence. The Shifta consisted of bands of Somali and Boran tribesmen who carried out desultory raids on villages and ambushed convoys and patrols of the security forces, under the guise of fighting for the independence of the Somalis of Kenya and the inclusion of their land into the Republic of Somalia.

Eighteen days after their first romance, Boy and Girl again mated. They were absent for four nights and returned early on the evening of the fifth. Ugas was present and promptly tried to take possession of Girl. There was a fight between him and Boy, the worst yet. I quickly jumped into my Landrover and drove it between them. Boy had received a bite in a foreleg and Ugas one under the ear. After this, Ugas seemed to accept the situation and made no further attempt to interfere. All going well, Girl would be due to have cubs towards the end of October.

Boy and Girl were now two years and nine months old and a very handsome pair in perfect condition with beautiful shining coats. Boy was well over nine feet long from nose to tail tip, taller than Ugas but not so heavily built, although he would fill out considerably in the course of the next two years.

All the lions are fond of sitting on rocks or other vantage points from which they can obtain a good view around. Since there were no rocks at my camp, my lions would sit on the Landrover. In order to preserve the little paint work left, I built a platform eight feet off the ground. It immediately became popular and at times all seven of the lions could be seen stretched out on it. One evening Susua, who was always the most inquisitive and venture-some, took a flying leap off the platform over the wire and on to the roof of my main living hut. As the roof had not been designed to withstand the impact of a lion landing on it, the structure collapsed, depositing Susua on the top of the manuscript of this story which was on my writing table below.

In August, the cubs had their first birthday; they now spent most of their time hunting together with Boy and Girl. Girl was their undisputed leader and I felt confident that in a few more months they would form a first-class hunting team. Soon after dawn one morning I found the spoor of Boy and Girl and the cubs heading towards the river four miles away. After following for a mile, I met the cubs hurrying back and casting nervous glances behind them. They hardly paused to greet me and made for the hill. Some way farther on I met Boy and Girl. They also seemed nervous and kept on looking back but stayed with me. Presently I heard two lions roaring towards the river and drove on to investigate as I thought one of them might be Ugas. They turned out to be Black Mane and Scruffy, both of whom had caused me many sleepless nights in the early days. Scruffy, when last seen, had been in the company of Girl as described earlier. Both of them showed little fear of my car and were staring intently in the direction of the place where I had left Boy and Girl. Looking back the way I had come, I saw Boy and Girl approaching and, perhaps emboldened by my presence, Boy was giving vent to ferocious roars. Suddenly, Black Mane and Scruffy turned and made off at a fast trot, they did not pause until they had crossed the river where a few minutes later I heard them roaring. Either of them might have been more than a match for Boy. Certainly he and Girl would not have stood a chance against the two. Why then did they retreat? I think the answer involved territorial rights. Black Mane and Scruffy knew they were trespassing.

About a week later, Ugas had been missing for two days and I went to look for him. I stopped my car at a little stream and was casting around for spoor when I heard growling and a few moments later two lionesses emerged from the bush closely followed by Ugas who, in turn, was followed by Boy and the four cubs. Next morning, Ugas was seen mating with one of the lionesses while Boy sat rather disconsolate, under a tree a hundred yards away. This went on for the next four days by which time neither Ugas nor Boy had had anything to eat for over a week. Finally, Ugas turned up at camp but not Boy. Whether the latter had taken up where Ugas had left off, it is hard to say. The following night there was tremendous roaring close to the camp, Ugas and a wild lion trying to out-roar each other. The four 'Ss' (the cubs were now too big to be called 'cubs' any longer) were much frightened and made for the hill. After a pause, I heard the wild lion come running past behind the camp: a few moments later Ugas trotted past after him. There was renewed roaring and I recognised Boy's gruff voice. Back came the wild lion with both Ugas and Boy in pursuit. This was another case of my lions seeing off an intruder.

A fortnight before the November or short rains started, black-headed weavers (Layard's black-headed weaver) arrived at the camp. The males always come first and with much chatter and quarrelling over nest sites commence a frantic building programme. In a few days the branch ends of the large acacia tree over-shadowing the camp were festooned with pendent nests. They always chose the leeward side of a tree and as far as possible, hung the nests over the roofs of tents or huts. This close association between the weavers and human habitations must go back to the distant past when the birds learnt to take advantage of the protection afforded by the proximity of man.

A fortnight after the arrival of the males, the first females put in an appearance. This caused great excitement among the males who redoubled their efforts at building and quarrelling. The females calmly went from nest to nest, evidently inspecting the premises, while the males, each hanging head down from the entrance of his nest, performed an excited dance, flapping their wings and swaying from side to side. A female approving of a nest would add the finishing touches, this consisted of lining the brood chamber with acacia leaves and the silky flowers of grasses. Mating would then take place and the serious business of egg laying and hatching begin.

The activities of the weavers attracted the unwelcome attentions of arboreal snakes, notably the deadly boomslang and the non-poisonous African egg-eating snake which has a skin pattern resembling the highly poisonous carpet viper. Early one morning, I was roused by a great commotion among the birds over my hut and saw a large boomslang about five feet in length attacking the nests. Already it had swallowed a chick and was being fiercely mobbed by the weavers who were diving at it in relays and buffeting it. The snake was extremely angry and striking at the birds with the fore-part of its body distended. Before it could do any further damage, a 22 bullet put an end to its career.

I was in the habit of feeding the weavers and other birds with millet which attracted rats and mice at night who, in turn, attracted more snakes, including a very large spitting cobra. As dawn was breaking one morning, my brother Terence, who was staying with me at the time, was getting ready to go off to shoot meat for the lions. He called to Korokoro to fetch a tarpaulin from the store. As he brought it to the car, an evil-looking head appeared from the folds. Luckily, Korokoro reacted instantly, dropping the bundle and springing back. The spray of venom just missed his face. The cobra was quickly despatched; it was a deep salmon pink in colour and its stomach contained a rat.

Shortly before the weavers arrived, a solitary bull elephant, for reasons best known to himself, developed the habit of making frequent calls at my camp and would feed off bushes within a few feet of the compound. Several times, after clearing the supper table, my cook had to wait for him to move away before he could reach his sleeping quarters. At first the four 'Ss' seemed to think it was their duty to try to see him off and would spend hours harrying the old gentleman who, losing patience, would utter a hoarse trumpet and charge, sending his tormentors scurrying. But after a few encounters the game palled and the lions and the elephant ignored each other to such an extent that the elephant would feed a few yards away from the sleeping lions. At times there were plenty of elephants near camp but none showed the same familiarity.

Lions are sensitive creatures and dislike being stared at. To look directly into the eyes of a lion for any length of time causes the animal visible discomfort. For this reason I always avoided looking my lions in the eye for more than a fleeting glance for they hate finding themselves in undignified situations.

On one occasion Ugas was riding on the roof of my Land-rover as I started to cross a steep-sided little stream. He slid off the roof and landed with a mighty splash in the water. My uncontrolled laughter did nothing to mollify his injured dignity. He walked away with his nose in the air, completely ignoring my sympathetic overtures.

Sometimes, when all the lions were feeding together on a carcase, one of the cubs would dispute with an elder over some delicacy and receive a painful cuff, or nip, for its boldness and cry out with pain. If I happened to be near by, the cub would come running to me and lean against me, moaning for sympathy. Often too cubs are inclined to be over-effusive in greeting an elder who will quickly let the offender know that it has exceeded the bounds of good manners.

Lions attach the greatest importance to territory marking and will never pass a chosen bush without stopping and going through the marking ritual which consists of backing up to the bush with tail raised and subjecting it to two or three powerful jets of urine and at the same time raising the nose and rubbing it against a branch just within reach. Sometimes, when I brought a carcase to the camp, one of the lions might be away, and rather than see any of the meat wasted, I could go in my Landrover to look for him and fetch him back sitting on the roof. As soon as we got to one of these bushes, I would have to stop and wait until the marking ceremony was gone through. This might entail four or five stops before camp was reached.

At the age of thirteen months, the three females Suki, Sally and Shaitani started to shed their milk teeth and grow the second teeth. It was not until six weeks later that the male Susua, followed suit. I had noticed the same among Elsa's cubs and have no doubt that it is normal for females to develop their teeth earlier than males.

About this time I had a strong suspicion that the four 'Ss' had made a kill on their own, probably the young of some animal. All the lions were becoming increasingly nocturnal in their habits which made it more difficult to keep track of their activities and to check on the number of kills made. One night Boy and Girl and the four 'Ss' killed a young eland and there were several other occasions when, judging by their appearance, they must have killed. Usually on these occasions Ugas was not present being too preoccupied in his quest for wild lionesses. One morning I happened to be out with him about a mile from camp when suddenly he became alert and following his gaze I saw three rhino slowly approaching. Ugas took up an ambush position while I retired to a strategic situation with my camera. On they came with Ugas crouching tensed to attack. At fifteen yards he made his rush. The rhino startled, turned, and ran. Quickly, he caught up with the hindermost, a three quarters grown calf and reared up on to its back. It began to squeal; promptly the mother turned back and charged Ugas, who very wisely took to his heels. Had the mother not been present, I believe Ugas would have killed it. I managed to get pictures of Ugas crouching for the attack and making his rush but for the most exciting one of all, of Ugas on the rhino's back, the film had finished, much to my disgust.

EARLY IN SEPTEMBER, about fifty days after mating with Boy, Girl showed the first signs of pregnancy by a slight swelling of her teats. Six weeks later the movements of her unborn cubs could be seen plainly when she was lying down. The gestation period of a lioness being about a hundred and eight days, she was due to give birth on or about the 26th of October. I was looking forward with great interest to the event and intended to keep her under close observation near her time. About a week before the cubs were due, I set out to the western boundary of the game reserve to shoot meat for the lions, a distance of about fifteen miles. I shot a zebra and then went on to look for another and on the way met three Meru who said they knew where there were some. Leaving my Landrover and taking a light rifle only, we set off on foot. After an hour's walk, not having seen any zebra, we turned back. While still half a mile from the car we came on a small herd of buffalo. I fired and hit one of the animals in the shoulder. It went off hard hit and leaving a blood trail which we followed cautiously for some three hundred yards until it was lost. As we were casting around to pick it up again, the buffalo, who had been waiting for us behind a tuft of long grass, suddenly charged from a few feet away. I put up my rifle to shoot and as I pressed the trigger, the head of the buffalo hit the muzzle of the gun and jerked it up, the bullet passing harmlessly over its back. The buffalo hit me in the ribs on my left side, knocking me to the ground. It then tried to hook me with its horns, fortunately without success although it gave me a black eye and trampled on a foot in the process. It then left me and went and lay down about forty feet away. One of the Meru crept up and picking up my rifle handed it to me and helped me to my feet. The buffalo, hearing the clatter of the rifle bolt as I reloaded, got up and looked as if it was going to have another go at me. But, much to my relief, this was its last effort and it collapsed and died. I was in a lot of pain and could scarcely breathe but with the help of the Meru I managed to stagger the half-mile to the car where, after a short rest, I felt slightly better and determined to return and secure the buffalo meat, which I had gone through so much woe to obtain. So I drove to the scene, rather to the disappointment of the three Meru who were expecting to have a whole buffalo to themselves, and after collecting the meat made my slow and painful way back to camp across country and over bumpy tracks. Luckily, there was a small 'Walkie-talkie' radio set in camp with which I got in touch with Charles Moore, the Warden at the Game Reserve Headquarters at Leopard Rock Camp who arrived a few hours later together with Joy. Next morning I was flown to Nairobi hospital where X-rays disclosed a few fractured ribs and a small bone broken in the foot.

I can remember several occasions in the past when I have earnestly advised young, aspiring big game hunters never to venture out after dangerous animals inadequately armed and then I go and do just this and, to add to my folly, leave my heavy double-barrelled rifle in the car. By which the reader will quite rightly gather that I am better at giving advice than taking it. It was particularly annoying being knocked out just when Girl was due to have her cubs. Fortunately, a young Indian, Arun Shama, was able to take charge of my camp during my fortnight's absence and Charles Moore kindly provided meat for the lions.

According to Arun Shama, Girl appeared at camp on the evening of the 24th October looking as if her time was very near and after eating a little meat went off towards Mugwongo Hill. She was not seen the next day but returned on the evening of the 26th obviously having given birth. After a large meal she disappeared towards the hill. Early next morning, Arun Shama and Korokoro followed up her tracks to the top of the northern spur of the hill where they started to call for her. Almost immediately she appeared from behind a low rock, and took the meat and water they had brought for her. With the most

Boy and cub

Myself, Girl and cubs

remarkable trust and good nature Girl permitted the two men, who were taking a considerable risk, to approach within a few feet of the birthplace until they saw two little cubs. Both male, easily distinguishable as the bigger one was light coloured and the smaller much darker. Girl's behaviour was the more remarkable as Arun was a comparative stranger to her. Elsa would never have allowed such a liberty; indeed, when Joy and I approached her cubs when they were a few days old, she made it very plain that we were not permitted to come any closer.

On the 2nd of November, having returned from hospital, I climbed up the hill (with a certain amount of grunting and groaning as my ribs were still sore) and saw the place where Girl had given birth. Later she moved the cubs into the confusion of rocks and vegetation and I could not locate her new hiding-place, but the following morning, with the help of Arun and Korokoro I found them under a flat rock where they were completely sheltered from the weather and well hidden. They were in excellent condition and their eyes were open. Although as yet unable to focus objects clearly, they immediately became aware of my presence and wrinkled their noses in snarls. During the next month Girl moved the cubs five times about the hill, always choosing sheltered places under overhanging rocks. Frequently, she left them on their own for a whole day, causing me to worry about their safety. In the evening, if she was dilatory about returning to her young, I would set off calling her to resume her maternal duties and literally shame her into following.

I am not sure exactly when the four 'Ss' discovered that Girl had cubs but a few days after my return I found them lying-up within a few yards of the latest hiding-place. They seemed quite fascinated by the babies and obviously longed to make contact but Girl would have none of it and would drive them away fiercely if they attempted to approach too close. She had, however, no objection to my presence and even permitted me to touch the cubs. The only other creature who was allowed the same privilege was the proud father, Boy, who showed surprisingly little interest in his sons. Then, one evening when I went to visit the lair, I found it empty. The next morning we searched all likely hiding-places in the vicinity without success. On our way back to camp late in the morning we found Girl within two hundred yards of camp with one cub only. She seemed much agitated and kept looking towards the hill; she would go in the direction for a few hundred yards and then come back, loath to leave the cub. For the next three days we carried out an intensive search of the hill and every likely-looking place within half a mile of its foot but never found any trace of the missing cub. Almost certainly it must have been taken, probably by a leopard, while Girl was carrying one and before she had had time to return for the other. It was the larger and more venturesome of the two which had gone. I had been strongly tempted to bring the two little cubs into the safety of the camp, but it would have defeated the object of letting them grow up wild and might have interfered with the exercise of Girl's mother-instincts. What happened was a tragedy all too common in the wild, particularly with a first litter. It was sad to think that the surviving cub, whom we called Sam, would not have his brother to play with.

For the next week Girl kept Sam within a radius of five hundred yards from camp, moving the lair several times and on two occasions bringing Sam into camp. She now permitted the other lions to play with him and it was touching to see how gentle they all were, Ugas even allowing the black tuft on the end of his tail to be stalked and 'killed'. In particular, the four 'Ss' seemed devoted to the little cub and would spend hours playing with him. Often when Girl moved the hiding-place, it was impossible to locate the cub unless she was present. Left alone, Sam would creep under cover and remain motionless without making a sound for hours on end, even when hungry, until his mother returned and called him by a low moaning sound, when he would at once answer and come out of his hiding-place.

One morning I went to visit Joy at her camp, leaving Girl and her son sleeping under the shade of a tree nearby the compound. When I returned in the evening Sam was missing although his mother and all the other lions were present. After some persuasion, she got up and set off with Arun and myself following, expecting her to lead us to Sam's lair. But after walking in a somewhat aimless manner for a mile, it became evident that Girl had no intention of taking us to her cub, and, in fact, her manner was strange. She would go a short distance and then throw herself on the ground purring loudly, usually in indication that she was coming in season. This was most disturbing and quite unnatural behaviour when nursing a cub. Already it was too dark to follow her farther and we returned to camp filled with foreboding. For the next three days, in spite of prolonged search, there was no trace of Girl or of Sam. On the fourth night Girl appeared at camp alone and on examining her it was evident that she had not suckled the cub for a long time and there appeared to be little milk in her teats. I felt convinced that she had abandoned or lost Sam, particularly as she had claw marks on a shoulder which suggested that she had been in contact with a wild lion. During the night she again disappeared and as there had been rain washing out all spoor, it was impossible to tell in what direction she had gone. I searched all morning without result and just as I was sitting down to a late breakfast, Korokoro said that he could hear Sam calling behind the camp. Arun and I went out and were met by Boy and Girl who gave us an exuberant welcome; a little way behind was Sam. He was a pathetic sight, he looked as if he had not had a meal for days and was scarcely able to stand from weakness. At this point Ugas appeared coming from the direction of camp. Promptly Boy went for him in a very determined manner and there was a tremendous fight, both standing on their hind legs and swiping at each other with either paw and claws extended. Any one of the blows might have removed half the face of a mere human being. I told Arun to run back to camp and fetch the Landrover, intending to drive it between the fighting lions. But by the time it arrived the fight was over and there was surprisingly little damage on either side, although Boy, for once, had seen Ugas off. I had never seen him in such an aggressive mood before. Also, the possessive manner in which he rejoined Girl and sat down beside her, in the shade of a tree, confirmed my suspicion that she was coming in to season.

The sound of battle had frightened Sam and he was nowhere

to be seen. Followed by Arun, I started to look for him and as we were passing close to the tree where Boy and Girl were lying, the former got up with a growl and without warning went for Arun and clawed him. Fortunately, I happened to be carrying a long stick and was able to beat Boy off before any serious damage could be done. I told Arun to get back into the car quickly while I faced Boy who then came at me. I hit him across the nose, making him pause, but only for a moment before he renewed the attack. 'This is it!' I thought, and struck him with all my might between the ears which seemed to bring him to his senses for he turned away and went back to his sister. Poor old Boy, he had never behaved like this before. It was simply that he was worked up over Girl's condition and his fight with Ugas and I should have had more sense than to go near him at such a time. Half an hour later he came up to me and rubbed his great head against me as if in apology.

Fortunately, Arun was not badly clawed but as a precaution I sent him off to a mission hospital forty miles away to get penicillin and anti-tetanus injections. He returned the same evening.

The incident taught me that even with my own lions it was not safe to go near them when they were sexually aroused, particularly in the presence of possible rivals—although, on the first ocasion when Boy and Girl mated I was standing beside them. In the Serengeti National Park, while searching for Elsa's cubs, I came on a mating pair of wild lions and when approached to within thirty yards, in my car, the male at once became aggressive, making me retire hurriedly.

It was now obvious that if little Sam were to survive, I would have to adopt him as his mother was incapable of feeding him. Also she seemed to be losing interest in him. In fact, there had been a marked decline of interest since the loss of the other cub. I found Sam without difficulty asleep under a bush and brought him to camp. Within an hour he had taken his first bottle of milk, sucked through a rubber teat. Thereafter there was no difficulty in feeding him. I used an ordinary baby's bottle filled with diluted Ideal condensed milk, a teaspoon of Farex and a

Ugas in my tent

Operation on Ugas's eye

Feeding Sam

Sam lying up

Girl with Sam

Sam with his parents
Girl carrying Sam
Sam plays with his mother

Girl's hiding place for her second litter

One of the cubs 18 days old

Girl with both cubs

couple of drops of 'Abedec' given five times a day or whenever Sam wanted it. In a few days he began to put on weight and gained in energy.

During the day, whenever his mother appeared and called for him I would hand him over to her care but keep a careful watch on her movements until I was satisfied she intended spending the day lying-up close to camp. On these occasions the four 'Ss' were usually in attendance and even if Girl left I could safely leave Sam in their charge. At night he slept in an open box beside my bed and would not stir till daybreak unless he heard the lions outside the wire when he would rush out to greet them. When the big lions roared, Sam would join in the chorus with a voice surprisingly powerful for his size. In a short time all of us were under his spell. Joy made special visits just to see him and I could tell that she longed to take him over.

It was my intention to allow Sam as much contact as possible with the rest of the lions and as soon as he was big enough to keep up with them, to set him free, which I thought might be possible when he was six months old. Meanwhile, I started to take him out for walks in the mornings.

Three nights before Christmas Sam was as usual asleep in his box beside my bed. About three a.m. I was woken by the rattling of the compound wire behind my sleeping hut. Thinking it might be one of my lions trying to get in, I got out of bed, noticing that Sam's box was empty and went to the back door of the hut. In the light of my torch, I saw a lion inside the compound, reared up against the wire, trying to get out. He had Sam in his jaws. At first I thought it was Boy who had forced his way in and was trying to carry Sam out: I shouted at him. The lion turned with a growl. It was Black Mane! I dived back into the hut to get my rifle and as I returned, the lion forced his way out, dropping Sam, who lay gasping in a spreading pool of blood. As I picked him up he died, bitten through the neck. It was unbelievable that an adult lion should kill and carry off a little cub.

There was a lot of roaring going on. I could identify the voices of Ugas and Boy and Black Mane and his friend Scruffy. I got out my Landrover and drove towards the sounds. First, I came on

Scruffy, close to camp and drove at him; he escaped across a gully. Next, I heard more roaring near the hill and discovered Black Mane and Girl together; they were mating! As I approached Black Mane started to run. I chased him and gave him a good buffet in the rump with the fender of the car before he disappeared into the darkness. Just as dawn was breaking there was further roaring on the opposite side of the hill and on reaching there I found Girl together with Black Mane and Scruffy. The former did not tarry but Scruffy, perhaps taking advantage of the situation, mated with Girl, who it seemed was distributing her favours equally. Between matings, she actually came and sat on the roof of the Landrover. I might have taken some interesting photographs but felt too sick at heart at Sam's death to think of using my camera.

Back at camp, investigation revealed that Black Mane had come over the wire netting at the back of the compound, gone through the store hut and picked up Sam close to the back door of my sleeping hut. No doubt Sam, hearing him outside, had gone out to greet him as he always did with my lions.

Twenty-five days after Sam's death, Girl again mated with Boy. On this occasion the romance lasted five days and during this time Boy was almost unapproachable, particularly if Ugas happened to be in the vicinity. But as soon as the period of mating was over, Boy reverted to his good-natured self. It is interesting to note that Girl was not affected in the same way and retained her friendliness throughout the period.

In May 1967 Bill Travers came out to Kenya and I went to see him. I was anxious to get back as soon as possible so as to be in camp when Girl's cubs arrived. The rains had started but after I had called at Joy's camp and was returning to my own, I found the water so deep at the ford at Kenmare Lodge that there was no chance of getting across. I therefore drove back to a place where there was a dilapidated, sagging bridge; it looked to me as though it would stand the weight of the Landrover, but the approach to the bridge had been partly washed away. I built a ramp with some stones that were lying around, and began to creep across in low gear. I was two-thirds of the way over when there was a crashing and rending of timbers and the bridge collapsed. The car came to rest perched precariously across the two ends of the bridge. It was heeling over at an alarming angle, and teetering. I tried to get out of the door, it was jammed; after a struggle I managed to get out of the window. As I was single handed, there was no question of my being able to do anything about the car other than secure it to a tree by a cable.

When I had done this it was dark, and I had a rather nerve-racking walk back to Joy's camp accompanied at a distance by a lioness who seemed to be taking a lot of interest in me, at least until I shouted at her and threw a stone. Later we set off in the 'Elsa' 4x4 Bedford five-tonner, a tractor and Charles Moore's Toyota, complete with winch, ropes and a gang of fifteen men, but when we got within two miles of the bridge all three vehicles became hopelessly bogged. I was convinced that the river would rise and carry away the remains of the bridge and my car. It was three a.m. before we managed to get the Toyota mobile and struggled through to find that my car was still there. We rescued my belongings, secured another cable to the car and started back to Leopard Rock Camp in pouring rain and darkness.

We had to wait until the following afternoon before the rain stopped and we were able to return to the bridge. Night was again falling by the time we managed to get my car out. When I got back to my camp I found that Girl was obviously very near her time. Next morning I had to go off to shoot meat for the lions and when I returned my old cook told me that Girl had gone off towards the hill. It rained heavily all that night but cleared in the morning when I went out to look for Girl, feeling sure that she had given birth. Of course all spoor had been washed away by the rain, but I searched her favourite places without finding a trace of her.

Sometime after midnight I heard her roaring at the back of the camp and got up to look for her, but she had gone away without touching any of the meat. Shama, Korokoro and I spent the morning searching for her in a northerly direction without success. Next day (the 10th of May), I searched to the west and found her close to the place where she had given birth to her first litter last October. She had two little cubs, both females; they must have been born during the early hours of the 9th. They had certainly been deluged with heavy rain, but nevertheless looked in fine shape and so they do today, as I write the last lines of my book.

Originally it was the intention to leave the lions to their own devices as soon as it was felt that they had become capable of fending for themselves. This stage has now been reached and the experiment of rehabilitation fulfilled, in so far as the lions kill for themselves, animals three or four times their own weight. They battle successfully against wild lions to maintain their territorial rights. They mate with wild lions. In fact, in every respect they are living the lives of their wild kind. Yet in spite of their independence, they remain friendly and trusting towards man. Why should it be otherwise? They have never been ill-treated by man.

I cannot look upon my lions as so much material for a scientific experiment. To me they are living beings with their individual characters and personalities and my friends whom I am under an obligation to care for. It is something remarkable that creatures which are traditionally man's enemies and among the strongest and fiercest on earth, can through kindness and understanding respond with unbounded trust and affection while leading their normal lives.

It is my hope that I may be permitted to continue my association with them indefinitely and perhaps share a little of my experience with other people. Not only for personal reasons but also because the relationship existing between us is unique and not to be found anywhere else in the world. It is a valuable asset to the Meru National Park which handled properly could prove a tremendous attraction to visitors from all countries as well as providing a field for continued scientific study into lion behaviour and the better understanding of our fellow wild creatures.

Often I am asked why I have committed myself to the lions. There is no material gain for me in the project. In spite of financial assistance from the Elsa Trust it is rapidly using up my slender resources. The answer lies in my great regard for these noble animals. I cannot bear to see these highly intelligent and sensitive creatures treated as so much merchandise, shipped here and there over the world, mothers parted from offspring, brothers from sisters, friend from friend, regardless of their feelings and happiness. For what? To provide profit for dealers and entertainment for humanity. They too are living beings with emotions akin to ours. If I can bring happiness and fulfilment for a span into the lives of a few and perhaps set the pattern for future rehabilitations, it will have been worth while.

Lions in the wild lead hazardous lives; a false move or ill-judgment in attack or defence may lead to serious injury or death from the horns and hooves of their prey or teeth and claws of their own kind. But it is their life, unchanged for millions of years, long before the ancestors of man learned to walk upright.

This night I bring my story to an end. If it has the good fortune to interest any who may read it, they can rest assured that whatever accrues from this tale will go to aid my friends the lions.

According to Korokoro the lion's roar translated into English goes: WHO IS LORD OF THIS LAND? . . . Who is lord of this land? . . . I AM! . . . I AM! . . . I am! . . . I am! . . .

Index

For index to lions in Parts III and IV, see p. 320

320   INDEX

Wakamba tribe, 167
Wamba, 81
Warrgues Mountain, 90
Watamu, 264

Yala river valley, 41-2
Yusuf (cook), 27, 44-7, 56-8

LIONS IN PARTS III AND IV

Astra, 254-6, 262-3
Bisleti cubs (four 'Ss'), 282-4, 286-7, 288-91, 293-5, 297-8, 301-2, 305
Boy, 256-7, 259, 264-7, 272-82, 286-9, 292-5, 298, 301, 303-6
Elsa, 219, 221-3, 226-36, 251, 254-6, 262, 271, 286, 301
Girl, 256-7, 259-60, 264-7, 272-82, 286, 288-94, 298-304, 306-8; second litter, 307-8
Gopa, 231, 252
Henrietta, 259-61, 264, 267, 268, 278
Jespah, 231, 237, 249, 252
Juba, 254-6, 262-3
Little Elsa, 231, 245-6, 249-53, 283
Mara, 257-60, 264-7, 278
Sam, 302-6
Ugas, 261-2, 266-7, 276-81, 282, 284-8, 290-5, 297-8, 302-3, 305

Moyale

Buna

El Wak

Guguxa

MARSABIT
RESERVE

BORAN TRIBE

SOMALIS

Wajir

SOMALI

REPUBLIC

dera

Kom

Merti

Gubato

Lak Dima (CAMP)

Habaswein

SOMALIS

Dif

Sabena Wells

Akhalar

Magardo Crater

Lorian

Garba Tula

Swamp

Kinna

BORAN TRIBE

SOMALIS

J

RESERVE

Melkalone

Mugwongo

MP

Kore
1449

Mbalambala

Garissa

tana

Galole

Ijara

Kionga

Rubu

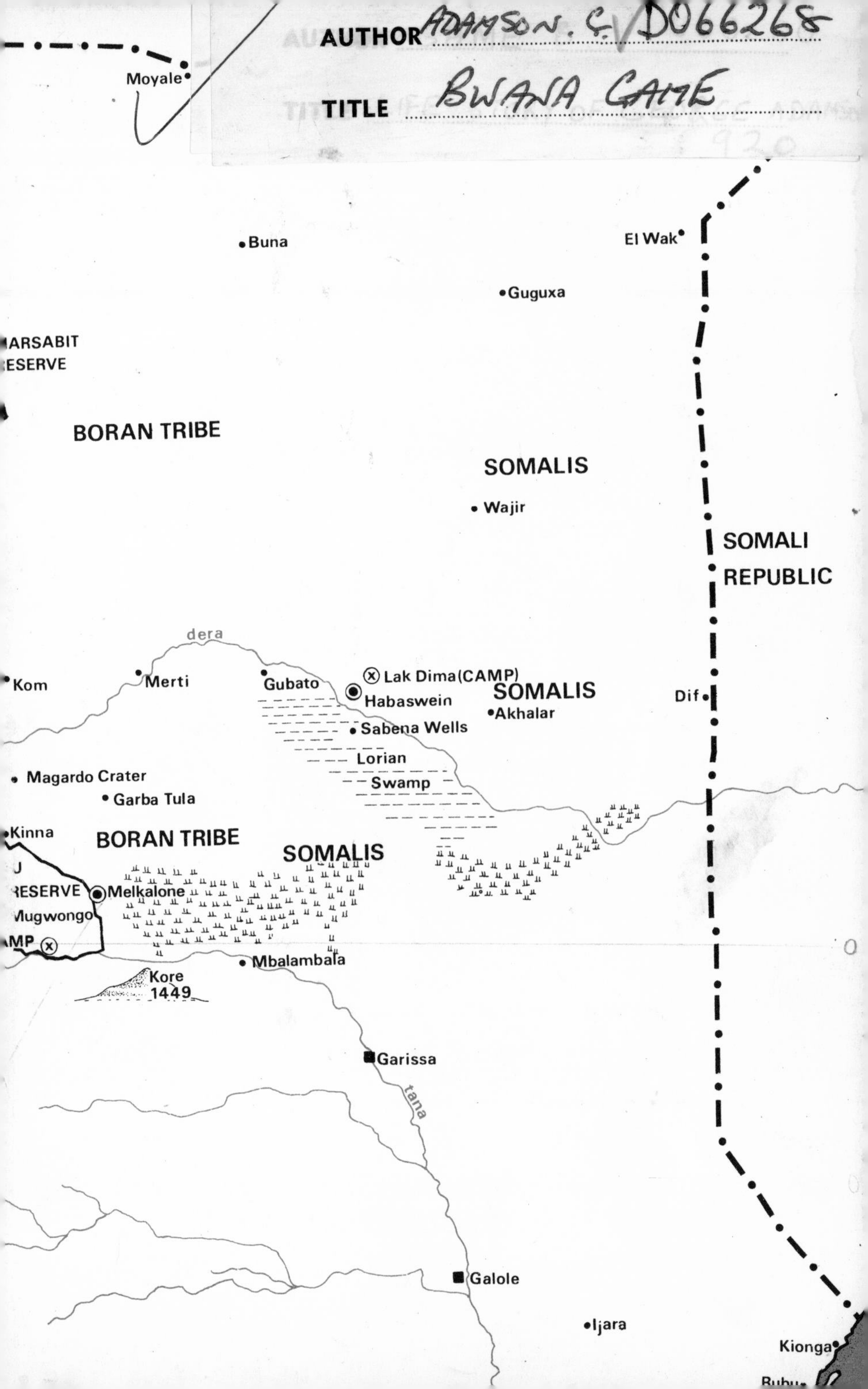